THE
GOSPEL
OF
WELLNESS

THE GOSPEL OF WELLNESS

GYMS, GURUS, GOOP, AND THE FALSE
PROMISE OF SELF-CARE

Rina Raphael

HENRY HOLT AND COMPANY

NEW YORK

Henry Holt and Company
Publishers since 1866
120 Broadway
New York, New York 10271
www.henryholt.com

Henry Holt® and Ⓗ® are registered trademarks of Macmillan
Publishing Group, LLC.

Portions of this book originally appeared, though sometimes slightly different,
in the following publications: *Fast Company*, the *Los Angeles Times*, and
Medium's *Elemental*.

Library of Congress Cataloging-in-Publication Data is available.

ISBN: 9781250793003

Our books may be purchased in bulk for promotional, educational,
or business use. Please contact your local bookseller or the Macmillan Corporate and
Premium Sales Department at (800) 221–7945, extension 5442, or by e-mail at
MacmillanSpecialMarkets@macmillan.com.

First Edition 2022

Designed by Omar Chapa

Printed in the United States of America

1 3 5 7 9 10 8 6 4 2

The names and identifying characteristics of some persons described
in this book have been changed.

Contents

Introduction

Santa Monica, California

It's a sunny spring day in Southern California. Two thousand women are gathered on the wooden planks of the famous Santa Monica Pier. Seagulls are squawking overhead, but the women pay them no mind. They're busy saluting the sun from a rainbow of colored yoga mats in perfectly spaced rows, spread out over a half mile of the pier. A yoga instructor's commands blare at them from a stage's loudspeakers: "The universe is calling and your right leg is going to answer." The women extend their legs in unison, with military precision.

Usually, after a yoga class, everyone grabs their stuff and walks to their car, maybe chatting it up a bit with fellow classmates. But not here. The loudspeakers switch to club music, and the yoga class morphs into a rave. Women bounce up and down and headbang to Robyn. Their stainless steel water bottles become percussion instruments. Nobody is drunk, or high, or rolling—the only thing they've consumed recently is complimentary kombucha. Also: it's eleven o'clock in the morning.[1]

This is Wanderlust, a traveling wellness festival that bills itself as an "all-out celebration of mindful living." It goes from town to town, setting up pop-up outdoor fitness events like revival tents, drawing women together to bond, set personal goals, meditate, and revel in collective namaste vibes. Wanderlust is Coachella for healthy living, and like the famous desert concert, Wanderlust sells both tickets and sponsorships.

On the far side of the pier is an Adidas-sponsored lounge with an interactive art installation where you're invited to post a mantra to their website. A blond woman wearing Tory Burch workout gear offers her own: "To feel whole again." She then slips her Chanel handbag over her arm and proceeds to the yoga shopping fair.

New York, New York

The scents of bergamot and frankincense flow through a minimalist spa. White walls, light birchwood floors, soft gray furniture. Succulents in sparse pots. WTHN is not an East Coast radio station—it's a word that's pronounced "within," and it's the name of this soothing spa. Though "spa" isn't exactly the right word for this place. WTHN is the Drybar of acupuncture.

Traditional Chinese medicine is now as chic and as easy to book as a blowout. I've been afraid of needles all my life, but WTHN has made this ancient practice into a modern luxury experience, with women lining up to be pricked and prodded by a copious number of them. While a pampering acupuncture session for "mind + body relief" is the main item on the menu, WTHN also offers a blend of Chinese herbs to prevent stress and boost energy so you can "keep calm and rock on."

Several thirtysomething women crowd WTHN's bustling lobby. It's a weekday afternoon in January. Some are dressed in work attire, others wear stylish black wool coats. "I mean, *who isn't* exhausted?" says one woman, running her freshly manicured hands through her honey-highlighted hair. Several ailments brought her here: constant headaches, groggy mornings, and pervasive anxiety. An attendant calls her name, and she stands up, excited.

As the staff lead her to her own private cubicle, her voice echoes down the hallway. "I'm off to be relaxed!" The rest of us, waiting for our turn, are left to browse the impressive display of supplements.

Palm Desert, California

It's early fall and I'm at Ganja Goddess Getaway, a women-only weed retreat about a half hour outside Palm Springs. This self-described "stoner girl slumber party" is held on a rented equestrian estate where the event organizers expect you to be high the whole time. Most of the guests sleep in tents on the grounds; I get to sleep in a horse stall in the stable. (Don't worry—it's furnished like a hotel room.)

Weed is available, in large quantities and in many appetizing forms. There are cannabis-infused cotton candy machines, waitstaff holding trays of pre-rolled joints, cookies and brownies, and something you use for "dabbing." There is also an open snack bar in case you get the munchies.

It's a diverse crowd. At night, by the campfire, a young Black mom in her thirties trades parenting advice with a retired white trucker in her fifties. A twentysomething Latina decked out in athleisurewear talks politics with a sixtysomething former hippie. At dinner, I mention to a twenty-five-year-old at my table how refreshing it is to hang out with older women. "Yeah," she says, exhaling pot smoke. "They're chill." Then someone else excuses herself from the meal, explaining "My edible just kicked in." Everyone else nods in solidarity.[2]

At one point a soothing voice comes over the public address system. "The belly dancing class will start on the great lawn in five minutes." Then the voice adds, "I love you." A pair of millennials in bright tank tops sway lazily down to the lawn with a gray-haired woman in a floral housedress. Several women have crowns of flowers in their hair. One middle-aged mom gives up early and retires to lie down in the grass, where she sprawls and looks up at the sky in amazement.

"I feel like we live in a society that requires a lot of charging ahead, getting things done, and going on autopilot in order to accomplish a lot of tasks," the co-founder of Ganja Goddess Getaway told me. "We need this kind of a moment where you slow things down and really just focus on yourself."

• • •

These women—from the designer-attired Wanderlust participant to the cannabis campers—are just a few examples of the millions of women contributing to the $4.4 trillion wellness economy. Far beyond yoga classes and veganism, they are modeling their entire lives—from where they live to whom they socialize with and how they parent—on the wellness lifestyle du jour.

What is "wellness," exactly? At its most basic level, it's the active pursuit of well-being outside the realm of medicine. It's more than just avoiding sickness; it encompasses prevention and maintenance: nutrition, fitness, sleep, community support, and stress management. It's the choices we make to feel better physically, mentally, socially, and spiritually.

Does it all sound a bit general and vague? That's because it is. There is no agreed-upon definition of what "well" is, and it's one reason why the wellness industry has grown so big. Plenty of companies have their own idea of how to get there—what you need to do, buy, or think—which is why the term "wellness" has devolved into an ambiguous marketing term that can just as easily mean activated charcoal toothpaste as it does mindfulness. Wellness can mean almost anything.

In many ways, wellness is whatever you need for your health. There's no one right path; wellness requires awareness of the uniqueness of your experience. It's about what you, the individual, can do for yourself to get through this thing we call life.

Entire industries have suddenly popped up around the desire to get healthier and live longer. Small boutique fitness studios now comprise 40 percent of the gym market and have become *the place* for women to exercise and hang out. Sales of organic food top $60 billion a year. Once a fringe practice, meditation has seeped into mainstream American culture (to create a multibillion-dollar industry). Two-thirds of American women devote half of their closets to athleisurewear.[3]

Wellness has taken over beauty, tech, and even housing and alcohol. Vitamin IV drip services are wait-listing customers; nightclubs serve booze-free herbal tonics; spiritual healers sell out workshops; real estate developers rush to build "wellness communities"; and Silicon Valley is pushing psychedelics as a mental health therapeutic. Even our language has changed. People say things like "I need this for my self-care," "I'm on a cleanse," or "I'm practicing gratitude." These slogans weren't around fifteen years ago. Now they're repeated by celebrities, business founders, suburban moms, and many a Gen Zer.

Of course, people have always bought things to help their well-being, but what we're witnessing today is an unprecedented cultural and historical moment. Wellness is a movement now. According to *NielsenIQ*, health and wellness was "the single most powerful consumer force of 2021."[4] Never before have we seen this level of focus on self-improvement, with U.S. millennials labeled the most "health-conscious generation."[5] We have become a self-care nation, though arguably one that still lacks the fundamentals of well-being.

Being "healthy" once meant going to the doctor regularly. Now it means you should rarely need to see a doctor. Wellness, in its current form, is almost an aspirational obsession for some and close to religious dogma for others. The average American believes adherence to popularized methods can overcome sickness, unhappiness, and even death. A strict overhaul of diet, movement, and thoughts is hailed as the new messiah. In wellness, it seems, we trust.

• • •

When athleisure seized fashion in 2014, it coincided with other lifestyle trends of its time, like the proliferation of boutique fitness studios and cold-pressed juice bars. Back then, I was a thirty-one-year-old digital news producer at NBC News in New York City. I had an inkling that a cultural phenomenon was coming into place, which I chalked up to holed-up, tech-addicted millennials craving physical movement. But by 2017, when I began to cover the wellness industry full time as a business magazine reporter in L.A., I saw the emergence of far more trends—clean eating, "forest bathing," meditation retreats—with more age groups joining the fold. Suddenly, it wasn't just your New Age pal in Venice Beach raving about bone broth. It was most of your friends too. Sometimes it was your mom. Or your boss.

Women flocked to these trends with urgency and intensity. They went fully organic, bought ClassPass subscriptions, and replaced dairy milk with soaked almond water. This wasn't just something they did, but something that soon came to define them. All these new habits and products made them believe they could change things. In their minds, things weren't good—and they hadn't been in a while.

I know. Because, you see . . . I am one of these women.

I mean, who doesn't want a bit of aspiration in their lives? I know I did. I wasn't any more immune to the industry's charm than any other adherent. My life was consumed by wellness. It determined how I spent my weekends, picked where I vacationed, dictated which restaurants I frequented, and prescribed my "natural" medications. I spent, on average, hundreds of dollars a month bolstering my health—a good chunk of it on expensive boutique fitness classes.

My pantry, meanwhile, was stocked with "natural" wine. My diet incorporated "superfoods" and organic vegetables. These items elbowed for room in the fridge alongside sparkling cannabis beverages and egg-free Vegenaise. Even my dog was on the trend: I sprinkled his dry food with canine-approved bone broth. (In my defense, it was on sale.)

Today I own five crystals, an interactive smart home gym called a Mirror, and an entire shoebox of skin care facial masks. Twelve pairs of yoga leggings—half of them accompanied by matching sports bras. Two aromatherapy devices. And six different kinds of bath salts. (I don't even own a bathtub. I used to bring them with me on vacations, filtering hotels according to tub availability.) It's all a bit odd because, by all accounts, I was never technically sick: I have no chronic diseases or disabilities, and I receive a clean bill of health every time I visit my general practitioner. So why all these rituals? Why all this stuff?

Because at the time I started down this path I didn't *feel* good.

Rewind to thirty-one-year-old me in New York City circa 2014. From afar, it sounded like the dream: single, living in a big city, and working for the *Today* show, the number one morning show in America. It was the kind of thing you could tell people at a cocktail party and they were often excited to hear more. "Do you get to meet every celebrity?" they'd always ask.

The truth of it was less than intriguing. I worked long, fast-paced workweeks tied to a desk in a windowless office with no real lunch break. By early evening, I was utterly depleted. At one point during my seven-year tenure, I had to undergo four months of physical therapy for a painful bout of tendinitis (which I feared would cost me my job). Typing nonstop for eight to ten hours a day left my wrists in agony, to the point where I could no longer massage shampoo into my hair.

Exhausted by stressful workdays in a 24/7 news environment, I'd order Thai food to my poorly heated studio apartment, then cuddle up on the couch to watch *Downton Abbey*. Most nights I was too tired to see friends, let alone make new ones. Loneliness became as routine as a bum radiator. I was also in my thirties, getting older, and increasingly nervous about my vanity, or more like, nervous about what losing my looks and figure *meant*. I saw how both higher-weight individuals and the aging were treated in the media industry and dating scene—and it was far from kind.

Ageism, unfortunately, is prevalent within journalism. I was at the *Today* show when it booted a tearful Ann Curry as co-host to make room for a peppy Savannah Guthrie, fifteen years her junior. It was eerily quiet in the newsroom that morning, the producers fearful to talk lest they say something they'd regret. Then came the commands to start scrubbing

Curry from the website. Photo albums, talent holiday recaps . . . it was as if she'd never existed.

Not too long after, my boss and mentor was forced out after her maternity leave and replaced by a younger, less experienced manager who was promoted while subbing for her. Although it seemed like blatant discrimination, she was told by her attorney she would have no luck with a lawsuit. The rest of us got the message: Don't age. Stay young. Keep your job.

It was a brutal blood sport, and one I wasn't prepared to engage in. Probably because I was so tired.

And what did wellness offer? Solutions.

Wellness promised me food that could deliver more energy *and* keep me thin. Supplements dangled better sleep when I lay awake wondering whether I'd die alone. A fitness class hinted I didn't need to make plans to see friends—*they'd just be there*. Meditation advertised a silencing of all the "dying" journalism industry woes clogging my brain. Wellness said it could fix me, like a toy that was not so much broken as in need of new batteries. And I wanted to believe it.

It would be dishonest to say that I was wooed by wellness as much as I was searching for remedies. Too many things in my life started to feel diseased. I couldn't always put my finger on it, but I started to suspect there was something fundamentally unhealthy about the way I was living. The work stress, the greasy takeout food, the endless, soul-crushing dating . . . I was actively looking to manage all of it. I was open to alternatives. And wellness brands spoke my language; they understood full well there were real issues impacting people just like me. People who felt depleted, frustrated, isolated, and nervous. People who needed a boost.

My conversion didn't happen overnight. I fought this culture for so long. I rolled my eyes and teased pals about trends like mushroom coffee, yet soon enough I found myself at the cash register, admitting defeat. That's because it was no longer countercultural—*it was the culture*. As they say, it happened slowly at first, and then all at once. I increasingly became further consumed with my health, like some sort of lab rat awaiting testing. It was fun and seemingly vital: yoga felt good, but it was also a *very important* mental health tool. Could a fitness tracker help me move more? Let's try! Cupping reportedly relieved muscle tension, and heck, everyone else was doing it. Surely there's something there?

In 2015, I moved from New York to L.A. for simple reasons: I wanted warmer weather and I envied what looked like a healthier, chiller lifestyle. On the West Coast, I saw people jogging outside year-round. They gulped green juice the way my New York pals downed tequila at after-work happy hours. On weekends, Angelenos favored hikes in Runyon Canyon over shopping and brunching. (If they did shop, it was at Whole Foods.) It seemed, at the time, like a promised land where everyone felt better.

A little over a year later, I was writing full time for *Fast Company*, a progressive business magazine centered on innovation in tech, leadership, and design. I mostly wrote about fashion and food, but the more I got into the L.A. lifestyle, the more my pitches reflected my metamorphosis. So that same year, my editor agreed to let me cover the sector entirely, going so far as to let me launch a newsletter about the latest developments in wellness.

"Why is everyone guzzling kombucha, buying DNA kits, and downloading meditation apps now?" I wrote in the announcement for my newsletter, *Well To Do*. "Are these inventions and new pursuits actually helping people? Do they even work?" These are questions I would spend the next four years answering. Not only for *Fast Company*, but for outlets like the *L.A. Times*, the *New York Times*, Medium's *Elemental*, and wellness research institutes. I wanted to know why there were so many women just like me, looking to exhale.

Over the years, I tried out innovative ideas like a texting therapy bot. I investigated Facebook's war on alternative health groups. I profiled beauty brands selling "athleisure makeup," that is, mascara and foundation designed to be worn in the gym. I also tested out the more ridiculous—

including a "sleep robot" (which was more like a faceless Teddy Ruxpin for insomniacs) and, no joke, sleep-friendly ice cream. My job took me to brain optimization labs and to the flotation tank studios expanding across the country.

I got to know a lot of communities. In a remote ski resort in Utah, I got to spend time with the tech elite building the exclusive wellness community of the future. In rural Alabama, I spent a weekend at a utopian commune for women only. Another time, I attended an "overcoming death" conference where scientists and hopeful senior citizens believed they could crack the code on immortality (and which honestly felt like the sequel to *Get Out*).

I interviewed Gwyneth Paltrow, biohacking icon Dave Asprey, Peloton founder John Foley, and also femtech founders fighting to discover new medical solutions. I also spoke with women across the country who were suddenly doing things like shunning dairy, but they weren't exactly sure why. Others felt they had a new lease on life as soon as they found a gym they loved.

But a funny thing happened a few years in: my thoughts on the industry changed. Quite dramatically. What had first begun as fitness, nutrition, and stress relief increasingly gave way to muddy waters: crystal-infused water bottles, "detox cleanses," and shady workplace wellness programs. After interviewing countless founders and trying out every trend under the sun, I grew skeptical. Out of curiosity, but also out of journalistic duty, I started doing my homework. By then, I had left the hamster wheel of digital news production and was afforded more time to dive deeper into the issues that wellness brands raised.

I called up medical professionals to investigate health claims. I checked chemical concerns with scientists. I started asking everyone just how their CBD collection was working out. I read the fine print.

I began realizing I couldn't take many of these companies at face value. Their marketing promises didn't align with science. The evidence was paltry or, at times, wildly exaggerated. Influencers with market growth agendas jumped to fearmongering conclusions far too fast. More than that, they were instituting their own pressures on women. The wellness industry isn't quite what we are led to believe. And surprise, surprise, many of the "facts" we take for granted about what's healthy and what isn't aren't true.

That's because wellness is often treated a lot more like fashion in the media. It's not always pressed upon reporters to investigate wellness companies' claims.

It's easy to fall into the marketing over accurate science trap: so much of what a wellness company's PR department puts out *sounds* right. And I was working for *Fast Company*, not *Scientific American* magazine. My readers cared about investor funding. Market share. Creative campaigns. Forward-thinking design. The science wasn't ignored, rather it was just secondary.

But at some point, there was a more general reckoning with the mission statements of VC-funded brands out there to "change the world," and the founders we'd previously revered to godly proportions. The *Wall Street Journal* released its groundbreaking investigative report on the now defunct company Theranos and its deceptive practices, and we all began examining Silicon Valley leaders' claims more closely.

I'll level with you: you might not like some of the stuff I unearthed throughout this process. I say that because I too was hesitant. It can all be quite jarring if you've only ever been exposed to one side of an equation. I didn't want to admit what became increasingly obvious: we've been conditioned to accept certain wellness beliefs, cemented as conventional wisdom because they're ubiquitous. We're bombarded by wellness propaganda—in our magazines, social media feeds, and Sephora stores. Marketing has a far stronger power than scientific proof. Few of us follow scientists, but we sure as hell follow celebrities, influencers, and brands that are in no way health experts but sure act like them.

The more I learned, the more alarmed I became. As a reporter, I had to admit the obvious: the wellness industry isn't well.

. . .

In this book, I examine how and why American women were led down the kale-covered path of wellness. Part investigative report and part sociological analysis, this book dives deep into this booming movement, going inside the sprawling landscape of wellness to explore how and why it grew to be the behemoth it is today. I analyze the solutions it offers, and the dangers—but also the possible promise—it holds for the future of our health. Many people assume wellness is simply the desire to be thin or to purify our lives, and while there are aspects of that, such a simplistic interpretation would be naive. There are far more facets to this movement, each demonstrating long-simmering discontent and hopes.

This book is about commodified wellness: the big business of selling you health. The marketing of wellness has inspired a religious fervor—and not in a good way. This industry communicates the idea that with enough devotion, we can manifest only goodness and manage what feels unruly or threatening in our lives—an idea that works almost like a divine principle. This book's title is rather tongue-in-cheek, but it does allude to how health has emerged as a regulatory framework, much like religion, telling us *how to live*. Sometimes these comparisons are subtle, but at times blatant. But make no mistake: the gospel of wellness has its own commandments, its own morality, its own community, and its own rituals.

It also has its own false idols. These golden calves indoctrinate women with false beliefs: pseudoscience, distrust of medicine, and unnecessary pressures robbing them of time and energy. And we need to combat these beliefs before they devolve into a full-blown cult. In wellness, the cure occasionally becomes worse than the disease.

The gospel of wellness spans multiple sectors and draws on a complex web of cultural and political forces for its sustenance. This book could have been a multivolume set—there is that much to talk about. Many of my examples focus on the biggest pillars of wellness, including nutrition, exercise, stress management, and spirituality. But know that any of the specific examples I delve into from one area teach lessons that can be applied elsewhere.

It's a lot of ground to cover. While I understand wellness is a fast-growing sector now spreading to multiple communities and income brackets, the majority of this book focuses on the groups most adoptive of commodified wellness—namely women. This is not to say men aren't also participating, just that women are more heavily represented, for reasons such as gender equity gaps and the specific roles of women in society. Naturally, not every reason discussed will apply to every woman—wellness is a massive, vague umbrella term with numerous sectors, so some might be more relevant than others to any individual woman. But if it doesn't reflect you, I bet it sums up someone you know.

This book traces not only the many segments of the industry and how they got here, but also the historic trends that planted the seeds of what was to come. You'll see sidebars that delve into a related historic episode in line with each chapter's theme. History shows that so many of these issues and solutions aren't anything new: we've been dealing with the same problems (and like-minded gurus) for centuries. Everything that seems innovative today possesses a long, rich history.

Here's what we do know: Wellness—in all its many forms and bizarre rituals—springs from universal truths. Everyone just wants to feel good, and that's becoming harder and harder as modern life becomes more chaotic. Too much feels out of control: a poorly constructed medical system, tech overload, a tumultuous news cycle, lack of community, *you name it*. We live lives that demand too much of us. Wellness, which spans both real, groundbreaking solutions and total bunk, is the direct response to genuine complaints in this country. Something is rotten in the state of Denmark, and wellness, we believe, might heal it. The question is whether what we're being sold is delivering. Can wellness truly solve these issues?

At the end of the day, I come neither to bury nor to praise the wellness industry. My goal is to help sort the wheat from the chaff, to distinguish the legitimate benefits from the marketing copy, and to identify those which only add more stress or sickness. In the quest to minimize what bothers us, wellness has both empowered and enslaved women. The more effectively we can disentangle the good from the bad, the more promising a future we can create for the movement—and for our well-being.

This is more than a book about a rapidly growing industry. It's a book about American women's search for a cure to all that ails them—and their journey to regain something they believe they've lost. They've discovered a new agency to chart different paths and search for better solutions. They are reimagining community, medicine, even faith. They are standing up to say, *The status quo isn't acceptable.* There must be a better way through.

Chapter 1

Why the Hell Is the Advice Always Yoga?

Can you remember the last time you felt *free?* Do you recall a time in which you weren't consumed by text notifications, computer install updates, grocery lists, school pick-ups and drop-offs, work emails, the news, and shedding "those last ten pounds"? Remember giving less of a shit? Being psychologically unburdened? And relaxed?

Neither do many other women. Modern life, for all its comforts and privileges, can feel wildly overwhelming. To be a woman today is to be stuck in a loop of unrelenting maintance.

I am, by all accounts, not a chill person. Type A is a more accurate description. My husband likes to motion for me "to take it down a notch" whenever I'm riled up by politics, line cutters, or nonsensical fashion. This is partially due to my own makeup but partially bred out of a chaotic career existence. And yes, let me preface all this by saying that I am overall a very fortunate person who is housed, fed, and not stuck in a war-torn country. I am lucky, 100 percent.

But by my midthirties, I'd become loaded with stress, even for Type A me. I worked as a full-time reporter at *Fast Company* with set hours and was expected to participate in Slack channels, conferences, news shifts, and company-wide initiatives. I even had my own newsletter and represented the outlet at industry conferences. But I wasn't granted any benefits, health insurance, or paid time off. For years I wasn't technically on staff even though I functionally was. Like many others, I'd become a gig worker with none of the "freedom" of a freelancer and none of the assurances of a staff employee. A permalancer. I had a contract stipulating a specific number of stories, but it could be canceled within two weeks' notice. This put me and my fellow writers in a perpetual state of job insecurity, of having to constantly prove ourselves to our "employer."

As a gig worker, taking a vacation or sick leave is out of the question. You aren't paid for any days you aren't working. Thinking about having kids? Forget it. If you can barely afford two weeks off, who is going to pay for your maternity leave?

Mind you, I wasn't about to start complaining, because by 2017, the journalism industry was in free fall as advertising money dried up. I was coming off previous positions where I saw budgets slashed, reasonable freelance wages disappear, and entire teams decimated. Site traffic—not necessarily quality—reigned supreme. Aggregation replaced original reporting. Ad sponsorship commitments steered content decisions. The sensational trumped the meaningful. *Be more like BuzzFeed*, we were told. *Churn, churn, churn.*

At those previous jobs, fewer bodies meant more work. It meant you had to be trendspotter, writer, editor, newsletter aficionado, sponsorship deal creative, contributor manager, media partner liaison, social media savant . . . an entire team in one body. And as digital journalism became more competitive, we had to follow our beats as soon as the "workday" ended. If I wasn't at my desk, I was on Twitter or on blogs trying to keep up with a twenty-four-hour news cycle. Sometimes I'd do my after-hours "research" while I was at the gym—one sweaty, slipping hand on the elliptical machine, the other scrolling my phone—trying to ensure that neither my career nor my body would fall by the wayside.

You couldn't complain. You were told you were fortunate just to have a job in journalism.

I was burned out at this point in my career. The stress was building, the anxiety seeping out sideways into other areas of my life. This was on top of everything else I worried about. As a Jew, I was anxious about rising rates of anti-Semitism. (By 2017, Jews were targeted in 58 percent of all religious-based hate crime incidents despite being just *2 percent* of the U.S. population.)[1] Then there was concern over reproductive rights, the growing political divide, and so on and so on.

It all kept me up at night. It was in my thirties that I'd stopped sleeping and shortly thereafter began suffering from anxiety. Which is how I found myself looking for stress relief—and major emotional release. Mind you, I was already dipping my toes in wellness at the time. This just heightened my need for it.

I found it one day tucked away on the third floor of a small and unremarkable brick building in Tribeca. Soothing neutral palettes and a wall of mirrors filled this airy fitness studio. Below one's feet, the wood floor rested atop a layer of rose quartz crystals. (Even if clients don't see the crystals, the hope is that they feel the "vibrational energy.") Right outside the studio doors, a bathroom boasted marble counters, modern gold-plated fixtures, and Chanel bath products. Inspirational tunes by Florence and the Machine set the pace for this class called The Class.

Thirty toned women in Lululemon sports bras and leggings stood silent, their flat tummies on display. Eyes closed, they placed their right hands firmly on their hearts. In this pose, they patiently awaited the command of their instructor, the fitness guru Taryn Toomey, who would lead them through a "meditation, just with your body."

This self-described "cathartic mind-body experience" serves as an unorthodox therapy session. Here, women are encouraged to yell, shout, scream, and express themselves while also doing challenging cardio moves. At other points, they're told to stand still and quiet the mind. The

Class centers around emotional management, which is why class names echo women's late-night venting sessions: I Love My Kids Just Not Right Now (give me a break!), F*CK Everything (when everyone and everything seems like the absolute worst), and the I Don't Wanna Workout (don't make me work out!).

Toomey, a blond, lithe, statuesque figure with the raspy voice of a Kathleen Turner, addressed the room while perched on a window ledge overlooking the Lower Manhattan skyline. "We're out of our bodies most of the day," Toomey said. "It's time for a reunion." The crowd nodded in agreement. Some looked genuinely touched.

Together, the crowd furiously squatted and shook, all while repeatedly shouting "Huh!" in tribal chorus. From there, the women contorted themselves into winged positions, their arms outstretched. They breathed heavily as their leader urged them to "rise up."

Midway through a medley of jumping jacks, lunges, and burpees, Toomey's voice intensified, taking on new gravitas. "What are your blinders?" Toomey demanded. "Your blocks—what are they?" Her voice got even louder, like a commanding priest. "What are they? What are they?!" As if hitting the crescendo at an opera, she shouted with gusto, "Feel! Feel! Feel!"

The room lost it. The session devolved into a rave as the Prodigy's electronic music anthem "Firestarter" roared over the speakers. Some class members moaned like birthing animals, while others shook their limbs with the spastic fervor of inflatable air dancers outside used car dealerships. One jumped wildly in place, tears rolling down her cheeks, as she yelled. Others frantically thrust their arms into the air, their $4,450 Cartier Love bracelets jangling. Rage, grief, and frustration were suspended in the sweat-mixed-with-Chanel-moistened air.

"This is a safe space," Toomey whispered.

Toomey at times can come across as a therapeutic healer, a cross between Deepak Chopra and Jane Fonda. "You start to realize that most of what's going on [in the body] is in the mind," Toomey told me. "And you know that you actually have a choice, and you can reroute it—that's what we do in The Class: we practice the ability to do that." That type of thinking is part of Toomey's appeal: a splash of the woo-woo grounded in the practical, incorporating her self-help messages within tried-and-true elements of mainstream fitness. She is completely aware that meta-physical and spiritual practices can seem foreign, and she makes the effort to render them more accessible to consumers without alienating her more Goopy fans. Her studio's crystal-embedded floors, for example, are alleged to "cleanse" bad energy. Despite spending thousands of dollars on them, Toomey will quickly label herself as a "pretty big skeptic." When asked whether she believes in crystals' supposed healing properties, she says she believes the most important healing element is the "power of intention."

Toomey created this new kind of workout after realizing she loved the meditative component of yoga as a way of connecting with her breathing but also craved the endorphin rush of cardio routines. The result is a mix of quiet reflection with bursts of fast movement. Sound is another component. She noticed that whether or not she vocalized what was bottled up inside made a difference in how she felt. Getting loud—*really* loud—was a catharsis of sorts.

Toomey built a cult following around this unique, visceral form of exercise—if you could even call it strictly exercise. Is it meditation? Athletic vocalization? Calorie-burning primal scream therapy? Celebrities like Naomi Watts swear by the $35 sessions. Ask New Yorkers to describe The Class, and they'll call it "a brain-body release," "an emotional workout," and "a spiritually orgasmic exercise." One participant simply explained it by saying, "Sometimes you just need to yell, ya know?"[2]

I definitely did know.

For almost two years, I was a regular at the L.A. outpost of The Class, surrounded by several dozen women who, by all accounts, seemed to have it together.

During one session, The Class took it up a notch. It was the Sunday following the Supreme Court confirmation of Brett Kavanaugh, who had earlier been accused of sexual misconduct by a former classmate, California professor Christine Blasey Ford. Liberal-leaning women tended to view the proceedings in a certain way: they saw a woman take the stand, be doubted by the public, then be torn apart. Acknowledging the week's news, the instructor led the entire room in a sing-along of the 4 Non Blondes song "What's Up." Participants thrust their arms forward and back—rowing without an oar—as the lyrics demanded,

And I scream from the top of my lungs
What's going on?

The room erupted in song, women shouting at the top of their lungs, turning their faces to the ceiling as if to summon the heavens to rescue them. Some pounded their fists in the air as though they were punching ghosts. "I pray every single day for revolution," they bellowed along with the 1993 hit single. The emotion was palpable. It was unlike anything I had ever seen, perhaps only rivaled by the kind of Christian revival faith healings I've seen depicted in movies.

After the class, I approached a few of the women about the intensity we had just witnessed. The Class skews older millennial—women in their thirties and forties, many of them moms or midcareer professionals. The atmosphere felt unreal, certainly not the norm for a nine a.m. workout class. "[The confirmation was] the last straw," said one woman in line at the studio's café. "We are broken camels."

How could it be, I wondered, that so many "privileged" women were so exasperated? What *was* going on? This was much larger than just my own anxiety. A simmering cauldron of frustration had come to a boiling point, and somehow it was exploding on a pastel-colored yoga mat. It couldn't just be the political situation inspiring such an outpouring. These women had evidently come to class to express their grievances, and no amount of sage was going to clear up that kind of toxic energy. But when and why did squats and burpees, among other wellness activities, become therapy?

Drowning in Stress: Not Enough Time or Support to "Have it All"

Women are overwhelmed. I hear it over and over and over again from folks across the country, on all sides of the political and social divide. They can be stressed by PTA meetings and ever-rising childcare costs or by a never-ending stream of work coupled with growing piles of laundry. They can be single, drowning in student loan debts and unbelievable housing prices. They might be college students, 40 percent of whom report being so stressed and depressed that "it's difficult to function," according to the American College Health Association. Or perhaps they're graduates hitting LinkedIn's virtual pavement (with little success) or moms struggling to find the time to "sneak in" a shower. Expectations continue to mount, yet they're barely able to tread the rough waters.

Of course, men are also overstretched, but women experience a particular strain of stress, and if recent surveys are to be believed, experience far more of it. Almost half of American women say their stress levels increased over the past five years (compared to 39 percent of men) and that anxiety keeps them up at night. And despite the benefits of coupledom, the legally bound seem to carry a heavier load: more than one-third of married women report managing "a great deal of stress" versus 22 percent of unattached women.[3]

The home is one of the bigger battlegrounds in the war between the sexes. The average woman spends two more hours each day than the average man cooking, cleaning, and caretaking,[4] and nearly two-thirds of women say they bear the responsibility for most of the chores.[5] They are constantly multitasking, holding a laptop with one hand and a Swiffer in the other. That unequal distribution of work affects them in multiple ways. Women have less time to focus on their careers, get involved in politics, kvetch to their friends, or heck, go to therapy. In one survey, 60 percent said the one person they never had enough time for was *themselves*.[6]

Stressed as they are at home, work, at least anecdotally, appears to also be one of women's chief complaints. Americans work the longest hours of all the industrialized nations, with the average workweek clocking in at forty-seven hours.[7] Germany, in comparison, averages thirty-five hours. The land of the free is also the only advanced economy that doesn't guarantee workers paid time off, whereas European Union members mandate at least twenty days of paid leave.[8] Three out of four women suffer from burnout, defined as emotional, physical, and mental exhaustion caused by excessive stress. Just how bad is it? One survey discovered that 48 percent of employees have cried at work, and while women are more inclined to break down in tears over stress, 36 percent of men also acknowledged crying on the job.[9] That's because day-to-day work is an exhausting obstacle course of stressors. Further, the stress often doesn't end once you leave the office: an "always-on" environment encourages bosses to email you at any time. Knowing a ping of anxiety could be incoming at all hours, there is no real end to the workday.

One might tell women to just find other jobs if their workplaces don't support them, but in this economy? It's not so easy. Few options are available in what's become a cutthroat race for well-paying, full-time employment with solid benefits. Job insecurity and a growing gig economy put the American dream ever-teetering on a pinnacle, always on the verge of tipping over. We're not hustling to get ahead as much as to just stay put and pay off our student loan debt—or the mortgage.

A wide cross section of women battle stress, though their wounds differ. Caretaking responsibilities within the office—organizing birthday celebrations, mentoring new hires, mediating disputes between co-workers—often fall to female managers with little acknowledgment. Childless women complain they're routinely expected to work longer hours than caregiving peers, and they feel insulted that management assumes they have no life after six o'clock. Maybe they too would like to leave at a reasonable hour so that they could tend to personal matters or just do whatever it is that fulfills them? Maybe they have a date?

Not that dating necessarily generates stress relief: many singles report they need to compete in a *Hunger Games*–like scene where individuals "swipe" their way through an endless supply of mates, where chasing "something better on the horizon" is as easy as ordering a pizza. Those wading through the dating circuit can get caught up in a shallow hookup culture, which some researchers link to lowered self-esteem. (Almost 50 percent of women report a negative reaction after a fling, versus 26 percent of men.) However you identify—gay, straight, whatever—casual sex may not always be as fun and carefree as *Sex and the City* would have us believe. While some do enjoy a buffet of one-night stands, others might experience depressive symptoms and loneliness.[10]

As for parents, the storm of stress elevates to a Category 5 hurricane: the average mom claims an 8.5 out of 10 on a scale of stress, positioning them somewhere between a Cathy cartoon and a ticking time bomb. A leading cause of stress is time. Sixty percent of moms say they simply can't squeeze in everything on their to-do list, which usually amounts to planning a nutritious dinner, helping with children's homework, organizing the social calendar, and oh, also staying fit and attractive. In addition to all that, 72 percent of moms are stressed about how stressed they are.[11]

Delving into why the American woman is about to burn down her white picket fence would undoubtedly fill volumes. But suffice it to say that one major reason is that she is in no way living the utopian dream envisioned by feminists past. Women are not equal in status nor immune from sexism, and they are still burdened by the domestic assumptions made by society. Our foremothers burned their bras and filed for divorce en masse, but that didn't release Betty Draper from pot roast duty. College girls dreamed of being Tina Fey or Ruth Bader Ginsburg, then found themselves soothing male egos in the boardroom or arguing with their spouse over whose turn it was to carpool.

While middle- to upper-middle-class women are technically liberated, for many their situation feels like further imprisonment: now they need to be both *Working Girl* and June Cleaver. Their life is nonstop emails and baby tantrums; they have two jobs but the respect of one. This is what the renowned sociologist Arlie Hochschild in 1989 termed "the second shift," by which Western women inherit a double-career life. They'll work a full day at the office, commute in traffic back home, hang up their coat, then run into the phone booth to transform into Superhousewife. The current hyperproductive and performative nature of American life is likely to blame. We're on a constant treadmill of doing way more than a normal human would have aspired to do until recently: attain career success, birth two kids, achieve a slamming body, cook like Ina Garten . . . You get the idea.

Futher compounding the issue, the days of living off a single income are long gone; as the cost of living increases and wages stagnate, both partners need to bring home the Beyond Meat bacon.

But again, there's the rub: as the average American increasingly needs to work long and sometimes unpredictable hours at demanding jobs, who is going to manage caregiving? When the workday doesn't end until six, who fixes dinner? How can you make partner at the law firm when you need to scuttle out at a reasonable hour? *Someone* needs to hold down the fort. Someone needs to take care of the kids. Not everyone has relatives nearby who can pitch in and provide free babysitting. And not everyone can afford paid childcare. This is not a predicament exclusive to women raising children with men. Same-sex couples also deal with one partner who inevitably needs to pick up the slack at home.

We may have fought the good fight for women's careers, but as Hochschild observed, "The workplace they go into and the men they come home to have changed less rapidly, or not at all. Nor has the government given them policies that would ease the way, like paid parental leave, paid family medical leave, or subsidized child care—the state-of-the-art child care, that too is stalled."[12] In essence, women changed, but many men, employers, and the government simply put up their feet. They see women struggle to scoot out of the office before children's bedtimes. They hear the exhaustion of those pumping breast milk in their cubicle. But bosses just put another meeting on their calendars. In 2019, a Pew Research survey confirmed what everyone already knew: half of employed moms say being a working parent makes it harder for them to get ahead professionally.[13]

The COVID-19 pandemic only intensified this workload, exposing deep cracks in the system. With schools closed, moms quickly found themselves juggling work Zooms while trying to help their first-grader log in to class. Mothers scrambled to monitor the kids, keep up with double or triple the dirty dishes, and then somehow appear alert during department meetings. In between all of that, they had to stave off a virus that kept them away from friends and family. A significant portion also had to manage eldercare for their aging parents. Their lives, like their wardrobes, began unraveling. They wiped their hands on their sweatpants, looked all around, and asked, *How?*

We might have hit a breaking point. By the fall of 2020, not even one year into the pandemic, 865,000 U.S. women surrendered and handed in their resignation.[14] The number was roughly four times more than the number of men, thereby further contributing to a gender disparity in corporate America. One mom, a friend of a friend, wrote on Facebook, "I've basically abandoned my career that I've worked for 15 years to build in order to care for my kids and give them an education. It's crazy."

An obvious fact that needs to be stated: some groups have it way harder than others, dealing with a wide array of stressors on top of the average American experience. One 2020 survey found that Latino and Black adults have experienced twice as much economic hardship as white adults during the pandemic. They also face more discrimination and greater mental health issues, and they do so with fewer resources.[15] As one co-founder of a meditation program for Black communities once told me: "We joke that [mainstream outlets] always try to get you to calm down in your commute. Our communities are dealing with a lot more things than just a hard commute."

Worn out by the daily grind and greater injustices, women seek solutions. During the last few years, breath work instructor Jay Bradley has drawn in far more female than male clients, many of them high-achievers who say they've tried everything to relax—pharmaceuticals, therapy, or "spiritual work"—but nothing's worked in the long term. These women are, by his account, depleted, demoralized, and discouraged. They are driven but feel unable to "accomplish it all." Bradley's clients are afraid if they let go *just a little*, everything will all fall apart. They express an "underlying unworthiness," says Bradley, who believes it stems from unhealthy boundaries surrounding work or family in addition to self-imposed expectations. This ongoing struggle leaves them "feeling powerful one day and then feeling powerless [the next]."

In his group sessions, Bradley acknowledges how well participants take care of everyone else. "Women, in particular, give, give, give," Bradley tells his class. He encourages clients to spend the session to truly focus on one person and one person only: themselves. Through breath work, they can hopefully release whatever worries occupy their headspace, maybe even practice some self-compassion. At the same time, says Bradley, they are "ready for something that will permanently shift them out of that fight-or-flight mode."

Women often voice that they need some time out, a Sabbath, a rest (though preferably not in a corporate nap room). They instinctively feel the urge to pull away and indulge in some self-care—a term that hit record Google searches in 2020. Some decide to waste a few minutes checking their Instagram, only to face an onslaught of clean kitchens and photoshopped bodies. What should have been a break turns into additional pressure. The same technology that was supposed to ease our lives is now arguably ruling them. Indeed, Americans who check their phones most frequently report the highest levels of anxiety. As soon as they wake up, they're assaulted by a barrage of texts, then spend eight hours or more staring at a work computer screen, followed by incoming emails and breaking news alerts in the evenings. It never ends. What's more, tech companies increasingly add more addictive features and design infinite ways to keep us hooked or "bingeing." I once heard Netflix CEO Reed Hastings deliver a conference speech in which he flat-out said he was competing not with HBO, FX, or Amazon, but with . . . sleep. "And we're winning!" he exclaimed to rapturous applause.

Well, guess what sleep deprivation causes? Fatigue, irritability, and stress.

Women are looking for *less* in their life. Less noise, fewer tasks, and reduced pressure. Self-care is marketed as the exit strategy. It's become so popular that the Instagram hashtag #selfcare grew to 60 million posts, and self-care is one of the top downloaded app categories. But what exactly are we being sold? And to what extent are these practices helpful?

Flashback: Running Free: "Exercise Is the Best Tranquilizer"

James Fixx had settled into the sedentary American lifestyle by 1967. The magazine editor took public transportation to work, where he was stuck in an office all day working long, stressful hours. To blow off steam, he smoked two packs of cigarettes a day. By his midthirties, he was unhappy with his weight and his habits.

Recognizing he was out of shape, Fixx tried running, and to his amazement, it made him feel significantly better. Running on an empty road became a therapeutic nirvana: quiet time to think, go at your preferred pace, and be free of distractions. In a domineering society, in which one is constantly being told what to do, wear, or think, running became an appealing way to assert some autonomy, to symbolically run away from "the chains of civilization."[16]

In speaking with runners across the country, Fixx noticed that many reported that anxiety, depression, and ruminating thoughts melted away as they hit mile after mile. Divorced men claimed it worked as "an ideal antidepressant." Women reportedly said they were "less cranky and bitchy." Fixx quoted one doctor who stated, "exercise is the best tranquilizer."

Fixx felt called to share his miracle cure, no doubt the work of endorphins and exercise's ability to reduce stress hormones. Soon enough, he inspired Americans to do something they'd never done before: jog. Before then, running constituted a gym class chore or an army requirement. In the late sixties, the activity was so unusual that police would stop running "freaks" for disturbing the suburban peace.[17] Bemused pedestrians hurled insults, and sometimes trash.

James Fixx changed all that. Considered the father of recreational running, his bestseller *The Complete Book of Running* became the bible of newly minted joggers. The handbook sparked a jogging revolution, prompting *People* magazine to label it a "craze" on a 1977 cover featuring Farrah Fawcett in gym shorts.

Was it just the stress relief and freedom of the road? Or something more?

Some historians have a different theory: Americans turn to fitness during stressful times.[18] They took up exercising in greater numbers during the Great Depression, throughout the tumultuous seventies, after 9/11, and during the COVID-19 pandemic.[19] Starting in 2002, boutique gyms exploded in popularity. Some industry experts believe the World Trade Center terrorist attacks spurred Americans into an existential crisis overnight. They wondered: Could being reminded of one's mortality inspire a desire to want to live longer, better? Does caring for our health make us feel more grounded? I've heard this idea from several researchers (as well as crystal sellers, who saw sales soar after 9/11).

Rhythmic exercise routines are indeed calming. Intentional repetitive actions can redirect focus away from anxious and depressive thoughts, lulling us into a relaxing trance. Researchers have also found that repetitive, ritualistic behavior can increase people's belief that they can manage situations that are otherwise out of their hands.[20]

In addition, as your body image improves, so do your confidence and sense of mastery. For women, this often also correlates with societal body size pressures. (Historically, women didn't have control over many aspects of their lives, but they could determine their size.) Perhaps it's a false sense of control, but people will grasp at whatever tools they have at their disposal.

"I felt more in control of my life," Fixx said. "I was less easily rattled by unexpected frustrations. I had a sense of quiet power, and if at any time I felt this power slipping away I could easily call it back by going out and running."[21]

Just Sweat Off the Stress?

"Your mobile phone is ringing. Your boss wants to talk to you. And your partner wants to know what's for dinner," reads the Mayo Clinic website. "Stress and anxiety are everywhere. If they're getting the best of you, you might want to hit the mat and give yoga a try."

The esteemed institution praises yoga's ability to help lower blood pressure, manage lower back pain, and "quiet your mind." The Mayo Clinic joins a wide array of outlets vouching for the workout's ability to modulate stress response systems. (Of the many different types of yoga, I am sticking to the mainstream American adaptation for the purposes of this book.) The wellness site *Well+Good* reports that when it comes to stress, "one thing that works *without fail* for almost anyone is yoga." The *New York Times* published a guide on "How to Use Yoga to Destress."

If you haven't read the dozens of headlines extolling yoga, then you've likely heard celebrities swearing by it. Reese Witherspoon relies on it before the chaos of award show season. Miranda Kerr says the daily practice keeps her grounded and calm. Lady Gaga does it in a thong. Yoga has become so popular that almost 37 million Americans hit the mat regularly, and of those, 72 percent are women.[22] They come across soothing fitness gurus like Adriene Mishler of the hit YouTube channel *Yoga with Adriene* and like what they hear. Instead of body transformation talk, all the approachable yogi asks is that you love yourself, find what feels good, and—like catnip to women—"make space." The space can be physical, mental, or emotional, but whichever kind it is, schedule in time for yourself, away from frenetic energies that consume us.

In fact, when Mishler asked her nearly seven hundred thousand Facebook fans what theme they wanted to honor for December 2020, she received an overwhelming response: "Myself."

Yoga has grown so very popular because it emphasizes emotional health in the context of mind-body union. In a society where we feel so disconnected from our bodies (and confined to a sedentary lifestyle), we need outlets that let us explore that union. Some also see it as a less competitive discipline that lets them go at their own pace, in stark contrast to hard-hitting cardio; slow, gentle movements act as a restful cushion from the rat race.

Of course, movement has long been recommended to release stress. Strong evidence shows that regular exercise is associated with lower levels of anxiety, and even just a twenty-minute stroll has been shown to clear the mind.

Frequent exercise is also an American tradition, albeit one historically more afforded to men. While nineteenth-century women prone to "hysteria" were prescribed bed rest or hysterectomies, men were handed a horse and told to head to the wilderness. At the time, "neurasthenia" became a catchall term for elite men's weakness of nerves caused by overly civilized life.[23] The cure for spending too much time working indoors was returning to the rugged outdoors. Teddy Roosevelt advocated a "West Cure": vigorous treks into the wild to build muscles while roping cattle, hunting wildlife, and exploring nature. Manly cowboy activities, he believed, could restore nerves sapped by an effeminate, coddling culture. (Some historians assert that the national parks owe their existence to the popularity of Roosevelt's therapies.)[24]

Today we have far more options than a fainting couch or a cowboy expedition. A host of self-care modalities promises to get you back on the Zen track, filling whatever gap you need filled: massages (touch), facial masks and manicures (pampering), meditation (being present), cardio fitness (movement), cannabis (relaxation), and so on.

To be honest, anything can be self-care provided it makes you feel better (although no real money can be made by telling people to go take a walk outside). Two prominent desires for women are the need to escape stress and the need to release stress. Sometimes one, sometimes the other, but often both. Fans of indoor cycling studios, for example, compare pedaling in place to a vacation from life. They speak of mentally transporting themselves to something more akin to a nightclub than the perceived hell they're living in. One SoulCycle devotee wrote, "I can shut out the world and my own thoughts for a while. There's no beep from my notifications, no expectations, no deadlines, no rules."[25]

With exercise, your worries completely shut off. Your brain is so intently focused on following the prescribed moves that you don't have time to fathom if you potentially chose the wrong career. You are jumping so hard that your shitty ex melts into the abyss. The absorbing repetitive motions occupy the space previously afforded to a ticking biological clock. Nothing else exists, for you have one task and one task only: complete the burpee. You are, for once, *present*.

Some use running quite literally as therapy. Jogging therapy is a combination of talk therapy with mindful movement. The unique workout has gained a small following in Silicon Beach, the L.A. region home to more than five hundred technology companies. Start-up professionals lace up their sneakers to join psychotherapists-slash-trainers who run beside them as they complain about their demanding boss or nagging parent. One jogging therapist's office has all the trappings of a Freudian experience—mid-century couch, end table topped with a tissue box—but also foam rollers, hand-sized FIJI water bottles, hair ties, and energy bars. A mini-gym of sorts.

"You're literally moving forward, *together*," the psychotherapist Sepideh Saremi, founder of Run Walk Talk, told me as I gasped for air while trying to vent and run at the same time. "That is a powerful experience for people to have when they feel really stuck in their lives."[26] (But only for those who can manage to talk while running.)

Solo runs prove equally powerful. One writer explained that she runs to break free of bad thoughts and to metaphorically pound frustration into the pavement. "There's a point during my run when I get this invincible I-could-run-forever feeling, as long as I keep running forward," Patricia Haefeli wrote for *Women's Running*. "But my runs are always large loops, and as I round the bend to head back, I'm reminded that you *can* run away from your problems—at least temporarily."[27]

Temporarily. That's a key point. We are briefly excusing ourselves from our lives and engaging in spurts of stress release before jumping back on the hamster wheel. And what you do, therefore, is sometimes less important than just separating time for yourself. Self-care can be snuggling puppies, watching *30 Rock* reruns, or stretching on a yoga mat because what often matters most is the disengagement from [fill in the blank].

As long as your mind is preoccupied with anything other than what would spur a meltdown, you're golden. But what happens when self-care doesn't cut it, or worse, is weaponized against us?

Stress Is Your Problem

Beatrice* graduated from nursing school at one of the most challenging times for healthcare workers. The upstate New Yorker was fast-tracked through her last semester of school so she could help with the COVID-19 relief efforts. In 2020, she found herself working full time at a frantic hospital, shuffling from one heartbreaking death to another. Any free hours were spent educating herself about the latest pandemic policies or visiting patients in the ICU, holding vigil under harsh fluorescent lights. Beatrice didn't complain. She knew full well these were extraordinary times that required extraordinary sacrifices.

As a healthcare worker in a short-staffed environment, Beatrice felt overstretched, though she knew her work was crucial in the "horribly stressful, grim" situation. At one point, she had a full-blown breakdown as she felt completely hopeless after "trying to follow every order to a T and people still died." It was defeating.

Following the holiday season, when COVID-19 deaths hit a new peak, Beatrice was summoned to a Zoom meeting with her team and supervisor. The nurses had been working massive amounts of overtime and were in desperate need of a break. They had voiced their need for backup support so they could take a little time off, or at the very least get some extra compensation to take care of all the errands piling up at home.

But Beatrice's boss didn't offer that kind of relief. Rather, the staff supervisor gave a presentation about employees' need to engage in self-care activities, asking them, "What are *you* doing to take care of yourself?" The suggested solutions were yoga, running, and drinking more water.

Beatrice was at first perplexed, and then furious. Why was the onus

---

* Throughout the chapters, you will notice that some people are referred to by their first name only. These are people who preferred to speak anonymously or whom I interviewed in a specific setting, not necessarily for this book—and as such, they are not fully identified or go by a pseudonym.

on *her* to fix a situation the hospital had put her in? Even a monetary bonus toward her student loans would have been more meaningful. When would the staff be able to exercise amid twelve-hour-plus shifts? How would sipping more water ease her anxiety? "It's patronizing that during a pandemic you're asking service workers to do so much more than they've ever been asked to do and then their employer doesn't absorb any of the responsibility . . . it's victim blaming," said Beatrice. "At a certain point, employers are morally responsible for what's going to [psychologically and physically] happen to their staff."

To Beatrice, the suggestions came across as taking further advantage of a gendered profession, since 90 percent of nurses are women. She felt they targeted what little energy women—forever society's caretakers—had left. "[Our employer] knows we would never go on strike," she fumed, "they know we care too much about our patients."

If you can't take the heat, the saying goes, then get out of the kitchen. But what if the kitchen is on fire? Telling overworked nurses to do yoga is similar to walking into a sweatshop and informing the employees they really ought to do something about all that stress. *Maybe they shouldn't be working insane hours.* Employers can dangle workplace wellness initiatives to offset the stress they create in part because we've accepted the concept en masse: it's *our* job to fix what's "wrong" with us. Consequently, employers are always suggesting more ways to get well, yet never offering less work or more substantial help.

My pet peeve is when companies offer "wellness days" but don't readjust the workload so that we can actually take advantage of them. Employees secretly work anyway, then resent their employers who pat themselves on the back for accommodating "work-life balance."

Or worse, companies offer nothing more than empty virtue signaling for press attention. In 2021, Nike publicly announced it was closing its corporate offices for a week in the name of mental health. Employees were told to "destress" and spend time with loved ones—a move rattled off in self-congratulatory statements shuffled out to reporters and applauded in

LinkedIn posts. But guess who reportedly didn't get time off? Warehouse and retail employees, proving that only white-collar workers matter to management. And you can be sure the company's burnout "break" didn't extend to all those hushed-about subcontracted factory workers abroad. The same goes for the athleisure darling Lululemon, which partnered with the United Nations Foundation to promote mental health for humanitarian aid workers and posts Instagram statements like "Everyone has the right to be well." That is, save for their outsourced Bangladesh factory's female workers who, in 2019, reported that they were beaten, overworked, verbally abused, and denied sick leave. These women said their paltry pay wasn't enough to survive on. They allegedly made roughly $112 a month, just $6 shy of being able to afford a pair of the very leggings they produced.[28] But you won't see that scrawled on Lululemon's feel-good mantra–covered tote bags.

I'm all for learning stress management techniques to aid us throughout day-to-day chaos. This is not a case against yoga. My point is that we should take a step back to analyze the root issues. Stress is rarely a matter of a broken brain or a poor "lifestyle choice" but often a symptom of the structural issues facing society. At times, wellness can serve as a disciplinary power whenever our emotions are unruly, or as horse blinders to keep us on track. We're instructed to revel in feel-good escapism, thereby tuning out the untouched problems. Instead of pointing the finger at management, we absolve them of guilt; we use self-care to become mentally bulletproof, the better to serve corporate needs. Mastering your stress, it would seem, helps toe the company's bottom line.

"[Burnout] is not a disease. It's not a medical condition," says Christina Maslach, a professor at the University of California, Berkeley, and a pioneer of burnout research. She created the Maslach Burnout Inventory (MBI), the most widely used instrument for measuring work-related stress. "To treat it as such means it's inside the person and the individual has more responsibility to take care of it on their own. It really misses a whole other part of what's going on in life, which is that there are stressors out there." Maslach is not opposed to relaxation tools, but there's a balance that's since been distorted. We believe our feelings are supposed to change while an imperfect system should remain as is.

The wellness industry stepped in to fill a void created by the unreasonable expectations that torment us. Self-care promised salvation, deliverance from the evils of stress. But if it's a toxic workplace, a meditation program isn't going to fix it. A fitness app won't solve the uneven distribution of housework within your marriage; CBD gummies will not enforce better childcare policies; bath salts won't stop late-night work emails. Buy whatever makes you feel good, but realize that these are short-term mental Band-Aids that do not ensure long-term redemption. Wellness remedies help, but the problem is that they're sold to the public as miraculous cure-alls.

We've somewhat butchered what "self-care" means. Historically, it stems from far more radical, activist roots. Marginalized groups in the 1960s adapted the medical term in response to the lack of adequate attention from mainstream medicine. Health care, they proclaimed, is a civil right—one that should be available to all, no matter one's skin color, ethnicity, or income. And if the powers that be failed to provide it, individuals would take it into their own hands.

In time, community members themselves took it upon themselves to serve their own. Hispanic civil rights groups set up programs to combat the lack of access to affordable health care; the Brown Berets, a Chicano activist group, founded the El Barrio Free Clinic in East Los Angeles. Likewise, the Black Panthers created and operated more than a dozen health clinics in underserved areas. These community-focused care centers offered a host of free services, ranging from food pantries to blood pressure screenings. Many centers were stationed in trailers or run out of storefronts and staffed by volunteers. But they all had a strong message: together we can take health into our own hands.

The Black activist and writer Audre Lorde expanded on the concept of self-care, viewing it as a radical vehicle for personal health in order to address larger societal issues. She wrote in 1988, "Self-care is not self-

indulgence, it is self-preservation, and that is an act of political warfare."
At the time, Lorde was battling cancer. Self-care meant survival—so that
she could continue to fight against racism, sexism, and homophobia.

Taking care of oneself was acknowledging your needs so you could
adequately push back against a system of social inequality. It caused one to
ask, "How can I fight injustice or overcome adversity if my tank is empty?"
Self-care meant standing up for yourself to declare, "I need more." I need
to protect my mental and physical health so that I can right what's wrong
not just for myself but for others too.

Self-care *today* is far more inward-looking—and dependent on a purchase. Not only that, but it hands the problem back to the sufferer, repack-
aged and tied up in rugged individualism. America has always treasured
the lone soldier who relies solely on grit and perseverance. But it seems
like we're giving up on communal change to cocoon ourselves, building
our own Noah's ark in place of petitioning God to spare the fate of our
fellow man. That's the new American way.

In this regard, we prioritize our inner private response over our potential ability to change situations via collective effort. By reimagining stress
as something that can be overcome individually—separate from social,
political, and economic influence—we are barring it from actual strategies
to fix it.

To be fair, we obviously can't tackle the root problems of all our stressors.
That mentality doesn't get us too far when we're stuck in traffic. But escapism
and consumption do not promise real change. Actual progress only comes
from engaging in whatever was responsible for the stress in the first place.
Self-care should move you toward a life you don't need to run away from.

Maybe We Should Use Stress to Get (Politically) Moving

One could say we need to jump off the Peloton and fight for change, which
is, of course, easier said than done. Structural transformations such as subsidized childcare or extended paid parental leave require complicated fights

that most American women can't afford to consider for many reasons—financial, emotional, and more. But certainly nothing will change if we lose sight of the real issues.

What would happen if we mobilized even just a little instead of performing so many downward dogs? Could we use all that energy to demand smaller but still worthwhile longer-term solutions? Wouldn't that be preferable to shoving issues under the frayed rug?

Not that everyone suffers from soul-crushing burnout; some simply battle everyday chronic stressors that add up over time. Changes like organizing your own hours or taking adequate lunch breaks might not sound significant or sexy, but they might eventually lessen the stress weighing you down.

I've been in workplaces where the women came together to demand extended maternity leave. I've witnessed managers give Friday afternoons off after several employees complained of burnout. I've been in a newsroom where the staff stood up and organized a union. We can collectively treat some structural issues: a human resources department can dismiss your individual request, but what about when it's a whole group—or a whole department—that's asking? That's a lot harder to ignore.

With more flexibility and fewer hours tied to a Herman Miller chair, mothers could make it back home for bedtime. Women could have time for physical movement in their daily schedule. Perhaps if we implemented these changes, we wouldn't be constantly exhausted and "sneaking" an hour of solo time. We could enjoy our friends and family and look after ourselves.

In other words, we'd have a life.

In a way, there's been a sliver of a silver lining to the pandemic, which inadvertently sparked a backlash to workaholism. Whereas in the past we may have believed stress is a good thing that builds character or resilience, now we're (hopefully) leaning into a healthier work-life balance. While we once battled employers who insisted corporate life had to be a certain way, social distancing regulations proved that we *could* do things differently.

Suddenly we discovered society wouldn't fall apart if we worked from home instead of commuting long hours and rarely seeing the kids. The office, we learned, wasn't essential.

We all came to the realization that many of our previous workplace mandates were unnecessary or burdensome or just plain dumb. We began insisting on better alternatives moving forward.

• • •

In a sick way, we're sedating women with consumerist self-care—or worse, silencing them instead of encouraging them to vocalize their grievances. I want to see headlines that read STRESSED? HERE'S HOW TO CRAFT A LETTER TO YOUR BOSS STATING YOU WILL NO LONGER CHECK EMAIL AFTER WORK HOURS or FIVE WAYS TO TELL YOUR PARTNER TO DO THE DISHES SO YOU CAN TAKE A SHOWER or HOW TO ORGANIZE YOUR WORKPLACE TO DEMAND BETTER BENEFITS. Why the hell is the advice always yoga? Weirdly, wellness is becoming almost as prescriptive as the medical industry. If we criticize some doctors for simply treating symptoms, why are we repeating the same mistakes with wellness?

The Class gave me the space to briefly reconnect and reset. But a few years into taking The Class, along with buying a host of other self-care products, I started questioning what was becoming a very expensive lifestyle. I had to ask myself: Was I significantly less stressed? How come the effect wore off shortly after? What else could help?

I also worry about how gendered this entire messaging has become. I spoke to one mother of a high school student who, along with her classmates, was resisting an elective offering. The curriculum mandated that boys would get to play team sports, while the girls would learn "how to relax" with a wellness course focused on yoga, meditation, and spa activities. Students complained that boys would learn team building skills, leadership abilities, and strength training exercises while the school presumed girls were so fragile that they needed a less demanding, soothing alternative. The mother described how the girls were required to buy "soft, pretty things." The boys just needed to show up in shorts.

In the nineteenth century, "hysterical" women were sent to an asylum. In the twentieth century, they were put on Valium or Xanax. Today, they're directed to a wellness app.

Stress exists for a reason: it's a mental state informing us that something is wrong. And yet we're constantly told this is something we should bury away. When women furiously pedal away on a Peloton to "silence their mind," you begin to ask: *Why should we silence our mind?*

Maybe my mind has legitimate complaints.

Chapter 2

The House Always Wins

Nearly every single lifestyle interview with a female celebrity sounds the same, as if they all rolled off the same conveyor belt. When asked about their daily routine, you get something like this: *I get at least eight hours of sleep because rest is so important. When I first wake up, I meditate before reaching for my phone (to practice gratitude, which keeps me grounded). I make sure to drink eight glasses of water (gotta hydrate!), then do yoga at least three times a week. And I always make sure to eat clean!*

It's like a game of health buzzword bingo, where at some point, the actress in question will comply and rattle off the revitalizing effects of whole foods. The questions might differ a bit, but answers remain the same: pure, unprocessed, *untainted*. Drew Barrymore eats "really clean and healthy" (along with doing an hour of Pilates four days a week).[1] Zoe Saldaña prefers "superclean" and "fresh" foods. And former vegan Olivia Wilde said she tries her best to eat healthfully but admits to the occasional Coca-Cola.[2] It should be noted that a decade ago, before the wellness revolution, magazines rarely asked celebrities to list their hour-by-hour health habits. Now it's standard practice.

"Clean eating" has become shorthand for eating as healthfully as possible, ascending to the crown jewel of the wellness industry's nutritional advice. Though lacking a clear definition, you're encouraged to fully recognize and pronounce every ingredient you put in your mouth—the consumption of food in its most natural state. That means whole foods such as vegetables and fruits, but no (or minimal) dairy, gluten, added sugars, or processed foods. It's a trend that's gained traction over time: In a 2015 Nielsen survey, more than a third of respondents reported they were choosing to consume fresher, more minimally processed foods.[3] By 2019, "clean eating" was the most widely cited food regimen, according to the International Food Information Council. The hashtag #eatclean has been used more than 60 million times alone on Instagram.

Clean eating is alluring because it is full of promises. Liquefied celery and various juicing programs assure you a sexy body, more energy, glowing skin, improved digestion, and the Tesla of immune systems. Heck, it may even be "the key" to balancing hormones and stabilizing mood swings. "Everyone's toolbox for optimal wellness looks different," Gwyneth Paltrow writes in the introduction to her cookbook, *The Clean Plate*. "For me, the most powerful reset button is food. I don't know any magic bullets, but eating clean comes close . . . There's a marked difference, for the better, in how I feel, and to a lesser degree how I look, when I'm eating at least fairly clean."[4]

I'm not surprised that many women and celebrities bask in the glow of turmeric-infused ginger shots, convinced that clean is the better way to eat. I've dabbled in it myself. It sparked my interest as a good way to get healthier and reverse a decade of ordering *pad see ew* for dinner. If I was constantly drawn to salty takeout, I reasoned, then I'd need a strict protocol to ensure I didn't drop dead from noodle overdose. In a way, clean eating felt like a protective barricade. With only lettuce and farm-fresh eggs permitted, I could seclude myself from oh so many greasy temptations.

I was intrigued when a functional medicine nutritionist wrote we only needed to shift our mindset to eat clean, *to feel our best*. "Food is medicine, and your mind is the cure," she wrote. Should we cave and give into mac 'n' cheese, it's because we use food "as a distraction, a reward, or to placate an emotion." Hence we needed to "dismantle" our reptilian brain's desire for a cookie at the end of the workday. That is, if we want "the vitality, clarity, and radiance that comes from consistently eating a clean diet."[5]

I did want vitality, clarity, and radiance. I wanted whatever Olivia Wilde was having.

Health was one part of the attraction. But if I was being completely honest, health took a backseat to another more pressing intention. Clean eating, like many other trendy food philosophies, hides ulterior motives—bad aims I wouldn't have necessarily noticed because they were hidden under glowing press coverage that made the idea sound so very appetizing.

But the hidden agenda is there. And it's as old as the diet it embraces. For clean eating isn't even all that new. Nor is Gwyneth Paltrow the first clean food influencer; she's heir to a long tradition—from the Atkins, South Beach, and Mediterranean diets to even more far-flung ancestors.

Flashback: The Moralistic Origins of the Graham Cracker

The mob of Boston business owners headed straight for the Marlborough Hotel front door, shouting and clamoring for blood as carriages rolled by. Butchers carried cleavers, bakers clutched rolling pins as their stained aprons flapped in the fall wind. Brawling their way forward, they came to collect the one who made that year, 1837, their poorest-performing one yet. Bread sales were down, and chunks of beef piled up in display windows. Their shops were on the verge of closing, and they knew who was to blame: a Presbyterian minister by the name of Sylvester Graham.

Barricaded in the hotel dining room, Graham and his supporters thought quickly. They ran into the kitchen, then dashed up the stairs to the rooftop. Staring down upon the crowd, they began pelting the rabble with bagfuls of limes, one after another.[6] The mob soon dispersed. Graham's life was spared.

What had caused such a literal food fight? How did a minister turn bakers into sworn enemies? Graham said something unremarkably common by today's standards but which back then constituted heresy: he told people not to eat certain things. And Americans, especially women, ate it up.

In the 1800s, Graham captivated a public terrified of the cholera pandemic. By Graham's account, sickness stemmed from an unsuitable way of life in which Americans consumed a heavy amount of meat and "unnatural" store-bought foods. A gifted orator, Graham lambasted American gluttony, claiming that overindulgence corrupted both body and soul. Salvation, he claimed, lay with rest, exercise, and a bland diet. (Flavorful condiments like mustard and ketchup, for example, could cause insanity.) He advocated "food in its natural state" not only to stay healthy but to reduce sexual tendencies.[7] It was clean eating with an added dose of repression. And like many fads to come, it mixed spirituality with pseudoscience.

Graham jump-started the idea that people can't fully trust that which is produced out of sight. At the time, some shops and bakeries packed their mass-produced products with fillers like chalk and clay, or what Graham described as "the most miserable trash that can be imagined." Homemade food was ideal, he advocated, as it ensured the purity of whole grains and fresh ingredients. Graham explained how to use unsifted whole wheat flour to bake plain, simple (or flavorless) bread. And hence the graham cracker was born, though far from anything Nabisco's Honey Maid produces today.

But Graham's philosophy also centered on how to attain a certain body size. "Grahamites" weighed themselves to assure they *weren't* losing weight because, at the time, a voluptuous body was fashionable. Some historians consider this diet the first to connect eating with weight, whereas before, food restrictions centered on spirituality or indigestion.[8]

The minister gained such a huge following that an entire collection of brand extensions popped up in the 1840s, like Graham hotels and boardinghouses. His popularity soon became an actual threat to the food industry. The press, however, was less than impressed, calling Graham "the philosopher of sawdust pudding." Ralph Waldo Emerson dismissed him as the "poet of bran and pumpkins."[9]

Graham passed away at the age of fifty-seven from, ironically, complications from several opium enemas. And Grahamism, like all fad diets, petered out. But a preoccupation with unwanted ingredients and "pure" food—a knee-jerk reaction to industrialization—would repeat itself in time.

Is Clean Eating a Front?

Today, a parade of wellness influencers—a substantial number of them lacking any nutrition science or medical credentials—have amassed millions of followers with their meticulous food regimens, seemingly existing on a strict diet of grapefruit and homemade nut milk. Almost every single wellness guru claims an identical origin story: they didn't feel well, realized they ate too many processed foods and swam in chemical-laden products, then repented. Like messianic messengers, they saw the light around "clean" and are now healed, which is why their lives are now so fabulous.

Unlike in previous eras, these crusaders have far more influence: social media allows for the rapid proliferation of clickbait in a way *Prevention* magazine or a best-selling diet book never could. They reach their fans every single day, sometimes multiple times on any given day. They do not live on your nightstand, waiting for a free, quiet moment to be read. They are in your pocket, ready to interact at all hours. Just click on the Instagram icon.

Their success isn't merely due to the ease of their availability, however. Like their counterparts from much earlier eras, what these influencers are selling goes directly to the heart of our aspirational selves. Because sure, I thought health was nice, I guess. But you know what I thought was even nicer? Looking good. Having a svelte body. For in 2015, I finally met a kind, honest, and intelligent man. We got engaged a little over a year later and I breathed a sigh of relief: I could get off the dating carousel and rest on the solid matrimonial bench. But as one stressor melted away, another quickly took root in its place. I felt I needed to shed a few pounds to squeeze into a tight Johanna Ortiz ensemble for my wedding in 2017. (It had sequined palazzo pants—it was really something.)

Clean eating, level one of wellness food regimens, looked like the ticket to ride. And I didn't make the connection between clean eating and thinness all on my own. It was served up on a biodegradable platter by everyone who professed concern for healthier living. For all the flowery language of "nourishing" your body with broccoli salad, influencers hinted at something almost every American woman wants: an "acceptable" weight.

It's not just that clean leaders were all thin. They also pushed thin ideals. Some posted "before" photos of themselves, back when they were eating processed foods, juxtaposed with "after" photos of their impeccable physiques from clean eating (often, right next to a $600 Vitamix blender). Successful entrepreneurs like Amanda Chantal Bacon, founder of the cult supplement brand Moon Juice, gushed about a mostly sugar-, wheat-, and dairy-free diet that emphasized whole foods. "I'm heavily rotating the watermelon rind and aloe juice," she generously shared.[10] Simultaneously, she sold us on $49 supplement bottles that, among other lofty ambitions, promised to control "stress-related weight gain."

Almost everyone would sooner or later mention, *By the way, you'll lose weight*, either subtly or overtly. They were right: the clean eating regimen itself is so very limiting that you're nearly guaranteed to shed some pounds. Because you're forbidden processed food, you inevitably end up staring at an arugula salad. When Nabisco cookies are supposedly toxic, you resort to cauliflower. It's as simple as that.

Mass media and brand marketing also play the disguise-diets-as-health game. If in decades past, women were told to slim down to get a "beach-ready body," now slimming down is couched in a new mandate: to "be nutritious." Instead of counting calories, you're weighing kale intake. Magazines will claim that they're anti-diet, utilizing positive self-love language, but then promote the clean eating "lifestyle," the paleo "philosophy," or how to be "keto-friendly" alongside photos of thin models. It's all the same concept, just different outfits. By invoking health (who can debate the importance of health?) the media masks what is actually involved—namely hard work and a restrictive lifestyle.

What had begun as a legitimate concern over more nutritious food has devolved into a more PC reincarnation of diet culture. For everyone talking endlessly about "health," what a portion is truly saying is, *I want a specific body shape and size.* Not all, of course (we'll get to that in a later chapter), but a good chunk.

Perhaps there's no better indicator of this than Weight Watchers officially changing its company name. When I profiled the company's "lifestyle rebrand" in 2017, their executive team told me that Weight Watchers, which usually sees a spike at the start of a new calendar year, saw a new low in 2015. When they commissioned a survey, they found that what once worked with generations past now felt old-fashioned and reactive. In this newfound era of feel-good campaigns, Weight Watchers learned that the term "diet" was rife with negative connotations, not in line with the growing body positivity movement. The general response, as one senior vice president told me, was: "You are a diet brand, and frankly, we are no longer willing to diet."[11] So the brand ditched the word "weight" to simply go by WW. Their new tagline? "Wellness that works."

Updating the terminology isn't just about conflating thinness with health. Far from it. It isn't necessarily about health at all. It's about money. A lot of money. Because here's the dirty secret of most diets: *they don't work*. The house, as we know in gambling, always wins. The majority of people quit their overly restrictive diets after three weeks, reports the *Shatter the Yoyo* author and clinical psychologist Candice Seti, who works with chronic dieters. "And then all of the impacts of that diet play out: the restriction effect, the overeating, the frustration, the self-confidence drop . . . all of these things that come from the deprivation take hold and we end up feeling like a failure," Seti told me. It's estimated that between 80 to 95 percent of dieters regain the weight within a few years, propelling them to try another and another and another.[12]

You'll see friends utterly devoted to a diet, be it Atkins, paleo, Whole30, or intermittent fasting. The next year, they moved on to something else, having entirely forgotten just how religiously they once protested a certain food group. You're tempted to remind them, Hey, remember when I needed to change my entire dinner menu to accommodate your adherence to the keto diet? This constant revolving door of hot new eating regimens is what makes diets hugely profitable.

The same goes for "detoxes" and "cleanses," short-term dietary regimens which claim to remove "toxin" buildup from human organs. These scams are everywhere. You can pick up "detox" kits at your local Whole Foods or just scan any wellness influencer's Instagram page for hawked products that essentially amount to water, lemon juice, honey, and pepper. It's an appealing idea: eat crap and party hard, then purify the buildup to "reset" the system. Spring cleaning for the body! You'll often hear how it worked for the influencer or brand spokesperson, ergo, we are to presume it will work for us.

If only science confirmed such a convenient process. The thing is, we already have an efficient detoxification system in place: a liver, kidneys, skin, and lungs. "You cannot detox, period," states Ada McVean, a science communicator with the McGill Office for Science and Society. "There is nothing you can do to remove more toxins from your body short of eating and drinking and taking in nutrients to support your liver and kidney function."

Our biological systems aren't perfect (otherwise, we'd never get drunk or poisoned). But popularized detox kits won't do much of anything except maybe extra hydration. These products don't help organs work better or help one recover faster.

That doesn't stop peddlers from peddling. Goop favorite Dr. Alejandro Junger sells a $475 three-week Clean detox program that gets raves from Gwyneth Paltrow, who claims it left her feeling "pure and happy and much lighter."[13] In reality, some of the detox reviews on the Clean Program website and other sites note that any weight loss program's mileage will vary by customer and might even pose dangers to those for whom the change is radical to their system. While some buyers express great enthusiasm after achieving desired weight loss, others attest to headaches, nausea, hunger, fever-like chills, and plain old disgust.[14] Dissatisfied customers are unable to make it through a few days of the strenuous diet, the deserted pills proof of hunger's victory.

I have met very few women who have done a "cleanse" out of serious concern for their liver. More often than not, detoxes are crash diets with heftier price tags and better cultural clout.

It's gotten to the point where it's hard to tell the difference between health and diet culture anymore. Wellness brands infuse body pressures into their messaging—a blur so successful that women often don't even think about whether something is being sold to them for health reasons or to play into their desire to look like an unattainable ideal. When consumers do catch on, brands defensively feign ignorance.

Take Rae, a trendy line of wellness supplements found in stores like Target and touted in women's lifestyle publications. "We believe nurturing your mind and body isn't just essential—it's your power," reads their website. In March 2020, the brand announced it was pulling one of its products off the shelves after "obsessed" teen girls popularized it on TikTok as a weight loss aid. The specific item? "Metabolism-boosting" tincture drops. The brand claimed it was for health, but it's hard to believe anyone wants to enhance their metabolism except for dropping pounds. Rae paused sales of the product because "it was the right thing to do" and because they wanted to "remind young girls that they are strong and beautiful just as they are." But that was only after *Vice* published a report on teen use and the product's ineffective ingredients.

Why do we keep falling for these pseudo-health scams? Perhaps because we are a pathologically optimistic nation, forever clinging to hope and exceptionalism in the face of crude reality. We just keep holding out for this rumored "perfect diet," always out of reach. But also, because we've been force-fed diet culture from every which angle: TV, magazines, social media, and targeted ads. Detox ads follow me from Facebook to Instagram to Google search results like some sort of virtual stalker. We're bombarded, even at the supermarket. We're sold on gimmicky "cleanses" and extreme regimens that only benefit the $192 billion diet industry.[15]

"What you have to remember is that it's not science dictating what's popular," says Bill Sukala, "but marketing." Sukala is a clinical exercise physiologist and nutritionist who regularly exposes wellness pseudoscience and deceptive marketing. He warns that we're getting used to the white noise of nonsense. We forget that health has been commoditized with ambiguous terminology and meaningless jargon. And what sells, swells.

Sukala is almost nostalgic for the good old days when all we had to worry about was a few fad diets. "Now the gloves are off and it's become an MMA fight for eyeballs and dollars. Wellness marketers have gotten brasher." If we once bought NutriSlim cans, now we scoop up "detox" kits. It's as if we traded one addiction for another.

While we might laugh off the Orwellian coded language games of "wellness" brands and media sites, disingenuous marketing practices have deeper ramifications. Sukala likens it to a single drop of water. One drop doesn't do much. But if you leave the leaky faucet unfixed long enough, eventually it carves out a big enough hole in the side of a mountain. The constant slow drip systematically erodes people's ability to separate fact from fiction. Or, worse, their sense of self. "Marketing zeroes in on your pain points—every emotional, mental, physical vulnerability that you have," says Sukala. The irony, of course, is that these wellness companies and outlets are supposedly trying to make people healthier, "but in many cases, they're just shooting everyone in the foot."

The tsunami of misinformation has gotten so big that science communicators worry whether the genie can ever be shoved back inside the bottle. The landscape has changed. Competing against an avalanche of overnight influencers and Internet echo chambers takes more resources than are available. "The gatekeeper has been chloroformed," says Sukala. "There are no gatekeepers anymore. The inmates are running the jail and anybody can say anything."

But even with all these inmates running amok, some influencers attempt to push back against the nonsense. More than a few previously healthy women are openly discussing the damaging effects of extreme wellness-dieting tactics. They speak from personal experience.

Taking It Too Far: Clean Eating Extremism

"In the last few weeks it's become clear to me how silly it is that I am so afraid to share this on the blog and in my life," began the post. "It's not healthy to feel guilt for listening to your own body—I should be thanking myself, not telling myself I've done something wrong. I have 'sinned.'"[16]

In 2014, a successful wellness blogger named Jordan Younger decided to publicly break up with clean eating. The blond, blue-eyed, svelte influencer, who went by the moniker The Blonde Vegan, broke ranks with devotees of the wellness creed. On her blog, she recanted her "entirely vegan, entirely plant-based, entirely gluten-free, oil-free, refined-sugar-free, flour-free, dressing/sauce-free, etc." diet.

The eating regimen that propelled her to Internet stardom had left her worse off. Her so-called "bubble of restriction" had devolved into an 800-calorie-a-day intake. Some days she had a green smoothie for break-fast, kale salad for lunch, and roasted veggies with quinoa for dinner. Other days, she'd live off juice cleanses. At age twenty-three, she suffered near panic attacks over restaurant menus, fearing one bad choice would "throw off" her system. Even juice bars made her anxious if their beverages had more than a tiny bit of apple, fearing the sugar would set her back.

One time, Younger ordered oatmeal in a restaurant only to realize it was cooked with cow's milk. She "freaked out" and threw a tantrum.[17] Occasionally she was so starved of energy she would binge on dates, one of her only sources of sugar. Then she'd beat herself up for going off-script. "I was so sick and upset with myself, the only answer was to skip the next meal and have a juice instead," she recalled in her memoir.[18]

As the months progressed, the blogger wasted away to a mere 101 pounds. In time, Younger's nutrient-starved body began rebelling. Her hair was falling out in clumps and her periods had stopped. Her skin was turning orange from eating too many carrots and sweet potatoes. These were foods she had promoted to her audience of seventy thousand followers with the hashtag #eatclean, alongside selling copies of her detox cleanse program. Younger (who has since changed her brand's name to The Balanced Blonde) feared the heresy of abandoning that which she had so wholeheartedly advanced. "I felt the pressure to remain vegan—it's what my readers and followers lived for," she later told the *Today* show. "I was worried my whole business would come crashing down."

In a blog post to fans, Younger finally admitted she could no longer abide by clean veganism, stating, "It's time to advocate a lifestyle that doesn't involve restriction, labeling or putting ourselves into a box . . . I ask for your support and acceptance." Her request was denied: Younger lost hordes of followers and received countless angry emails, including a few death threats. Irate customers demanded refunds for her hawked apparel, namely $32 T-shirts emblazoned with the words OH KALE YES!

Some expressed their disappointment that she lacked the dedication to be "clean." Others discredited her entire journey, skeptical as to whether she actually ate whole foods. Some went so far as to doubt whether she was even really blond. "You weren't eating enough fruit!" they launched from their laptops. "Now you're just boring," another added. "No wonder you're so ugly." A few seemed genuinely offended, protesting, "You're putting down the **best** diet on Earth!"[19]

That Younger was not a nutritionist seemed lost on a group who so willingly abided by her advice. The heretic was sentenced to excommunication, her influencing powers revoked. She had unknowingly joined the religion of health, never foreseeing she would be burned at the stake. Later, she would reflect on "this cult-like mentality"[20] that simply couldn't handle a defector, an affront to the holy consumption they so valiantly upheld. Fanaticism, she decided, just wasn't worth the toll.

An unhealthy obsession with healthy eating has a medical name: orthorexia. It's food pickiness on steroids, or more like nutrition taken to an extreme degree. And it's what Jordan Younger had suffered from. How widespread is orthorexia? Hard to tell. Those who take to clean eating seem most susceptible. As it's so new, it's believed that less than 1 percent of the U.S. population engages in orthorexic behavior, although small studies attest to its growth among younger women.

In fact, eating disorders as a whole are on the rise: a 2019 study published in the *American Journal of Clinical Nutrition* found that the prevalence of eating disorders doubled between 2000 and 2018.[21]

When reporters asked Younger how it all started, she answered innocently enough: she wanted to be healthy. Younger just wanted to feel good and look good, so she adopted the *en vogue* wellness trend of the day.* She hoped to lose a few pounds but she was also searching "for something more in her life,"[22] and a restrictive eating regimen gave

---

* A survey of more than 1,200 Americans between the ages of fourteen and twenty-four found that over half learned about "clean eating" through social media, online sources, and their peers.[23]

her, not surprisingly, purpose. The willpower (or more like starvation) made her feel extraordinary. It gave her an identity. But she was likely also impacted by our society's lopsided views on women's health and appearance.

"We are told from all different kinds of sources, that we are a body first and maybe a human second," says Katherine Metzelaar, a "non-diet" registered dietitian and nutrition therapist. Before becoming a nutritionist, she battled orthorexia from age twenty-two to twenty-seven. Metzelaar had cut out whole food groups, including gluten, meat, eggs, and dairy. Over time, her diet grew more and more restrictive, excluding "anything that wasn't directly from the ground." She consumed only vegetables, nuts, legumes, and very little fruit, though she was also spending a ton of money on costly supplement powders. "I was deeply afraid of foods causing me some kind of harm, but the irony was that undereating and restrictive eating was harming me significantly. All I did was think about food," recalls Metzelaar. All the while, multiple friends and family members showered her with compliments and exalted her discipline. They'd say she was amazing or "so strong" and ask her for advice. In reality, she was "quite sick."

Clean eating doesn't automatically lead to eating disorders, but the way we discuss and treat food can lead to an unhealthy fixation with what we consume. Your average clean eater may not go to the same extremes as Jordan Younger or Katherine Metzelaar, yet the thinking baked into the message given to an ordinary dieter has a disturbing amount in common with the extreme thinking of orthorexics. It's a slippery slope, and one that needs plenty more guardrails.

Promoting Promises Your Body Can't Keep

Like restrictions of yore, clean eating moralizes our daily choices. Certain foods are deemed "good" and "natural," serving as a "detox" of all the bad foods clogging our arteries (and supposedly stretching our swimsuits). Celebrities list their "guilty" indulgences or "cheat day" menus. Influencers refer to cauliflower bowls as "plant-based goodness" and call sugar-laden cereal "poison." This type of language taints daily decisions with unnecessary virtues and vices.

Christy Harrison, the registered dietitian and host of the popular podcast *Food Psych*, lambastes this new culture that's more about "performing a rarefied, perfectionistic, discriminatory idea of what health is supposed to look like." Nutrition matters, but the notion that food is medicine (or poison) can twist people into all sorts of knots. "It suggests that consistently making the 'right' food choices will heal or prevent all ills and that eating certain kinds of food will inevitably harm our health," she writes. "Putting too much emphasis on our day-to-day food choices doesn't lead to improved health at all, but to a preoccupation with food and panic about our health."[24]

Constant deprivation proves anxiety-inducing and can lead to over-indulgence, inspiring more shame cycles. As Judith Matz, the co-author of *The Diet Survivor's Handbook: 60 Lessons in Eating, Acceptance and Self-Care*, explains, even the thought that something's going to be taken away is enough to lead to people bingeing on it. If someone says starting tomorrow, you can never have ice cream again, what would you do? You'd hold the local Baskin-Robbins hostage. Psychologically, we want what we can't have. "There's nothing wrong with that—it's normal," Matz told me. "And abundance makes us calm down when we know something's available. Like water, you don't have to think about it."

Absolutist guidelines and cutting out whole food groups can also lead to nutrient deficiency. Low-carb followers, for example, might experience low energy and brain fog, since carbohydrates provide the body with energy. Or, as in the case of clean eating, dietary convictions can increasingly take on more and more militancy. The boundaries keep tightening: more food groups get the axe, potentially jump-starting compulsion. First, the enemy is highly processed foods, then it becomes meat and fish (making protein harder to come by), then dairy (potentially endangering calcium requirements), then all sugar . . . until you're left with cabbage and a grumbling tummy.

A pursuit of perfection is praised, even though many people on ultra-restrictive diets are practicing disordered eating. But pressure is to be expected when women's bodies are scrutinized from a young age, thereby making them more susceptible to messaging about food as they grow older. One can just look at how the media obsessed over Selena Gomez's weight fluctuation or the late Princess Diana's body (since she was nineteen!) to understand that women's size matters.

Also, we're influenced by cruel messaging consumed with individual responsibility. We're made to believe that should someone get sick or gain weight, it's because they did something wrong. They didn't try hard enough. "Bad eaters" of today are yesterday's smokers: *Maybe you deserve this.*

There's nothing wrong with wanting to eat healthier. The issue is when diets gobble up too much headspace. WW (formerly Weight Watchers) alludes to this preoccupation in a 2021 ad starring spokesman James Corden. After the TV host says that *just by looking at his body* you can tell he's a "bad boy," he admits his head is bombarded with SmartPoints, the brand's food tracking system. "All the time I'm thinking about points: How many points is that, I'm scanning points, I'm over points, I'm under points, I've got my free points," he rattles off to a clinical psychologist. "And I've realized I don't know what a point is. What are points?"[25] The comedian has been driven mad by an imaginary calorie calculator he never even fully comprehended.

Again, WW calls itself a "wellness" company, though that word has more or less become a synonym for diet. The title of this video—"How Has James Corden Lost 20 Lbs?"—makes its true subject, weight loss, clear. And in it we once again see a successful "wellness" company's triumph of marketing the thing that we'll continuously consume and which requires significant mental energy. Lost in the *Beautiful Mind* math of counting points, we forgo time spent on the pursuits of a healthy life. We'd almost certainly be better off using the headspace to finish a long-term project, join a book club, or be more present with our children. But if the company sold us that, who in their camp, as the saying goes, would benefit?

The Skinny on Fat Myths

Clean eating doesn't just moralize our daily food choices, it moralizes our weight, period.

We're conditioned to look to weight as *the* telltale sign of health. But you can't predict medical outcomes just by looking at someone. Some higher-weight individuals are completely healthy, while some size 4 women harbor all kinds of illnesses. And vice versa.

The reality is that an individual's size is not the sole or even leading determinant or predictor of health.

This is not to say that weight doesn't play any role, but rather that weight is overemphasized in our skinny-obsessed culture. In conversations focusing on obesity, there is often a glaring omission of other elements that may lead to future sickness: genetics, poverty, stress, pollution, nutrition, and limited access to health care, physical activity, adequate sleep, or social support. If you live with ongoing poverty, wouldn't chronic stress impact your health? If doctors discriminate against your size, would you be more reluctant to seek medical care or go to checkups?

We don't know the effects of all these factors, and yet some health aficionados automatically, instinctively, jump to weight, partially because it's measurable. How can you, for example, quantify stress?

It seems we're constantly lectured about body size, specifically: how to shrink it. The diet industry, wellness gurus, "war on obesity" . . . they all disproportionately zero in on weight as an independent causal factor. The discourse is counterproductive, explains Paul Campos, the author of *The Obesity Myth: Why America's Obsession with Weight Is Hazardous to Your Health.* We have not figured out a way for people to successfully lose and keep the weight off, "at least not at a statistically significant level," says Campos.

One study of 22,000 adults who followed one of fourteen popular diet programs such as Atkins found that most weight loss is regained within one year.[26] Weight loss might not be achievable for a number of reasons. Maybe it's genetic. Maybe people don't have access to healthy food. Maybe they don't have a support system. Or maybe they need professional advice tailored to their unique situation. Also, human biology is not wired to shed pounds easily.

There are, of course, people who lose and keep off the weight, "but you can't focus social policy around outliers," says Campos. Society constantly scolds people that they *should* be thinner, but we've seen that they often *can't* be thinner. It's like telling teens from underprivileged backgrounds they ought to go to Princeton; it's easy to say, right? So too, the vast majority of people who are in the "overweight" category of the BMI (body mass index)—which is nearly one-third of all American adults—are being told to aim for a BMI range between 18.5 to 24.9, which is unrealistic. By setting people up to fail, we inevitably cause tremendous psychological damage.

"The emphasis on weight instead of health actually makes people sicker," notes Harriet Brown, the author of *Body of Truth: How Science, History, and Culture Drive Our Obsession with Weight—and What We Can Do About It.* "The level of shaming and stigma that is directed is a deterrent, not an encourager for better health behaviors."

And what about the physical health of these chronic dieters? After all, it's bad enough spinning through bouts of self-loathing, fearful eating habits, and stress—all of which have long-term consequences. But the news gets worse. Far from optimal health, research indicates that yo-yo dieting (also called weight cycling) has negative effects: chronic deprivation and fluctuating weight gain are associated with increased risk of heart conditions,[27] strokes, increased insulin resistance, and, naturally, feeling shitty when you just want a damn sandwich.

Despite all the "thin glamour," it's sometimes better to forgo struggling to hit a "normal" weight, experts note. "Each time you lose and gain weight, you double the risk of diabetes," says Dr. Kamyar Kalantar-Zadeh, a professor of medicine at the University of California, Irvine, who has led a study on obesity's impact on kidney disease. Dr. Kalantar-Zadeh will advise patients to change their eating patterns if, say, they have high blood sugar levels. But in general, he encourages patients to focus on healthier habits and weight stability, noting, "massive weight loss and weight gain [are] usually detrimental."

Dr. Kalantar-Zadeh joins other medical researchers in reexamining our de facto strategies. UCLA researchers analyzed thirty-one long-term diet studies, only to conclude that most dieters "would have been better off not going on the diet at all. Their weight would be pretty much the same, and their bodies would not suffer the wear and tear from losing weight and gaining it all back."[28]

Dr. Fatima Cody Stanford is an obesity medicine physician, scientist, and policy maker at Massachusetts General Hospital and Harvard Medical School. She believes in encouraging better nutrition choices without dictating restrictive diet rules or suggesting a target weight. "I never ask my patients the number of calories that they are eating," Dr. Stanford told me. "It has minimal importance when compared to the quality of what they're eating."

Throughout all this discourse, we continue to rely on the BMI as a measure for what's "overweight." The BMI is an outdated height-to-weight ratio tool that many researchers have called out for overly simplistic calculations. It does not account for muscle mass, bone density, genetic makeup, age, or body composition and variation. Not to mention that it was based on white European men and does not account for racial or ethnic diversity (as different populations can have different body compositions). It's ludicrous to assume such a one-size-fits-all measurement method can dictate an "ideal" body weight.

"This hyperfocus that we are all the same human, and we all have the same target, is just flawed," says Dr. Stanford, who prefers a personalized approach to nutrition. The BMI was never intended to measure individual health, and yet it's used to judge millions. To give you an idea of how faulty the BMI is, celebrities who are technically "overweight" include Matt Damon, Will Smith, and Tom Cruise. As Keith Devlin, director of the Stanford Mathematics Outreach Project, has concluded, BMI ratios are "mathematical snake oil."[29]

But the more people are labeled "overweight," the more we can churn out diet consumers. That's more opportunities for diet programs, "detox" hawkers, and wellness gurus. And, historically, for insurance companies to charge higher rates for individuals with a high BMI.

I don't want to give the impression that there isn't a valid debate about body size. Researchers are certainly divided about weight's exact role in medical outcomes. And yes, studies have shown that individuals with severe obesity do have a higher risk of health complications like diabetes and heart disease.[†] Extreme weight—at both the high *and low* ends—is associated with medical issues. But the focus should be on encouraging healthier, sustainable habits.

Bottom line: it's clear that the relationship between weight and health is highly individual. A question we need to ask is, Even if we agree obesity carries risks, why do we think restrictive dieting is the answer? The evidence suggests that not only does it not work, it often causes harm.

Maybe it's to be expected in a country that proclaims a "war" on obesity not by targeting the culprits (stress, financial constraints, lack of time, sugary drink advertising) but by pointing the finger at individuals. People are responsible for fighting an uphill battle to eat nutritiously in our society, then shamed for a lack of "discipline."

Anti-fatness is woven into our cultural fabric, and by some reports it is slow to remedy. A Harvard University study analyzed millions of Americans' implicit and explicit biases, spanning sexual orientation, race, age, and other factors. In 2019, researchers discovered that overall, the country was demonstrating progress toward a less bigoted society. (An anti-gay

---

[†] While restrictive diets can be problematic, that doesn't mean all weight loss attempts should be shunned, especially if medically necessary. "Often, weight loss is required to reduce harmful fat storages," explained Bram Berntzen, a postdoctoral researcher at the University of Helsinki who studies lifestyle factors and their effect on obesity and related metabolic disorders. "However, we don't yet know how to do this effectively [on a large population scale]."

bias, for example, decreased by 33 percent in a ten-year period.) That is, save for attitudes directed at higher-weight individuals. Implicit weight bias—that is, pro-thin, anti-fat—increased 40 percent between 2004 and 2010. "We think the increasing attention to the health benefits of lower body weight and concerns about the obesity epidemic may be responsible for the increase in bias," writes the *Harvard Business Review*. "Additionally, the perception that body weight is always under one's own control (race, sexual orientation, age, and disability, on the other hand, are not) may lead to harsher attitudes toward those who are overweight."[30]

I am the first to admit I have internalized thinness culture and that I have been working on reversing its damaging effects for years now. But at the very least, let's not kid ourselves that ongoing rounds of dieting constitutes healthy behavior or that cleanse after cleanse is real wellness. Because the research just simply doesn't support it. This is the commodified wellness-diet complex, subsisting off skewed marketing to distort real principles of health. We may prefer a specific size, but as Candice Seti notes, just be mindful as to whether it impairs your mental well-being: Does it cause dysfunction? Does it in any way interfere with your personal or professional life? Does it cause extra stress?

These are questions I wish I could answer with a straight-faced "no." And I know I am not alone in that.

Combating the Guilt-Driven and Exploitive Dieting Psychology

Food can quickly become a guilt-generating machine. Too many blame themselves when they can't hit the goal, especially once weight factors in. "Good" eating then becomes less of a choice and more of a reflection of self-worth. And with that, we strip food of its original purpose—not just sustenance, but pleasure. Gosh, remember that? Remember *enjoying* food?

Professionals such as Matz and Metzelaar work to unpack clients' Santa sack–worth of food guidelines collected over a lifetime. Although clients don't follow a fraction of them, the weight of it all subconsciously affects their relationship with food. It's just as much about unlearning as it is about learning. Clients often mourn the loss of dieting culture and ask themselves: Who am I without this preoccupation? How can I be in a better relationship with my body? How else can I connect with women in a way more meaningful than debating almond butter brands?

An anti-diet philosophy called intuitive eating has gained traction as we've come to learn more about the harmful effects of cyclical dieting. The buzzed-about approach advocates listening to internal signals of hunger and fullness to guide eating choices, rather than subscribing to rigid rules. The idea is that humans have all the answers inside them once they unburden themselves of food anxiety. Peeling back the layers of harmful "good or bad" ideas that infiltrate one's relationship with food can help us reconnect to it without guilt or negativity. You don't need to eat "perfectly" to be in good health, as no one food will kill or heal you. You can have that damn cookie.

Elyse Resch, the co-creator and co-author of *Intuitive Eating*, points to the political climate, which has exhausted women to the point of seeking a more freeing lifestyle. They feel disconnected from their bodies, yearning for a more natural connection to their appetites. "[They are] really tired of being told how they should eat, how they should look, and are rebelling against that kind of oppression," she told me in 2021. (Of course, intuitive eating became such a popular idea that Gwyneth Paltrow co-opted the terminology to suit her empire: in 2021, the Goop guru began promoting "intuitive fasting," which is just structured starvation.)

Intuitive eating doesn't mean people don't overeat or choose McDonald's every so often, especially when stressed. Rather, it means food doesn't possess any moral significance: you don't beat yourself up for foods our culture demonizes, like pizza (which, while high in fat and sodium, is also actually quite nutrient-rich). "Having a healthy relationship with food is different than only eating healthy foods," clarifies Matz. "A healthy relationship with food allows you to eat all types of foods in a way that supports your body." This approach also accounts for the fact that each body differs in how it metabolizes food and nutrients, owing to factors varying from genetics to exercise levels.

Intuitive eating is not without its critics. Some assume it's only about hunger and fullness cues, while others argue that because it gives you free rein to eat whatever you want, it potentially will lead you down a path of overindulgence. This is an incorrect interpretation of intuitive eating, which does touch upon balanced nutrition in its ten principles (not rules). The criticism leveled at this movement is also quite telling: it assumes that as soon as you take your eyes off the prize—the scale, that is—you will devolve into a bonbon-munching maniac. (Our bodies seem to require constant vigilance and self-surveillance.)

But the nutritionists I spoke to say that's not the case. People will usually self-regulate once they pull away from a fear-based relationship with food, which triggers an avalanche of "taboo" cravings and overeating. In time, they choose a balance of nutritious foods, along with some "play foods," simply for the pleasure they provide. "It's about listening to what your body needs, listening to how your body feels based on what you choose to eat," clarifies Resch.

While intuitive eating may not be the right approach for everyone (and is certainly not an overnight process), experts say it's a good step for some in overcoming a fraught relationship with food. And unlike plans hawking shakes or products, there's not much to buy here—you can read about it for free online—nor are there promises reminiscent of exploitive diet culture. It's at least one potential way to escape bad habits.

• • •

More moderate solutions are surely welcome. As it turns out, clean eating ends up being remarkably difficult unless you're a forest rabbit. There are only so many roasted cauliflowers and salads you can eat before wanting to burn down a vegetable patch. In my clean eating days, I hallucinated Pepperidge Farm cookies. Rage became as familiar as hunger. I hated my husband for enjoying a frozen pizza in my presence. I was hungry.

It became so difficult to prepare appetizing "clean" meals that I did something nuts. I was reporting on the upsurge of fresh baby food delivery start-ups—imagine HelloFresh for rug rats. Companies sent me samples of pureed squash with spirulina and quinoa or mashed red peppers with black beans, avocado oil, cumin, and cilantro (all very highbrow for a baby). But I didn't just test them. I started living off them. I would empty several baggies of soupy pulverized beets for lunch. It was just way easier than cooking all those vegetables myself.

It all came to a head when my husband stumbled upon my newfound snacking habit. Every afternoon, I would buy a pack of Sour Patch Kids. But I wouldn't eat them. I would only permit myself to lick the sugar off, leaving a heap of sticky gelatin carcasses. That's how desperate I was for sugar. I lost five pounds and quit the regimen shortly thereafter, but my husband still speaks of the time his partner lost her damn mind. "Women do some *weird shit*," he'll remark while looking right at me.

I wasn't the only one throwing in the towel after succumbing to tempting wellness marketing. Even celebrities come around after having been around the hungry block. Olivia Wilde certainly had her own revelation. One day, just like Jordan Younger, the actress/director gave up being a "hardcore" vegan. Following a stressful period in her life, Wilde was done. "Fear of carbs, of gluten, of everything—we've distanced ourselves from the beauty of food, the art of it," Wilde told *Allure*, adding, "it makes me sad when people say, 'Oh, I don't eat gluten. I don't eat cheese. I don't eat this. So I eat cardboard.'"[31] Wilde's life was too hectic—and short—to shun food. If she craved chocolate or onion rings, she was going to help herself to it. She, like many women, had just about had it with denying herself what she wanted.

And what we want is quite simple: to eat in peace.

Chapter 3

Is My Face Wash Trying to Kill Me?

On a chilly March morning in 2018, one hundred women—two from each state—marched up the steps of the Capitol Building. Clad in sleek power suits and designer sunglasses, they topped off their look with bold red lipstick. Balancing handbags in one hand while taking selfies with each other, they laughed and posed for loved ones back home. The side of one of their charter buses was emblazoned with the motto THIS TIME, IT's PERSONAL.[1] Their palpable energy was like that of an army before battle. Or teens exiting a limo on prom night.

These women represented the billion-dollar "clean beauty" company Beautycounter. And they were on a mission: lobby Congress to nix harmful chemicals from personal care products. Specifically, these women came to support the Personal Care Products Safety Act, a bipartisan bill to promote industry transparency and strengthen cosmetic regulations. They were there to educate politicians on "clean beauty," a relatively new (and shifting) term that refers to products free of any proven or suspected "toxic" ingredients. They wanted to remove "bad" ingredients—be they synthetic or "natural."

These women were representative of many more. Beautycounter counts more than sixty thousand independent salespeople—called "brand advocates"—who are drawn to the company's mission. Beautycounter employs a direct retail marketing model (or what some might call multilevel marketing) that could be described as an activist twist on Avon. Consultants sell the products online and peer-to-peer within their communities, persuading others to buy a face wash and also telling them why they need clean beauty. The latter is what inspires many women to get involved. Their mission feels important, as if the power to prevent sickness (or impact legislative change) lies in their ability to off-load an eye shadow palette. It gives them a sense of pride. As one Alabama-based brand advocate—or salesperson—explained, "The example I am setting for my children is immeasurable. When I returned home from D.C., the first thing out of my daughter's mouth was, 'Mommy, did you change the world?'"[2]

"Empowerment" is a word thrown around a lot with this group. The more I learned about these consultants, I could see why. Show up at your neighbor's door hawking Mary Kay cosmetics, and they presume you've merely found a new side hustle. But show up with a whole awareness campaign on women's health, and suddenly you're Maria Shriver. Blurring the lines between advocacy and salesmanship, Willy Loman got a socially conscious makeover.

Beautycounter founder Gregg Renfrew led this battalion of concerned women who had little or no political experience. Renfrew, with her honey highlights, minimalist jewelry, and understated makeup, exudes effortless professionalism. Think jeans and a striped T-shirt topped with an open blazer. With a high-wattage smile, she rattles off stats and political facts at breakneck speed, made digestible by her ease and optimism. Laughter comes easily to her. She's enthusiastic, but not too enthusiastic. The kind of entrepreneur young women of that era aspired to become.

Beautycounter hopes to change the landscape through activism, deploying an arsenal of charcoal facial masks and lipsticks as a Trojan horse for personal care product reform. "It was never about getting beauty products into the hands of everyone," Renfrew told me. "It was about getting *safer* products into the hands of everyone."

Which brings us back to that energized morning in D.C. As a reward of sorts, Beautycounter flew in a hundred of their top-performing brand advocates to enjoy a weekend of fine dining, champagne, and socializing. They enjoyed a dinner at the National Portrait Gallery before knocking on politicians' doors. They regaled elected officials with moving personal anecdotes, cancer recovery stories, and hopes for their children's health—their passion rubbing off like red lipstick on a shirt collar. Just as the sign on their bus proclaimed, their mission was *personal*. "[Our community] believes in being part of something bigger than they are as individuals," says Renfrew. "Given all that's transpired [since 2016], women have woken up to the fact that maybe our voices haven't been heard as loudly as we would like."

Now their voices *are* being heard. The fight to guarantee beauty product safety has gained momentum on a national, state, and even local level. Shoppers want to know what's in their moisturizer just as they want to know what's in their Goldfish crackers. I see it everywhere. Facebook friends post on how to banish parabens and sulfates from bathroom cabinets. Acquaintances declare they want to "feel good" about what's seeping into their skin, "the largest organ in the body." Friends imagine a *Psycho* shower scene of a shampoo bottle stabbing us with invisible chemicals. Many of their concerns could have come straight from a Beautycounter ad.

But Beautycounter isn't the only firm selling us "clean" and raising an alarm about chemical exposure. If you've read any women's magazine in the last decade, you've likely come across the following stats: Some studies suggest these chemicals play a significant role in early puberty, obesity, cancer, and infertility. Activists say thousands of personal care products contain synthetic chemicals known as endocrine disruptors, which mimic and therefore confuse the body's natural hormones.

That's in addition to all the publicized lawsuits. In 2019, Johnson & Johnson recalled 33,000 bottles of baby powder due to accusations centered on traces of carcinogenic asbestos. Claire's pulled makeup products after the FDA indicated the possible presence of asbestos fibers.[3] WEN Hair Care settled a class action lawsuit after they received thousands of complaints, some from people who claimed their hair came out in clumps. Headlines like these left me skeptical of the government's ability to regulate chemical safety. Was it Big Tobacco all over again?

By the time Beautycounter went to Capitol Hill, I too was "aware." In the Sephora beauty aisle, I began checking out the "clean" skin care products and second-guessing my Pantene conditioner. When I received a bottle of a Bath & Body Works shower gel as a holiday gift, it sat in the corner of my bathroom for months. Finally, I emptied it into the guest bathroom hand soap dispenser, rationalizing, *Visitors will only use it once or twice a year. How much chemical damage could it do?* My husband watched from afar, not fully comprehending the switch-and-bait occurring within what had now become a soap caste system. He freely and merrily continued using his Kiehl's soap and Mitchum deodorant. "I really don't think about that stuff," he shrugged.

I started writing articles about how and why millennials were flocking to "chemical-free" alternatives. I named Beautycounter as one of *Fast Company*'s Most Innovative Companies of the Year. I also started shopping. A lot. Suddenly, my bathroom shelf exploded into a mini apothecary of Goop-approved products. If I was already spending money, I thought, why not drop a bit more cash and get the *better* option. Why take the risk of convenience store sushi when you can go to Nobu?

Renfrew had been ahead of many of the other corporate players now crowding the clean beauty space. Starting the company wasn't Renfrew's first rodeo. The serial entrepreneur had previously found success with her bridal registry company, The Wedding List, which she sold to Martha Stewart Living Omnimedia in 2001. She was itching for a new project when she watched *An Inconvenient Truth*, Al Gore's documentary on global warming, in 2006. "It was really jarring," reflects Renfrew. "A real wake-up call. It was the first time that I began to contemplate my own life and how it was impacting the earth."

Many of Renfrew's friends were dealing with fertility issues and diagnosed with different types of cancer in their thirties. Others had given birth to children who had health problems or couldn't leave the house without an EpiPen. Reading up on the links between substances that are harmful to the earth and also to human health, she zeroed in on toxic chemicals in everyday products. She started washing her floors with water and vinegar. Nonstick cookware was thrown out in favor of stainless steel replacements. Plastic containers got the boot to make way for glass.[4] But when it came to purging her beauty cabinet, she was hesitant: Could anything less "toxic" really meet her high bar for skin care products? Where was the Clinique for Whole Foods shoppers?

Renfrew didn't just want to build a beauty company. She aimed to address the alleged systemic issues at play. "This isn't just shopping your way out of the problem," says Renfrew. And so the company continues to lobby Washington each year and to date has conducted more than 2,000 meetings, made 16,000 calls, and sent 200,000 emails to lawmakers. Renfrew hobnobs at political parties while her consultants host meetings with congressmen in their hometowns.

Beautycounter is fighting for the whole beauty sector, because without regulatory support from the government, clean beauty is still very much out of reach for the average consumer. Clean beauty basics generally cost quadruple the price of a drugstore equivalent. A Beautycounter foaming cleanser runs $35, in comparison to Neutrogena's mass competitor at $5.29. Beautycounter's red lipstick—the same one worn by the Capitol Hill marchers—costs a cool $34. Their aluminum-free deodorant, beloved by Jennifer Garner, goes for a whopping $28. You won't find these at your local Food 4 Less. Hence, Renfrew hopes to represent all consumers in the marketplace through the company's efforts. "Safer products should be a reality for everyone," says the founder. "This is about all people."

Indeed. Though presumably we want to be sure we're steering people in the right direction.

Flashback: Women as House Managers:
Foot Soldiers for Health

Boston, Massachusetts, 1870. The faculty at MIT were at a standstill. The chorus of mustachioed men, dressed in varying hues of gray and black suits, were huddled to debate the admittance of a female student. One by one, they addressed the potential issues. Could the applicant keep up? Would this compromise the institute's standing? Did women even have the intellectual capacity to study science?

The student in question was Ellen Swallow (later Richards), a Massachusetts farm girl with a bachelor's degree from Vassar College and a passion for sanitary chemistry. Despite the initial discrimination, Richards prevailed to become the first woman admitted to MIT. A true trailblazer, Richards studied popular packaged foods of her day, in which she found sugar mixed with chloride or cinnamon powder full of sawdust and sand—a discovery that would later inspire the Pure Food and Drug Act of 1906, which prohibited the mislabeling of food and medicines.

At the time, Americans faced a rapidly changing environment: new diseases, new technology, and new public health challenges. Before the advent of advanced sewage systems, illnesses like typhoid fever killed 20 percent of those infected. As germ theory seeped into the national consciousness, how to limit disease in an easily contaminated environment was a popular topic.

As a fierce consumer advocate, Richards acknowledged the need for government and industry oversight of commercial products, but she also encouraged homemakers (and their domestic servants) to oversee their surroundings. She instructed women how to wipe down floors, purify water, and safeguard food. To Richards, chores were "a fine action, a sort of religion, a step in the conquering of evil, for dirt is sin."[5] The man would come home from the factory dripping in evil germs, and the woman's job was to scrub them all away. This art of protection was deemed "domestic science," which we now know as home economics.

Richards believed that a successful housewife "was constantly asking herself what could be better, healthier, cleaner, or more effective in her home."[6] Under this newly intense scrutiny, home-care grew fraught with anxiety. It was up to women to ensure that their children were not carried out in tiny caskets. Then companies began to realize they could capitalize on the fear. A slew of brands marketed a wide range of disinfectants under the guise of sanitary adherence. Women who had been lured to professionally study the science of sanitation with hopes of educating their peers soon found themselves hired to market the latest household appliance or cleaning agent—some of them fraudulent or unnecessary.[7]

What did their tactics look like? To sell iceboxes (nonmechanical refrigerators) in the 1920s, they emphasized the importance of fresh food while invoking gendered and exaggerated fears. Cold storage meant less contamination and thus fewer children's deaths, they claimed. As one fridge pamphlet warned: "When a baby's health hangs in the balance the intelligent mother will see to it that the ice supply never runs too low."[8] Women had become both corporate foot soldiers for health and household safety leaders who couldn't afford *not* to rely on consumerism.

Marketing to Women:
"Shopping Right Will Set You Free"

Fear is a potent marketing tool. Today, as much as at the birth of domestic science, women are frightened into taking responsibility for family safety. "Asbestos. Formaldehyde. Lead. Not exactly the words you think of when you're purchasing your favorite personal care products," reads the website of the Environmental Working Group (EWG), an advocacy group popular within wellness circles. "Sadly," the EWG notes, "toxic chemicals in our cosmetics, sunscreens and skin care products have gone unregulated as far back as the Great Depression."[9] The EWG's solution for such paltry regulations? Becoming your very own inspector, supplied with lists of chemicals to avoid and a guide for interpreting product labels.

This practice is called precautionary consumption. As with housewives of yore, the goal is proactive oversight. It falls to you, the consumer, to vigilantly protect yourself and your loved ones from chemical dangers.[10] When you shop at the market, you are expected to recall all the restrictions to ensure safety. If you need a new bodywash, you must scout for a list of "dirty" ingredients. When buying a new moisturizer, you calculate, *Will this product cause cancer?* Each time you see an organic chicken sitting alongside a normal one in the meat section, you are forced to reckon, *How much am I willing to pay to keep my family healthy?* All the small decisions add up.

There's a lot we're told to to worry about. Women on average use twelve personal care products a day, exposing themselves, according to brand marketers, to 168 unique chemical ingredients. The average man, in comparison, uses six personal care products a day. A Beautycounter brand ambassador on Facebook assures: "With all the craziness surrounding us, it's nice to know that the products I'm using are significantly safer . . . giving me one less thing to worry about." By purchasing the right facial cleanser, one brings structure and order to a chaotic world.

The media joins the circus by asking women to evaluate every nook and cranny in their home and handbag. *Women's Health* tells readers to "green your beauty routine with these 5 natural makeup swaps" and warns that toxins are everywhere. Even our nether regions require vigilance: WARNING: YOUR VIBRATOR COULD BE MADE WITH HARMFUL CHEMICALS, one headline proclaims. In contrast, male magazine readers are fed features on fitness, diet, work, and biohacking their way to Chris Evans's abs. The word "toxic," if ever used, predominantly refers to an unhealthy relationship with one's boss.

Renfrew acknowledges that the clean movement was primarily built on women. "If you light the fire under the asses of women about something they care about," she says, "they're going to fight tirelessly," whether it's Mothers Against Drunk Driving or child safety initiatives.

Companies also target moms because they still bear the brunt of decision-making in the family, upholding the legacy of the woman's domain. Branch Basics—a line of all-natural, nontoxic home cleaning products—showcases a smiling woman washing her hands with her child in a pristine white kitchen, alongside the caption CREATE A HEALTHY HOME: EVERYTHING YOU NEED TO REPLACE DOZENS OF TOXIC CLEANING PRODUCTS. The Honest Company, which primarily focuses on moms, promises customers can "rest easy" knowing their products are made without "health-compromising chemicals."[11] The brand's campaigns and social media posts show mothers happily cuddling their children, including founder Jessica Alba. The actress turned entrepreneur claims there are "a lot of toxic chemicals in everyday products" and especially in baby products. With her line of products, however, moms don't have to choose between "what works and what's good for you."[12]

In a way, not much has changed since the 1930s. Back then, as the American historian Roland Marchand writes, advertisers believed women possessed a "greater emotionality" with "inarticulate longings."[13] Manipulating women's emotions continued for decades to come, as the feminist writer Betty Friedan expounded on in 1963's *The Feminine Mystique*. And the tactics continue today. Precautionary consumption plays on women's vulnerability and demands our vigilance. Made fearful of "hazardous" ingredients, our intense risk aversion manifests into a bible on what we can and cannot consume. Some items are forbidden to us, hence we scout for a kosher "clean" symbol ensuring we're on the right path.

Shopping becomes a layer of protection, but at a cost. Personal purity mandates drain time and resources—a limited commodity in an already hectic existence. Women still do more laundry, grocery shopping, and household cleaning than their male partners, regardless of any recent discourse on gender equality. Now they need to do it even better and *safer*, with noxious chemicals peering over their hunched shoulders. Adding to their sense of urgency, their children's lives could presumably be in peril; cancer and chronic conditions loom on the periphery.

In time, women might come to blame themselves should they fail to buy their way to healthy freedom. Dafna, a marketing consultant and mother of three young children in New Jersey, considers her home "clean." She buys strictly nontoxic cleaners, consumes only organic produce, and counts seven natural deodorants on her nightstand. Plastic bottles are banned, as is most processed food. "I'm basically the CDC of our household," Dafna explains. Naturally, she was shocked when her eight-year-old daughter showed signs of early puberty, including breast development. Her pediatrician's tests confirmed follicle growth on her daughter's ovaries.

The discovery sent Dafna into a tailspin that caused her to fault her diligence, believing if she'd just *tried harder* and completely banished all synthetic chemicals and GMOs, her daughter wouldn't be in such a predicament. She joined parenting groups and read health sites that stressed the need to eradicate anything that didn't grow straight out of the ground.

"It's so easy to lose yourself in these forums, you don't know which way is up," Dafna recalls of the avalanche of information. In detoxing her home, the worried mom threw out any items that she believed could be contributing to her child's unwelcome development. Dairy was replaced with almond milk (much to her husband's dismay), and the perfumes were shelved away. "Could I have protected her better?" she asks with a strained voice. "I *thought* I was doing a good job."

The hectic mom likens herself to a smartphone running twenty apps at once—likely to crash—versus her husband, running just one. "It's not that my needs come last," she sighs, "it's that they don't come at all." Dafna doesn't blame her spouse: he doesn't encounter even a tenth of the information thrown her way. In frustration, she framed a quote—Michelle Obama's response to Sheryl Sandberg's *Lean In* philosophy: "That shit doesn't work all the time."

Dafna is not alone in her frustrations. It's neither cheap nor easy to carry the safety burden. For those unable to afford the expense of clean products, questionable chemicals will simply have to do. Lacking the disposable income to assemble a pure bathroom counter, most women continue to worry about ingredients as the media warns they'll jeopardize their future health. Meanwhile, it's not like women can opt out of the entire system: our labor market demands a certain level of hygiene and beauty. Women need to smell nice, look good, and be "presentable" not only to get a job but to keep it. A female professional cannot simply forgo consumption; she might feel as if she cannot stop dyeing her hair (with products made from ammonia and peroxide) unless she's willing to be subjected to ageism.

Although "clean" is a relatively new concept, it has hijacked women's anxieties, not only about beauty but about food, household cleaners, and even over-the-counter medicine. Suddenly we're all terrified of chemicals. Justifiably? Perhaps. Or not.

"The Real Thing": A Return to the Natural Order

"Clean" isn't the only buzzword taking over your local Sephora. "Natural beauty" exploded in popularity alongside it, propelling luxury brands like Tata Harper into an industry worth billions. The naturals market is defined by products made from naturally derived ingredients stemming from plants and minerals, presumably free of synthetic chemicals. Think botanical ingredients that are usually in a fruit salad but somehow end up in your facial toner.

The appeal of nature is obvious, if not nostalgic. Nature worship has deep roots in American culture. (The naturalist John Muir, for instance, wrote that "nothing truly wild is unclean.")[14] By the more religious, nature is regarded as God's handiwork; therefore, the closer we get to it, the closer we are to godliness. In nature, we feel stripped down, minimal, and pure. We're clean in the most fundamental sense. And maybe that's a logical desire in a society in which we're divorced from nature and tether ourselves to tech in our artificial environments (like our cubicle offices).

We long for that which we feel missing, and what we're missing is minimalism. Everything feels overdone, overstimulating, and overwhelming. Less—as Marie Kondo tells us—is more.

A return to the natural order of things can presumably undo modern brutality, all the man-made "toxins" polluting our space and our world. More to the point, it signifies an awakening to the unhealthy environment around us. We want remedies and products to reflect our values: local, small, or handcrafted alternatives. The farmer's ideal. We long for days of yore, romanticizing village life when we personally knew the pig that ended up on our dinner plate.

Roughly 75 percent of millennial women say "natural" ingredients are an important factor in their purchases.[15] Consumers are drawn to naturals because they're "the real thing," believing that their bodies intuitively reject synthetic chemicals. They appreciate the authenticity of ingredients that have been "crafted" by nature, extracted from the beautifully evolved plants of the wild. Some women from ethnic communities use herbal remedies to reconnect to their cultural heritage, a link to a long maternal history. Likewise, people are attracted to the foreign, exotic, and ancient—centuries-old cures assumed to contain wisdom.

Corporate behemoths have flocked to this natural flame, eager to cash in. Clorox bought Burt's Bees, Colgate-Palmolive acquired Tom's of Maine, Unilever scooped up Schmidt's Naturals. Retailers built up entire "natural" and "organic" sections. Chemicals are out, "natural" is in—even in fashion. By late 2020, Gwyneth Paltrow could be found walking around her Brentwood neighborhood in a $100 white sweatshirt adorned with a single word: NATURAL.

All of this marketing does make you wonder: What even constitutes "natural"?

The Natural Fallacy

In 2019, the natural skin care brand Herbivore Botanicals advertised their $44 jars of Pink Cloud, a moisturizing cream reportedly made without harsh chemicals. "Everything we make is natural, chemical-free, non-toxic and entirely good for you," reads their website. The pretty, minimalist jars, inspired by the soft pink clouds of a Hawaiian sunset, quickly sold out. *Allure* posted a story to announce when it was restocked.

Alas, some who had scooped them up in time opened their jars of coveted loot only to encounter clumpy, funky-smelling goo. Their promised clouds of moisture? The texture of yogurt. A portion of Herbivore's naturally formulated products turned out to be moldy, and a recall was issued at Sephora.[16] As it happens, some "natural" beauty preservatives don't always work as well as their traditional "chemical" competitors. "Natural" preservative substitutes, if ineffective, can allow more contaminants—bacterial spores, yeast, and others—resulting in something more akin to a third-grade science experiment.

Herbivore wasn't the only company to experience this problem. The FDA increasingly recalls beauty products over bacterial contamination resulting from less effective preservation. And since "natural beauty" took off, dermatologists have reported an increase in patients reporting itchy red rashes, bumps, swollen areas, and other allergic reactions.[17] Such products often contain high concentrations of botanical extracts that can also be skin irritants. Not to mention that many "natural" ingredients are far less effective when it comes to results-driven skin care (aimed at wrinkle reduction, moisturizing, acne treatment, and other remediation) and lack the same rigorous level of clinical research. That means people are potentially paying a premium for inferior ingredients that not only underdeliver but (in rare cases) might irritate them.

But isn't natural supposed to be better than chemical?

Personal care products are all, technically, made of chemicals. The term "chemical-free" perpetuates science illiteracy because *everything* is composed of chemical compounds. Just because a company arbitrarily labels a product "natural," doesn't mean it isn't chemical. As one irritated Twitter user once tweeted at me when I wrote a story on the popularity of "natural" fragrances, "natural essential oils are complex chemical mixtures."

"[Beauty products] are all processed in some way," explains Perry Romanowski, a cosmetic scientist and formulator who delves into these complicated issues on his podcast *The Beauty Brains*. "You cannot go out into nature and pull a bottle of shampoo off a bush. There are no lipstick trees." A chemical is a chemical is a chemical; only its source and synthesis differ. But corporations love misusing the term "natural" as a way to distinguish their products, as if their concoctions are yanked right out of a garden.

The narrative surrounding chemicals in beauty products reminds me of a famous 1983 April Fools' Day prank. The *Durand Express*, a Michigan weekly newspaper, reported that dihydrogen monoxide—"a chemical known to cause death" if inhaled—was discovered in the city's water lines.[18] How terrifying! After paragraphs alerting readers to the chemical danger, the joke was later revealed: dihydrogen monoxide is simply the chemical name for water, literally H_2O. The lesson? Everything sounds scarier if you identify it by its chemical terminology.

There might be less confusion if the use of the label "natural" to market products was clearly defined and regulated somehow. But although there have been efforts to establish a standard for the term "natural," uniform definitions simply don't exist. Any brand can slap "natural" on a label regardless of the ingredient list. These distinctions are often false advertising, offering consumers nothing more than a pricey placebo and a way to satisfy conscientious shoppers despite negligible botanical content.

"Natural," by definition, means existing in or caused by nature. Anything beyond that is conjecture. In fact, many natural substances (e.g., arsenic, asbestos, mercury) are more toxic than man-made ones. Even the seemingly most benign of naturally derived products can be harmful if used in the wrong way. This includes "natural" remedies like essential oils, which can act as irritants and allergens—or worse. Our illogical deference to Earth's bounty has become so widespread that researchers had to give it a name: the "appeal to nature fallacy," which occurs when we automatically assume something is better just because it's natural, and likewise, worse if it's not.

When I interviewed scientists to get their perspective on the natural product press releases flooding my inbox, I learned that the issue is not about synthetic versus natural, but whether the ingredient is safe and effective for use in the way intended. But *why*, I pressed, do brands continue to push a skewed beauty narrative? Why incorporate incorrect terminology?

Because it works. Over 90 percent of consumers believe natural beauty ingredients are better for them, according to a survey.[19] "If that kind of marketing wasn't effective with the people that are buying cosmetics, they would do other things," says Romanowski.

This is Branding 101. To create a need for a product, one must differentiate it from its competitors, as Douglas Atkin explains in *The Culting of Brands: Turn Your Customers Into True Believers*. One must create a mythology that marks a clear distinction and flatters the shopper through shared values.[20] Much as Apple fans buy in to the notion that their hardware purchase makes them "think different" than humdrum Microsoft drones, natural products make consumers feel good, educated. You know something others don't, and your face wash reiterates your inherent authenticity and environmental concern. Only "normals" buy in to the mainstream system. But not you: You know what's up. You are not satisfied with the status quo. *You care.*

Brands and influencers capitalize on legitimate yearnings. But they sometimes take it up a notch, assigning to nature fantastical traits and inherent virtue. They lean in to near-religious associations to sell nature as "purer" and "safer" (often without scientific backing) or to claim unsubstantiated superiority. Nature becomes something to worship. In some cases, you could easily substitute the word "God" and the copy would read like any devotional dogma. "Get rid of all of those harsh chemicals and come over to greet Mother Nature. She always has your back," reads an ad for the skin care brand Allure of Nature. Fiddler's Greens tinctures, composed of extra virgin olive oil and cannabis, are described as "just Mother Nature giving us exactly what we need."

Nature now possesses all the wisdom once afforded a bearded man up in the clouds. Trust that nature has a plan, brands state, while ignoring the earthquakes, tsunamis, pandemics, famines, and poisonous mushrooms plaguing this troubled earth. Nature, as science shows, does not signify goodness: nature is brutal, relying on survival of the fittest. And yet it's exalted as a higher power we can put faith in or that can transport us to a more wholesome era.

Shoppers gravitate toward this trend because of how cleverly it's been marketed. "Natural" is mentioned alongside words such as "pure," "authentic," "good," "real," "honest," "fresh," "wholesome," "worry-free," "gentle," and "safe." Compare that to demonized synthetic chemicals, which are regularly called "fake," "unnatural," "harsh," "toxic," "harmful," and "man-made." Juxtaposing chemical versus natural creates a narrative that these two categories are at odds with each other when in reality that's a false dichotomy.

"Household CDC" Dafna admits that highly publicized product safety scandals drove her to natural products. "In this fake world, you want fewer steps away from the source," she explains. "It feels a little more innocent, less consumerist." Having children also sparked a greater interest in what she describes as instinctual, innate womanhood. "You want to be in touch with nature."

But when Dafna finally visited a pediatric endocrinologist for her daughter's puberty spurt, she was advised to refrain from using lavender oil, which some studies have suggested may be a factor in premature breast development. Dafna was aghast. She used lavender oil every evening at bath time and rubbed it on her daughter's feet because wellness websites suggested it as a "safe" alternative to most drugstore moisturizers. "For eight years, I've been buying all organic, natural, beautiful organic shit to protect my kids, and then this. How fucked is that?" seethes Dafna. "You can't win." This is not to say one can identify what caused her daughter's early puberty. Studies have found associations with stress and obesity, among other potential factors (not to mention the randomness of genetic or hereditary traits). The point is that natural ingredients can potentially harbor the same concerns as "chemical" alternatives.

So why are we being told "alternatives" are always better?

A Clean Beauty Revolution or
Marketing Confusion?

When I started writing this book, I called a cosmetic scientist who told me the clean beauty "movement," for all its promises of revolutionary change, is decidedly murky and chock-full of pseudoscience. His claims felt a bit inflated. So I called another. Same thing. Then another. Again, the same hesitance. By the fourth call, I began to accept what they were saying.

It's all marketing, they said.

Several additional calls later, here's what I learned about clean beauty. For one thing, it's complex. There's no simple answer here. But what is clear is that the science, as it stands now, is not being communicated to the consumer.

How so? For one, ingredients' presumed effects are often exaggerated, especially in cases in which topical use of an ingredient is equated with ingesting it. (You aren't eating your skin cream, right?) In addition, it's also common to cite studies conducted on animals exposed to high doses of the ingredient under question, significantly higher than the amounts any human encounters. These studies' findings therefore aren't immediately applicable to humans, who are much larger and have far different biology.* And if you think that something harmful to an animal is automatically problematic for us, then perhaps you also think we should stop eating chocolate because it's toxic for dogs.

In general, most ingredients in question are often used in amounts that are considered safe by toxicologists. Ingredients are studied for how much can be used, and cumulative exposure is accounted for. Toxicologists often repeat "The dose makes the poison," which means that at a high enough level, even water can be toxic. The result depends on how an

---

* However, toxicologists can establish safety for humans based on animal studies. The safe dose for humans based on animal toxicity studies is determined by its own science-based process.

ingredient is *used*. Focus shouldn't be placed on the potential dangers, but on the actual exposure, much as you shouldn't equate a splash of water to a tsunami. Water is not inherently dangerous, but it can be in the form of a fifty-foot wave.

"Toxicologists distinguish hazard from risk, wherein risk is the likelihood that a hazard will occur," explains the toxicologist Jay Gooch. "The fear game that is played is one where you simply mention the hazards that sound the scariest."

For example, lead is a natural element that can get into cosmetics, including lipsticks, at very low levels from a variety of sources. Beautycounter warns that lead poses health risks such as neurological effects, thyroid dysfunction, and reproductive toxicity in exposed adults. In response, the brand puts forth their own lipstick formulation, attempting their best to reach "non-detectable" heavy metal standards.[21]

But the level of lead in most conventional lipsticks is so minuscule and the exposure is so inconsequential that it can't be measured in routine blood testing, explains Perry Romanowski. "You could chew lipstick every single day for a year and you're not going to get lead poisoning."

We're not being given the full picture. "With a lot of ingredients that have been used for many years, there's still no strong link between these ingredients and any long-term health effects," says Michelle Wong, a cosmetic scientist who runs the popular website Lab Muffin Beauty Science. Contradicting the popular myth that "60 percent of skincare ingredients get into the bloodstream," Wong explains that the skin is a very tough barrier, with very few ingredients possessing the right properties to penetrate it in significant quantities, which is why most drugs are administered orally. For the overwhelming majority of molecules to get through the skin, you generally need some sort of penetration enhancer, because the skin's job is to keep the environment out. (I guess that's why we don't fear jumping into a chlorine pool.) Skincare formulations are crafted to stay within the first few layers of the skin. Beauty products are actually quite low on the list of potential hazards in comparison to something like air pollution or drinking water.

"The beauty industry is largely male, and they've largely ignored women's concerns about these [ingredients]," says Wong. "And because they haven't been addressed effectively, it's made it really easy for pseudoscience to take hold and get ingrained into our consciousness."

Often reporters believe in clean beauty's exaggerated claims because they are, like many unsubstantiated theories, based on real, existent anxieties. "The problem is that we humans, as a whole, have an inclination to believe negative information," explains the cosmetic chemist and formulator Esther Olu, who runs an Instagram account called The Melanin Chemist to combat misinformation in the beauty industry. We're more inclined to prick up our ears when faced with terrifying tidbits than we are when presented with science. Humans are built that way, evolutionarily hardwired to focus on threats.

Olu, along with Romanowski and others, is part of an emerging class of science experts producing content through podcasts, Instagram, TikTok, and YouTube to share a more nuanced take on the beauty industry. Cosmetic formulators and scientists were once quite content to work on their craft and leave beauty writing to underpaid twenty-six-year-old magazine writers. But as the clean beauty campaign ballooned, they became motivated to peek out from the lab and address false information and oversimplified arguments. Remember, it's not toxicologists running the beauty industry. It's marketers. And even dermatologists cited in articles might be incorrect because they do not necessarily specialize in toxicology and might not grasp the complexities of formulation as an experienced cosmetic chemist would.

In speaking to these cosmetic science experts, you pick up on hints of annoyance and weariness, of having to explain basic fundamentals for the hundredth time. They sound a lot like public health experts in 2021. *Tired.*

The Prickly Parabens Debate

One topic that can reliably get these scientists fired up is parabens.

Parabens are preservatives used to prevent the growth of bacteria and mold in everything from shampoo to shaving cream to mascara. They are probably the most rigorously tested ingredients in beauty. But some researchers hold that parabens may mimic natural hormone function, harm fertility, or increase the risk of cancer, and therefore have no place in personal care. The EWG cites animal studies in which certain parabens impacted female reproductive development and human studies that show a potential association with negative effects.[22]

But a blanket targeting of parabens is like saying *all* animals are dangerous. Which ones and at what level of exposure? Toxicologists I interviewed say the most commonly used parabens at their usage levels are *not* dangerous. The FDA, whose scientists continue to review any new paraben studies, states there is no proof that parabens' cosmetic use has an effect on human health.

Some critics mention the fact that parabens are found in urine, which doesn't sound great. But that doesn't necessarily prove harm: our bodies are meant to expel parabens from our systems. Not that parabens should even be assumed to be the devil. Parabens are derived from para-hydroxybenzoic acid (PHBA). Hydroxybenzoic acids naturally occur in some fruits and vegetables. The ones that show up in your skin care are synthetic versions of that.

The dispute over parabens is a complicated issue that took off after a highly contested 2004 study published in the *Journal of Applied Toxicology* discovered parabens in breast cancer tissue. However, in this study, the tissue was taken from samples of just twenty patients and not from a control group (that is, the researchers didn't test healthy breast tissue).[23] And, as critics have pointed out, "they didn't know if any of the people who donated tumor tissue used paraben-containing products."[24] The study did not demonstrate that parabens cause breast cancer, according to scientists I interviewed.

Some researchers challenge toxicologists on these matters, stressing that several studies suggest certain chemicals can be harmful at low doses. This is especially true of endocrine disruptors, since our hormone systems are activated at very low doses. Subsequent studies have suggested a possible link between parabens' estrogenic properties and breast cancer development.[25]

Heather Patisaul, the associate dean for research at North Carolina State University's Department of Biological Sciences, is a neuroendocrinologist who studies endocrine disruptors and says that they might be more subtle. "There can be this more insidious harm, like one could lose their fertility or could become obese," she explains. "It opened up this complicated dialogue about [if we are] harming ourselves in a way that's harder to see and evaluate than 'Oh, I just had a major stroke because I got massive exposure to a pesticide.'"

Discovering exactly what is going on is difficult because the impact is rarely immediate. "We know that the incidences of many diseases are going up and up too fast to not have an environmental cause, but it's incredibly challenging to establish cause and effect," explains Patisaul. It could be, she argues, that there are significant mixture effects. "What if it's parabens + phthalates = higher breast cancer risk? Or parabens + high sun exposure = higher skin cancer risk? . . . Those questions are rarely asked, let alone tested."

Perry Romanowski agrees that some chemicals can be harmful at low doses, but reiterates that cosmetic ingredients are tested for safety at low dose levels. As for potential harm, he asks, where is the proof? "Lots of things could be true," notes Romanowski. "Eating pizza could result in infertility. Exposure to soybean oil could cause birth defects. It's simple to dream up potential problems . . . These things have been studied. There just isn't any evidence to support the claim that cosmetic ingredients are causing 'insidious harm.'"

So we're always stuck with these questions: What do we do when the information is seemingly inconclusive? It's a complicated field of science, and one that, like all areas of health science, continues to evolve and incorporate new information. Experts call for more scientific research.

It's especially complicated when a host of other factors might play in. Take deodorants, many of which contain parabens. Because breast cancer is found near the armpit, deodorant is often blamed. But both the National Cancer Institute[26] (the federal government's principal agency for cancer research) and Susan G. Komen[27] (the world's largest breast cancer organization) state there isn't sufficient evidence to support this claim. And why blame the parabens when there are more likely candidates? The American Cancer Society notes, "Although parabens have weak estrogen-like properties, the estrogens that are made in the body are hundreds to many thousands of times stronger. So, natural estrogens (or those taken as hormone replacement) are much more likely to play a role in breast cancer development."[28]

One reason breast cancers grow not far from the armpit is that tissue is denser in that region and dense breast tissue is linked to an increased risk for breast cancer, suggests the University of Pennsylvania Health System. Denser tissue is also more difficult for doctors to detect via mammograms.[29] "So far, studies have not shown any direct link between parabens and any health problems, including breast cancer. Many other compounds in the environment mimic naturally produced estrogen," concludes the American Cancer Society.[30]

Isolating one culprit is extremely difficult because we are exposed to so many chemicals in our environment. Finding the smoking gun is nearly impossible because of the large number of chemicals we encounter each day in the air, the soil, and our frizz-free hair conditioner. For that reason, medical researchers (a conservative bunch) err on the side of caution in presuming culprits. Correlation does not equal causation. But that answer isn't definitive enough for some consumers.

A final note on parabens: the entire purpose of putting parabens in products is to avoid the growth of funky bacteria and fungus. So sometimes there's a weighing of risks. And we shouldn't always err on the side of nature, because nature isn't necessarily safer. In fact, parabens have been far more tested in comparison to newer, more "natural" substitutes which have less data. Parabens have thousands of studies assessing their safety. They also remain one of the least allergenic preservatives.[31] That might be because "natural" preservatives, which aren't as effective, need to be used in *higher* concentrations. "The reason that parabens are so difficult to replace is because there's no other preservative that works that good and is that safe," says Romanowski.

But ultimately, even when the body of evidence heavily leans in a particular direction, it's a tough call for the average consumer. One might think there is no concrete causal evidence, but who's to say they won't find it down the line?

Even if we concede there's a debate, the inconclusiveness doesn't stop companies from exaggerating probable harm. Some brands tout a refusal of fourteen hundred ingredients already banned by the European Union, in seemingly stark contrast to the United States, "which has banned or restricted only thirty [ingredients]."[32] These numbers give the impression that the oversight process is an indiscriminate free-for-all. But the majority of those fourteen hundred "questionable" ingredients—like rocket fuel—never end up in beauty products, so restricting them is unnecessary. Just as banning Legos from food production is pointless.

Some clean brands love to say the United States hasn't passed a major federal law governing the cosmetics industry since 1938, implying that regulators have sat on their laurels for eighty years. This accusation is disingenuous. The framework is the same, but the FDA regularly updates regulations. Potential issues can and sometimes do slip through, and the FDA could certainly do more. But claiming that nothing is regulated is an exaggeration.[†] "It's just taking little points out of context and then confusing the marketplace," says the science communicator

---

[†] The FDA has the ability to require a company to recall or halt sales of any product deemed unsafe. It's also illegal to knowingly sell an unsafe product.

and formulation chemist Jen Novakovich, founder of the podcast and blog *The Eco Well*.

Most conglomerates and well-known brands, such as L'Oréal and Unilever, are obligated to take safety very seriously. Plenty of toxicologists point to their Scrooge McDuck–size budgets to research ingredient efficacy and safety. Big brands, especially in our highly litigious society, generally (though certainly not always) try to ensure safety because the consequences of not doing so can be very costly. If they face a class action lawsuit, they know they need to substantiate safety, and if they can't, they will have to pay out millions, if not billions, of dollars. This is why many also push for cosmetic regulation bills—because they already abide by many of the requirements proposed for legislation.[33]

What about all those lawsuits? If it's all just pseudoscience, how are lawsuits being won against big companies? On this front, the wellness shopper's concern is understandable. Product fiascos have left us wary of major manufacturers. But there's not always a simple answer—even for incidents that seem like a done deal. Thousands of women sued Johnson & Johnson, claiming the company's talc baby powder caused ovarian cancer due to naturally occurring asbestos contamination. Johnson & Johnson was ordered to pay over hundreds of millions of dollars, while other juries have ruled in favor of the pharmaceutical giant.

Johnson & Johnson denies their product was liable, and indeed some scientists say there's no conclusive evidence to suggest a causal link between talc and cancer development. A few experts I spoke to accused law firms of aggressively recruiting clients for class action lawsuits. But then other scientists defend women's claims. Studies are mixed, with some suggesting moderate risk and others unable to establish causality. In 2020, a study of a quarter million women was unable to find "a statistically significant association" between talc-based powders and ovarian cancer.[34] It's an ongoing scientific debate, one with worried consumers caught in the middle.

What does seem clear, however, is that J&J failed to disclose asbestos

by activists but detested by scientists," according to the American Council on Science and Health. Critics say the organization peddles "scientific half-truths and outright fabrications."[37] In one survey of nearly one thousand members from the Society of Toxicology (an association of professional toxicologists), nearly 80 percent believed that the EWG overstated the health risks of chemicals.[38] Some scientists I interviewed have accused the EWG of depending on obscure, flawed, or dated studies with minuscule sample sizes—cherry-picking those that support their theories—and misinterpreting data to their liking.

The EWG cannot even be described as an impartial party, as it has a lobbying arm and receives heavy financial backing from the organic food industry, corporate brands, and "clean" beauty, including Beautycounter. The EWG also participates in affiliate programs (like Amazon's) and sells a certification label to make money off the very same products it recommends.[§] If you go through their tax forms, you'll find folks like Michelle Pfeiffer, founder of the "clean and transparent" fragrance brand Henry Rose, who paid the EWG for ingredient guidance.

The EWG instills fear, then pushes certified products that will make it all go away. "So many people forget how much money they've made by doing the certification programs for brands," says Olu.

• • •

When clean beauty companies say they opt for "safe" ingredients, they imply that the competition doesn't. But toxicologists reiterate that the personal care aisle is not oozing slime, and that the body of evidence should be communicated to the consumer. Marketing cannot claim your face wash is out to harm you without being able to back the claim up. This is no longer even limited to small clean brands. Even conglomerates have pivoted to get in on the trend of the day because that's what the consumer responds to. They just give in to what's fashionable—exploiting doubt, fear, and guilt—regardless

---

§ An EWG representative noted that many nonprofits receive corporate support and sponsorships.

of the science. It's why you'll see CoverGirl promoting its "sulfate free" clean pressed powder even though sulfates wouldn't make their way into such a product. I'm surprised it isn't also labeled "fat-free" or "cage-free."

Still, with ingredients' impacts being debated, more research is required; perhaps that's what we should be lobbying for, considering beauty doesn't receive as much research or funding as other sectors. Although one thing is certain: we are worshipping a golden calf of misinformation. Novakovich and others would love to see the word "clean" removed from the beauty lexicon altogether because it perpetuates so much undue apprehension around safe products. The term reinforces the idea that if someone experienced bad effects or poor health, it's because they didn't buy the right products. It's fueling a culture of self-blame. "*That's* toxic," she says.

Don't get me wrong: I still buy Beautycounter (specifically their lightweight cleansing oil that dissolves makeup faster than any other cleanser I've tried). But I don't buy it out of fear, as though it's some magical amulet protecting me from chemical demons. I buy it because it *works*. And I like it. Maybe we can return to a space where we enjoy our products without fueling unsubstantiated assumptions. As the back of my Beautycounter cleansing oil informs me, "beauty should be good for you." Agreed. Perhaps that should apply to our psychological health as well?

The teachings of clean and natural beauty can cause bigger problems. Instilling an irrational fear of "chemicals" and claiming that nature reigns supreme—in other words, science illiteracy—can change the way we think about a whole lot of other stuff beyond lipstick. Some women take those simplistic lessons and apply them elsewhere. Because confusion or distrust over what's inside a package isn't just an issue with beauty. This concern reaches far beyond our bathrooms and extends to so many of the products we depend on. More and more women are asking, What's in my food? What's in my medicine? What's in my vaccine? *What's in everything?*

Chapter 4

Gym as Church

On the screen before you, a darkened stage is awash in purple neon lights. At the center of a circular podium sits a woman decked in a purple sports bra and leggings set. She is beautiful. She is hard-bodied. And she draws thousands of viewers on any given weekend.

Welcome to Sundays with Love, hosted by the Peloton fitness instructor Ally Love. This streaming stationary cycling class can gather seventy thousand viewers—what Love sometimes calls a "movement." A movement mostly, that is, of customers who put down anywhere from $1,745 to $2,495 for Peloton's connected bike.

Our fitness instructor begins with her eyes closed and hands in a casual prayer position. As the beat of an R & B tune kicks in, Love opens her eyes and stares directly into the camera. Extending her toned arms, she invites you—the audience—to join her. We are here, she explains, for a thought-provoking and spiritually grounding experience. "It's a celebration of life," Love offers.[1] In the background, the faint R & B song grows louder. It's Samm Henshaw's "Church," an apt title for this morning's work: "Mama said we in the church / You best believe this ain't no hotel."

"Today's virtue is honesty," Love proclaims. Honesty is supposedly the foundation of all other worthwhile virtues, and today we will hone this craft. Love then strengthens her voice to the uptempo beat: "Twenty-five to forty on resistance!" she shouts as you fiddle with your resistance control. "Welcome to your three-and-a-half-minute warmup."

Love pedals forward on her stationary bike, a makeshift pulpit. Bobbing up and down, her gold necklaces motion left and right like ping-pong balls. Five minutes in, she is ready to share more of her wisdom: What's the reason people are dishonest? Why do they shun this virtue? They fear embarrassment, want to avoid awkward situations, or simply hope to evade punishment. If you feel like you've committed any of these transgressions, it's okay, Love empathizes, pausing for effect: "Add one or two on resistance if you've done it."

You could call Love the patron saint of modern workouts. Incorporating religious lingo and pop psychology, her classes are motivational sweat sessions dripping with nondenominational faith. Sundays with Love begins with a mini-sermon centered on a chosen "virtue," like determination, honor, or courage, which Love peppers with moving personal anecdotes. This high priestess on handlebars might technically instruct clients in physical movement, but her real goal is to elevate the stationary bike into a soaring Pegasus of self-reflection with our fellow man. (Peloton integrates live rides with a digital social experience where users can "see" and compete with other members.)

Ally Love wants you to feel spiritually fulfilled. But also totally ripped.

Love has ascended to celebrity status with this creation. Peloton even sells a Sundays with Love capsule fashion collection, including $88 purple branded leggings that "inspire you to push into each week with passion and purpose." In just a few years, the energetic model/dancer has amassed nearly eight hundred and fifty thousand Instagram followers and snagged coverage in publications such as the *New York Times*, *BuzzFeed*, *People*, *Vogue*, and dozens more outlets. Fans dress up as Love on Halloween, complete with branded tank top and highlighted wig.

Peloton describes her class as "creating a sensation of deep connection with yourself" and declares that Love offers herself "to be used as a ves-sel."[2] Even the class artwork evokes the idea of a prophetic leader: Love is photographed with her arm outstretched and purple auras emanating from her bike pedestal, like Jesus at a disco. That is if Jesus, like Love, had an advertising deal with Adidas. (For all those who demean the human-ities in college education, Love's success demonstrates otherwise. She seemingly got her money's worth from her theology program at Fordham University.)

Love is instantly likable, even inspirational. She offers up a dramatic origin story rooted in pain, perseverance, and ultimately independence. At the age of nine, Love was hit by a car as she walked away from an ice cream man. The horrific accident broke her hip and left femur. Love lay in a hospital bed for a week; the staff weren't sure she would make it due to massive blood loss.[3] She came out on the other side but to devastating news. Doctors informed her she would never be a runner, nor could she expect to ever be athletic. She was told to expect arthritis by the time she was fifteen.

Just a year after her accident, however, Love pushed the boundaries of her mortal body to overcome medical expectations. "I was able to defy those odds and decided that I really wanted to move my body," Love pro-claimed decades later.[4]

People adore Love. Nearly all the Peloton fans I interviewed for this book detail how she impacted them. "Peloton saved my life . . . I feel like myself again," declared Danielle, a working mom of two who overcame postpartum anxiety. During a time when the elementary school health educator had stopped showering and cried every day, Peloton came to the rescue: the combination of motivational "life lessons" and hard-hitting exercise proved stronger than her antidepressants (which she's since ditched). Each morning, Danielle logs on to Peloton's streaming fitness classes where she is surrounded by happy strangers joining her in this mass ritual.

Danielle finds she has sustained energy throughout the day, more hope for the future, and even more patience for her children. "I don't go to church, but I can imagine that's sort of what church would feel like."

Today, Peloton has more than 6 million members, surpassing the population of Ireland.[5] Peloton grew to be a market leader for several reasons, one being that it was far more convenient for overwhelmed Americans (especially parents) who struggled to commute to and from physical studios. Walking upstairs to the guest room turned home gym trumped driving to a boutique gym.

But we already had NordicTrack and many home fitness options, so what catapulted Peloton to upper-middle-class stardom? What did it offer that other brands didn't?

An intoxicating blend of community and motivational interactive content.

Peloton promises far more than cardiovascular stamina; it promises all kinds of things that have nothing to do with cycling—by way of stirring language. So to call Peloton a "church" on a bike or their classes "mass" would not be a stretch. In fact, the similarity is intentional.

In 2017, the Peloton founder and CEO, John Foley, gave a presentation at a tech industry event. In describing the need for his 140-pound exercise hardware, Foley said there's been a dramatic slide in people's association with organized religion, but "that is not to say that people do not still want that guidance and ritual and identification and community and music and ceremony and spirituality and reflection—that stuff that happened on Sunday morning at church or in your synagogue."

Foley went on to say that people want fitness *and they want something else*, before pausing for dramatic effect. The heralded solution? "Enter instructor-led group fitness classes. Replete with the candles on the altar and somebody talking to you from a pulpit for 45 minutes." He goes so far as to liken a Star of David or a crucifix draped around one's neck to a branded fitness tank top. "That's your identity. That's your community. That's your religion."[6]

It's not that far-fetched an idea. Going to a gym can be sacred depending on the meaning one gives it. Purpose, ritual, fellowship, discipline, and prayer all make their way onto a fitness bike. As the sociologist Wade Clark Roof once observed, religion is socially produced and is constantly being reproduced. Faith is always being creatively tinkered with and interpreted to fit people's heritage, environment, and cultural norms.* And the most successful faiths adapt to the demands of the day.[7]

The ultimate Peloton mission is "to better ourselves, inspire each other, and unite the world through fitness."[8] By this account, Peloton is something to *believe in*. If not talk of virtues, Peloton instructors share uplifting one-liners reminiscent of elementary classroom posters: "Anybody can give up, but you're not just anybody," or "Don't do what you can do, do what you should do." The body is something to conquer, to mold into something greater. Much like the concept of original sin, our bodies—as is—are weak, imperfect, and keeping us back. But with perseverance and labor, we can transcend the pitiful state we're in; we can change our destiny.

While Peloton's digital platform might be the new Vatican, it wasn't the first to market sweat-dripping faith. When it comes to mixing spirituality and group fitness, no brand is more on the nose than the upscale fitness studio SoulCycle. Though it may have forfeited its papacy to Peloton, its ascent explains a lot of current fitness trends growing stronger by the day. SoulCycle walked so that Peloton could run (or rather bike) to fitness domination.

Over the years, I've gone to SoulCycle more than a dozen times, and each time, I was amazed at how enjoyable it was. Class never felt like work. It felt like being taken on an interactive amusement park ride with a bunch of ecstatic women way too enthusiastic for morning exercise.

SoulCycle lived up to a term thrown around too easily these days: cult

---

* In 2020, I wrote a *New York Times* piece about how organized religion was turning to wellness to woo back audiences. Churches, synagogues, and mosques have begun implementing cardio classes, hikes, and even forest-bathing prayer programs.

brand. Fans built their work schedules around classes. Women rose before the sun for their favorite instructors. It even governed real estate choices. "I can never live anywhere where there's not a SoulCycle," one follower noted in a report on nonreligious communities studied by Harvard Divinity School students.[9] It went beyond being just a boutique fitness studio. It induced religious fervor.

So what exactly was in the sugar-free Kool-Aid?

Evangelists on a Transcendent Bike

Julie Rice was *over it.*

Her seemingly perfect Malibu life wasn't cutting it anymore, even though it looked like a Hollywood success story. For ten years Rice served as a talent manager to A-list stars at a well-known management company. Jennifer Lopez was a firm client, as was Will Smith. She took on Ellen Pompeo and Justin Long before you knew who they were, and you know who they are now largely because of her.[10] Rice knew everyone, was well respected, and negotiated deals with a lot of zeros behind the dollar sign.

But Rice was missing something. She flashed forward and saw a future full of long days with uninspired meetings surrounding the whims of demanding clients. She saw herself more like a prisoner with golden handcuffs than as a power player on a golden path. Rice didn't even want to stay in Los Angeles. She wanted to return to her native New York, "to keep it real."[11]

When she thought about her next pursuit, Rice kept thinking about the one thing she loved about Los Angeles—the city's active lifestyle. Like many Angelenos, Rice treasured weekends spent hiking with friends, reveling in the majestic mountains while chatting away. Or, if she wasn't climbing the canyons, she was engrossed in a local running club where camaraderie trumped speed. Her social life didn't revolve around drinking cocktails so much as it did around burning calories.[12]

When Rice moved to Manhattan, there was nothing quite like the social activities that filled her L.A. weekends. Acclimating to the concrete jungle, Rice joined big-box gyms, but they failed to provide the intimacy or awe readily built into California fitness culture. The instructors at a New York cardio class yelled at her to work harder, which wasn't exactly emotionally supportive. Going to work out felt like "part of the grind."[13] She missed the sense of connection. It was a real void.

So Rice turned to one pastime that New York has on lock: venting. She complained to her cycling class instructor that nothing felt quite right. She wanted to be dazzled, not bullied—or worse, ignored—by her gym's staff. The cycling instructor set her up on a friend date with another client who had expressed similar gripes. That's how Julie Rice met Elizabeth Cutler, her business soulmate.

Like Rice, Cutler came from an outdoorsy social culture—in Colorado. She too missed the bonding moments that came with hiking with friends. Without her mountains, Cutler had no social fitness outlet. She missed the ritual.

Cutler and Rice found themselves imagining their perfect gym over lunch at the members-only club Soho House. It would be an uplifting fitness "experience" staffed by life-changing instructors who nurtured a supportive community. The clients should connect, not compete. The studio should be a center for empowerment, with exercise treated like a theater production and fashioned as a "lifestyle." And unlike the membership model, they wanted a pay-per-class system to ensure that people had a reason to come back—the classes would have to be *that good*. So good that a brand wouldn't need to spend much on marketing; their users would automatically spread the word to their friends, co-workers, and family. And if their friends couldn't get in, they wanted them to feel only the most visceral Manhattan reaction: FOMO.

They wouldn't create clients. They would create *evangelists*.

"It was like we had the same exact idea, and we were just completing each other's sentences," says Rice of their fateful first meeting. "When I left lunch that day, before I even got in my cab, my cell phone rang and it was Elizabeth. She said to me, 'I'm going to look for real estate, and you look at towels. I'll call you on Thursday.'"[14]

Sure enough, by that Thursday, Rice's new best friend had found a 1,200-square-foot former dance studio on the Upper West Side ("which we found on Craigslist!" Rice proudly recalled years later).[15] It was perfect. Rice, who had a five-month-old baby at the time, went all in: she quit her job, locked away her credit cards, put her family on a $400 weekly budget, and signed the lease.

The very first SoulCycle opened several months later. The boutique studio offered an "inspirational, meditative fitness experience" in the course of a forty-five-minute indoor cycling class. Rice hit the pavement, traversing Manhattan with a baby stroller as she begged people to let her post flyers in their storefronts. If she saw someone open a door to an apartment building, she'd stick her foot in before it closed and then flyer-bomb the mailroom. It was, as she called it, guerrilla-style marketing.[16]

Within a year, SoulCycle sign-ups were crashing the server as New Yorkers rushed to snag a seat.[17] The studio's popularity was due in large part to how the brand trained its employees in hospitality. Instructors were hired full time and paid above market rate so that they could take the time to invest in their students—learning their names, sharing favorite songs, and chatting with them before class. "People felt seen . . . like they mattered," said Rice.[18]

Within a few years, what started as a need for social exercise turned into one of the hottest and most exclusive boutique fitness studios. Soul-Cycle earned a celebrity following and acquired the kind of status usually reserved for luxury fashion labels. How? By formulating a transcendent collective experience that women couldn't resist.

Boutique Piety for Mystic Sweat

At seven in the morning, a group of stationary cyclists furiously pedal to the uptempo electro-beat of a Britney Spears remix. The song is "Till the World Ends," an uncanny title given that the cyclists are there to find something akin to salvation. "How you do anything is how you do every-thing," calls the energetic class leader, readjusting her headset. "Hell yeah!" responds a member from somewhere in the back of the room.

Lights are dimmed to near blackout, save for a few grapefruit-scented candles in the corners of the intimate SoulCycle studio. You're cocooned in the darkness—a muted support system that lets you, the individual, shine. Working individually but in the reassuring presence of others, members can focus on themselves. There's an element of freedom despite being squished together like sardines, a closeness purposely manufactured. Rice, who along with Cutler stepped down after selling SoulCycle to Equinox in 2016, explained:

> When people were done complaining about "Can you believe they're going to charge $27† and I'm going to have to sit that close to somebody?" what actually happened was, the lights were dark, and people could all feel the music at the same time, and you could almost feel somebody breathing next to you. Your foot was on the same beat as their foot was on, and all of a sudden it became connected, and it became tribal, and it was dark, and there were candles. The music was amazing and an instructor is telling you that you could be more than you thought you could be . . . There's something about a moving meditation with other people that are rooting for you, that are holding space for you, that aren't there to compete with you, that are there to elevate you so that they can be elevated as well.[19]

Heavily contributing to this altered state is the combination of music with movement, similar to the way EDM concerts inspire euphoric emotions. Such strong emotions can spark a spiritual connection to something outside ourselves; we submit ourselves to see the world as something good,

---

† Note: It's now approximately $36.

beautiful, and powerful. And when we're deeply entrenched in something, like when we're wildly dancing at a party, the absorbing activity puts us into a near-trance-like "flow" state.[20] We shut off that nagging voice in our head (with all its to-do lists) and redirect our focus to repetitive rhythmic motions. Hence the term "losing yourself" in an activity: when you're so absorbed in pedaling, there's no room for intruding, ruminating thoughts.

The self, as you're accustomed to it, melts away. A "we" takes over. And suddenly you feel nothing but love and connection to your fellow rider. You look around the room and think, "we're all getting through this ride together."

Pedaling in unison takes on a powerful force, even in its digital equivalent, Peloton. But according to researchers at Oxford University, it is exercise's mood-enhancing endorphins and serotonin (nature's uppers) that might be responsible for some of those feel-good bonding emotions. In experiments where strangers were brought to row together, they discovered that moderately intense group exercise creates more meaningful social benefits than lower-intensity exercise. "It may be that experiencing exercise-induced natural highs with others leads to a sort of 'social high' that facilitates group bonding, friendship, and cooperative behaviour," wrote the study's co-author.[21]

Of course, much of SoulCycle's success also lies in its talent. (Before there were Peloton influencers snagging brand endorsement deals, there were SoulCycle star instructors, often known only by their first name, like Oprah.) The brand does not hire the average fitness instructor. It recruits charismatic *performers*. Dancers, cheerleaders, actors, models, Broadway veterans, and professional athletes audition in what Rice once called *"American Idol* on a bike." The company scouts for charismatic showpeople oozing star presence—the same kind of people who can lead a congregation. Fitness pastors, you could say. SoulCycle promotes talent as the main attraction, some of whom reportedly earn up to $1,500 per class. And they make sure to live up to the hype.

Instructors say they "strengthen faith muscles," supplying a kind of emotional catharsis for those in need of healing. As one teacher explained,

"I get them to a point where they are so tired that emotionally they are so much more vulnerable. They no longer rely on their physical strength; they have to go deeper. That is when the experience becomes more than a workout."[22] Instructors motivate, but they also exhibit a slice of vulnerability to connect with congregants. "Sorry I'm late, my four-year-old was sick," one instructor told a class. "If you thought I looked too young to have a kid, I also have a six-year-old, a ten-year-old, and a divorce."[23]

Plenty of SoulCycle instructors develop strong ties with repeat customers, who at times rely on them during moments of crisis—a divorce, a breakup, Barneys closing. Fans report that they'll text their fitness mentor when they're going through a rough patch or stop them after class to seek counsel on sensitive matters. This attachment is not unlike the dependence on self-help books, which some researchers say fill in the gaps once filled by organized religion or closer-knit female communities.

"It is possible that the emphasis placed on friendship in women's lives has diminished as we have entered the paid labor market in greater and greater numbers, as the division of labor has become more specialized, and as families have become smaller and more isolated," writes the sociologist Wendy Simonds in *Women and Self-Help Culture*. "All these trends may have helped to professionalize the giving and receiving of advice, at least among the rich and middle class."[24] What was once a mainstay of female friendships—of telling someone to dump their dumb boyfriend—has now been outsourced to "professionals" as a commodified service. One's psychologist or Peloton instructor has replaced a once ordinary exchange because we're all too darn busy or far away to be there for one another.

Fitness brands may have created new ministers, but people need more than just a priest. They need a congregation. People need people. And with those people, they need to *feel* something. SoulCycle emphasizes "community" as much as it does its impressive talent, and Peloton advertises working out "together" in your living room. As the beloved indoor cycling brand posted on Facebook in 2020, "Sun up to sundown, you'll never ride alone."

So exercise classes are group therapy and High Holiday services and country club social time all rolled into one. They are, as the sixties "seekers" sought, an experiential spirituality. Whereas once mankind shook at Sinai to bombastic commandments or participated in gleeful revelry with faith healers, now we get a spiritual boost from group cardio. There are now even wellness festivals where ten thousand or more people (80 percent of them college-educated women) join in mass yoga like a Zen revival tent.[25] Women are expressing a need for intense tribal gatherings. And Beyoncé goes on tour only so often.

Flashback: The Original Group Fitness Fad (with a Nude Twist)

The April 1937 issue of *Life* magazine was keen to investigate a new "body culture" taking the Western world by storm: a peculiar new fitness fad that had groups of women doing leg circles and spine twists in a classroom setting—and completely in the nude. Not only were they stark naked, but they were performing a medley of slow-moving exercises in between two mirrors.[26] Double the view.

Called the Mensendieck system, it was a set of functional exercise movements to strengthen muscles as well as improve posture. Its creator was Dr. Bess Mensendieck, one of the first female physicians (European-trained but American by nationality). She inspired a generation of women to gracefully move their bodies. She also exalted nudity, believing it "fundamental in enhancing body consciousness."[27]

In 1905, Dr. Mensendieck published the first of several books centered on gentle movements, with picture tutorials on how to properly iron or reach for an item on a shelf. (Since Dr. Mensendieck's exercise manuals featured photos of demonstrations in the nude, they initially were deemed too risqué to be sold in the United States.) Some exercises were in direct response to what she saw as society's increasingly negative effect on women's health—modern constrictions such as fashionable narrow shoes and corsets so tight they resulted in fainting.[28] The body required full physical freedom, she preached. These ideas stemmed from Victorian dress reform, an attempt to make fashion less suffocating and more comfortable. In place of constricting undergarments, Dr. Mensendieck advocated "nature's corset": exercises to strengthen abdominal muscles and align the spine.

Over the next two decades, Dr. Mensendieck would open schools across Europe, and eventually her teachings spread to New York.[29] Her gymnastic training became a worldwide hit, with a reported two hundred thousand students enrolled in her programs. Two-thirds of them were women. By 1937, Yale University was teaching her revolutionary theory. Elite private academies incorporated the nude classes, although teen girls were permitted to wear underwear if they had "the curse."[30] Hollywood took to the Mensendieck system too, with devotees reportedly including screen sirens like Ingrid Bergman and Greta Garbo.

On the one hand, fitness was still a relatively new idea: tending to one's own body was a foreign concept to those who were raised to care solely for others. Throughout history, women weren't afforded the same opportunities as men to build strength. Now they were encouraged to work on their own physical well-being. And to do so with other women.

On the other hand, Dr. Mensendieck's teachings—which mostly catered to upper-class women—overemphasized beauty and grace, flat-out equating appearance with health and virtue. Maintaining an attractive body, by her logic, cemented one's social standing. "Sculptors tell me they are in despair over the lack of models with perfectly proportioned bodies," she told the *New York*

Times in 1924. "I go to the opera or a bal masqué [masquerade ball]. I am ashamed of my sex when I see the backs and arms and torsos revealed by décolleté evening gowns."[31]

Exercise fads come and go. The Mensendieck system is rarely heard of today. Although, some historians believe she had an influence on Joe Pilates, who created one of the most popular exercise routines of all time; Pilates is now taught in group classes everywhere.

Craving Connection: Wellness Fills the Void

By now we're all aware many Americans are lonely, isolated, and increasingly detached from meaningful socialization. There is no shortage of literature on this. The seminal book *Bowling Alone* by Robert Putnam flagged the crumbling dissolution of robust social infrastructures. We've heard that loneliness is rumored to be as damaging to health as smoking fifteen cigarettes a day. We've read headlines on millennials who struggle to find friends and hear about new moms grasping for advice on message boards. And we've come across startling social media groups, like a 300,000-member-strong Reddit group titled NeedAFriend.

More telling: thousands join virtual and silent co-working groups, where they keep a muted collective Zoom on in the background just so they can feel the presence of others. That's how bad it is. That's how *real* it is.

Today, a vastly different landscape confronts the lone American from a century prior, thereby shattering communal bonds and in effect, their identity. If in decades past, we automatically inherited fraternity through our large families, walkable neighborhoods, and religious institutions . . . in the twenty-first century, we cobble together a hodgepodge of friends here and there and stay in touch via frantic text exchanges. Meaningful social activities have been replaced by paid services that rob us of the chance to connect: quick Amazon book deliveries stand in for local libraries while Grubhub replaces communal home-cooked meals. Consumed with convenience, career success, and independence, we never stopped to ponder whether all these advancements hampered our social health.

Tech is another double-edged sword. Many Americans feel isolated despite "friends" at their fingertips, just a text away. If anything, recent research finds that heavy social media dependency—those who mainly use it as a substitute for real, in-person connection—increases loneliness. One reason is because so much of online postings are situated around performance, status, and showing off what's going superbly well. It's a toxically positive exaggeration of real life. When everyone is posting only the highlight reel on Instagram, that might just make you feel only lonelier: *Does everyone have an amazing life but me?*

Loneliness adds stress, accelerates physiological aging, and increases rates of depression. But interestingly, strong bonds are a female superpower. Research suggests women, more than men, engage in something called the "tend-and-befriend" phenomenon. When shit hits the fan, they are better able to handle stress because they're more inclined to seek social support (versus the "fight or flight" response to a threat). Reaching out to others releases oxytocin, the "love hormone" that facilitates bonding and reinforces commitment to those in your group.[32]

Prioritizing support isn't that easy, though. Would people prefer to have friends over for dinner and get to know their neighbors? Absolutely. But working Americans are so pressed for time that they barely have the opportunity to cook a meal for themselves, let alone for the Joneses next door. On weekends, when they presumably do have time, they're exhausted, preferring just to veg out on the couch watching Netflix. Facing an ever-growing list of errands and pressures, they simply can't be bothered to socialize as much as they'd like. If they don't belong to a built-in community with scheduled events, like, say, a church, that means they'll need to make plans. And who has the patience to make plans?

That's where boutique fitness studios come in. Like church—which has long been a communal gathering place—you don't need to orchestrate brunch plans or figure out friends' availability: people are just there. There is a set time. It's a social hour programmed into your life. And so, it becomes part of your routine, *a habit*. And if you give fitness a sense of purpose, as many women do, it evolves into a ritual—one that brings meaning, if not a sense of belonging. It's why I hear so many women call their local studio their "tribe."

Turns out that despite all the loneliness, connection continues among women, albeit in altered forms and by virtue of new wellness enterprises. Maybe they're not chatting in the church pews or baking cookies together for the sisterhood, but they are creating new and useful models. Ones where they can ask: Why not reach and connect with someone while also toning that butt?

The wellness industry has succeeded in convincing consumers they can master their life—and solving the problem of isolation was no exception. Over the last two decades, boutique fitness studios marketed their intimate social settings, spurring rapid expansion over the last decade. Some studios host book clubs, holiday parties, even weekend retreats. These gym societies draw millennials with the allure of meeting new people. Instructors ask participants to high-five their neighbors and to hang out at post-class happy hours. Planet Fitness throws pizza parties where members socialize over a free slice and bodybuilding tips.

In a 2019 survey of two thousand Americans conducted by *Vox* and Morning Consult, respondents were asked what kinds of social or ritualistic activities regularly provide "purpose, community, or identity." More than book clubs, bar outings, recreational sports, or political meetups, people named . . . exercise classes. They hit the gym once a week or more.[33] In Los Angeles, you might find the young, toned, and athletic hitting up trendy gyms like CrossFit or Barry's Bootcamp. Type A Manhattanites join early-morning running clubs that meet in both sweltering and freezing temperatures. The Midwest sees rapid growth of Females in Action (FiA), a free and peer-led workout program for women in which each workout finishes with a prayer or secular intention.

Boutique gyms wax poetic on how their enterprise provides "family" and "connection." Promises sound like, "At SoulCycle, we are a pack—we look out for each other." As with any group dynamic, participants' reason for banding together sets the motivation: the why is just as important as the who. A shared passion or experience is the point. And naturally, no one wants to be merely with people; they want to be with their own perceived kind. This can be distinguished by race, class status, interest, or psychographics. No matter who these spaces cater to, they attempt to gather the scattered, anchoring them in a familiar place—a twenty-first-century Cheers.

Some say the communal benefits outweigh the primary health draw. A small Brown University study suggests that with instructor-led mindfulness programs, the social factor is potentially "more significant than the type or amount of meditation practiced."[34] The "with whom" may just trump the "how" because face-to-face contact has been shown to lessen anxiety, stress, and depression.[35] In interviewing more than a hundred participants, researchers found they frequently spoke about their relationships with fellow participants and the class instructor, notably "the expression of feelings and the installation of hope."

Others might question whether building your communal identity around the ability to perform push-ups rings hollow. They turn their nose up in favor of political movements, traditional religion, or more intellectual pursuits, believing them superior modes of communal power. But if the ultimate need is to connect, then whatever gets the job done is worthwhile. And if you are concerned with your health, then why wouldn't you seek out like-minded parishioners?

What Kind of "Community"?

Questions I've long had while peering into these newly established wellness spaces: How much of a community is it? What kinds of bonds are we forming? Perhaps things aren't as bad as they seem with this whole "loneliness epidemic."

From a macro view, wellness acts as a social signifier. When individuals see others carrying a yoga mat, it's a clear signal: *I'm one of you. We share the same interests.* So often I see women strike up a conversation with someone spotted in yoga leggings, sparking discussions on products or practices. It's a common language. That's one type of belonging.

Then there's the belonging to a specific gym. Boutique studios can truly act as a tight-knit clan, where members check in with one another and rally around a member going through chemotherapy. I've heard several remarkable stories about the close bonds forged within CrossFit gyms, a chain well known for welcoming people of all backgrounds and sizes. It all depends on the space or the leadership, which sets the tone for community engagement. Is there a sense of obligation to one another? Is there room to socialize? It also comes down to what you put into it. If you loiter around the water cooler, you have a better chance of making new friends.

The same goes for digital groups. There are over a hundred Peloton Facebook groups for fans to unite over a shared identity, hobby, or goal, some boasting hundreds of thousands of members. There's Peloton Riders for Christ, Working Moms of Peloton, Peloton Military & Veterans, and instructor fan groups that feel like rock star fan clubs. For the LGBTQ community, Peloton can feel like the church they were never quite welcome at. When instructors mouth Lady Gaga lyrics such as "I'm beautiful in my way, 'cause God makes no mistakes," they can feel seen in a way that feels nearly therapeutic, a radical acceptance in a society that doesn't always extend it. One superstar instructor told *Vogue* he helped students come out to their parents.[36]

Even the seemingly casual networks can foster real support and substantial dialogue. It's not uncommon to see issues of self-worth, feminism, and the meaning of a good life pop up on fitness platforms. Members boost up those in need of emotional assistance, like a new mom sharing her body image issues. Far beyond cardio tips and oatmeal recipes, these spaces become beacons of help for those in need.

One member of the Peloton Law Moms group—a group of mostly

young and middle-aged lawyers—told me that if someone posts about needing a job, another member will call in a favor or offer a referral. Another time, a member shared that her child was in the hospital, prompting Law Moms members to order flowers, food, and gifts straight to her daughter's ward. Maybe they weren't there in person, but their virtual support proved they were united by more than just $1,895 exercise equipment. "It's not superficial," this member assured me.

While sociologists debate the quality of virtual interactions, others hold that the structure of a community is changing. After the pandemic, we are not returning to a world where everyone counts on Sunday service or social clubs for socialization. So the question becomes: With this new reality, how can we make it the best it can be?

Critics worry that people only socialize with their own kind in these communities. Peloton's core demographic, for example, is college-educated, has a household income of over $100,000, and skews female. As Americans gravitate to smaller, single-purpose groups (like the Peloton Law Moms Facebook group), they retreat from a more diverse pool of people. We naturally tend to silo ourselves off into groups where others look like us, act like us, and think like us. As Putnam wrote, if once upon a time we came face-to-face with our disagreeable neighbors, now we opt for groups "purpose built to represent our narrower selves."[37]

That said, I also hear from plenty of Peloton riders who learn about different groups of people through fitness classes. Diverse instructors share their personal experiences of discrimination with their audiences. Gay instructors recount how they have struggled in a society that wasn't always hospitable to them. This is where, specifically, digital connection brings together people from all walks of life.

Maria Doerfler, an assistant professor at Yale University's Department of Religious Studies, is skeptical of digital fitness communities. Without suggesting that every person who purchases a Peloton or works for the brand is of a certain mold, there is a very strong overlap and strong homogeneity.

"It's a very curated sort of diversity—exactly the level of diversity that is tolerable for the lowest common denominator of consumers," Doerfler told me. "If that's the extent of your encounter with persons of different ethnic background than yourself, persons of different sexual orientation, of different gender identity, I think you're being sold a bill of goods."

Now, not everyone is looking to their gym to be their diversity outlet—or their community. In most cases, gym connections are loose and casual. Some just enjoy seeing the same faces every week, like their own little buff Sesame Street. I attended a cardio fitness studio two to three times a week for nearly three years. And though I adored my instructors, I bet none could tell you anything about me save for the fact that I love working out to Prince and hate doing burpees.

People might dismiss these "loose affiliations," but the pandemic proved how being barred from those acquaintances felt like a real loss. People spoke of how surprised they were that they missed schmoozing with the yoga studio receptionist or joking around with their fellow gym members. They often wondered what happened to that one guy they would high-five after class. Were they best friends? No. But it did mean *something*. We need both loose and strong connections, and the former might just even turn into the latter if you cultivate them.

But here's another question I have: While these gyms act like religion, feel like religion, and nearly market themselves as religion, should we expect them to deliver like religion?

Spiritual Leaders in What, Precisely?

Gym members might consider instructors their surrogate pastors, but the majority of fitness instructors are as trained in chaplaincy as Gwyneth is in gynecology. They're trained in showmanship. In SoulCycle's case, talent undergoes an *eight-week* training program where they learn cycling, DJ skills, and "how to be spiritual and emotional leaders."[38] Fitness instructors aren't necessarily equipped to handle a client's issues with divorce, trauma, or loss. They might not know how to navigate suicidal tendencies or spot dangerous downward spirals. They are potentially being put in positions that they're not ready for.

Fitness instructors also tend, inevitably, to be much more mobile than their pastoral counterparts, who are often stationed for life with a congregation. The result can be devastating for their flock. As one member lamented on Twitter, "my regular SoulCycle Instructor is moving to Southern California and I don't even know what to do." And vice versa: in the early months of the pandemic, SoulCycle furloughed or cut a percentage of their staff without severance.[39] One former instructor felt it was at odds with the company's preached ideals: "A brand that talks about honesty, transparency, community and supporting each other all seems to all be a big myth," wrote one former instructor of being let go with no severance, and by his account, no explanation.[‡]

Now, of course SoulCycle, like all companies, had to protect its finances during the pandemic's economic upheaval. But just like companies promoting social justice causes without practicing it in their hallways, SoulCycle's "community" evangelizing came to bite them in the firm ass.

In 2020, numerous reports found that not only did the company transgress its "family" ethos by unceremoniously dumping staff, but that top management turned a blind eye to inappropriate behavior. By boosting fitness stars to prophet proportions, SoulCycle inadvertently created untouchable gods. Clients and former employees accused top-performing instructors of sexist, racist, and bullying behavior. A *Vox* investigation unearthed a note that hung in an office, penned by a top instructor

---

[‡] A SoulCycle rep offered the following statement: "Like many organizations at the start of the pandemic, we furloughed a percentage of our employees and maintained benefits coverage. Whether someone impacted by a position elimination received severance was based on our severance eligibility criteria at that time. If not severance eligible, impacted employees received benefits continuation for three months or a stipend to cover benefits continuation for three months."

trainer: "If someone asks you if you are back on cocaine or if you have an eating disorder, you know you've hit your goal weight."[40] One popular instructor allegedly fat-shamed front-desk staff. Other instructors were accused of diva-like antics like hurling objects at fellow employees, berating staffers if they got a green-juice order wrong, or sexually harassing non-talent staff.[41]

But SoulCycle reportedly did nothing.[§] Why? Because, as former corporate employees attest, the instructors were just too valuable to the brand. They brought in too much money.

Gym-goers seem to forget one important point—at the end of the day, *these are businesses*; their goal is profit. Unless you're the Murdochs, "family" bonds do not report to shareholders. For although SoulCycle's IPO filing claims the brand intends to "help people connect with their true and best selves," it also states a very definitive goal: make gobs of money, as evidenced by plentiful income stats like "expanded total revenue from $36.2 million in 2012 to $112.0 million in 2014, representing a CAGR of 76 percent."

On one hand, SoulCycle claims its "mission is to bring Soul to the people." On the other, it proudly touts an intentionally exclusionary reservation system that "has created a frenzied experience . . . when approximately 30 percent of our weekly rides are selected within 15 minutes." Some classes had waitlists of over 400 people. In a 2010 *New York Times* report, one besotted member compared snagging a seat in a top instructor's class to getting a reservation at Momofuku,[42] which was then among *GQ*'s top five hardest restaurant reservations to score.

You also have to ask what a "family" entails when it relies on very

---

[§] In December 2020, SoulCycle responded with a statement, noting, "When we receive complaints or allegations within our community related to behavior that does not align to our values, we take those very seriously and have internal processes in place to both investigate and address them, as needed."

specific criteria. If your community membership is dependent on a level of physical ability or financial status, you're out of luck should either fall by the wayside. (A *Business Insider* investigative report alleged that one instructor booted a pregnant woman from her reserved front row seat to make way for a thinner rider.)[43] Here is where wellness spaces lack the infrastructure of more established institutions; a religious congregation, for example, spans multiple touchpoints versus one particular (ableist or financially dependent) touchpoint. And while organized religion also relies on money—as anyone who has paid a hefty temple membership fee can attest—it's usually better equipped to help those who have fallen on hard times.

Do you really think SoulCycle would let someone attend for free if they lost their job?

This is not a spirituality intended for the masses. Scarcity—or more like *exclusivity*—is the point.

Boutique studios are meant to be small, exclusive, and special to keep the Planet Fitness masses out. One former fan wrote that attending a Soul-Cycle session felt "more like going to a debutante ball than going to the gym."[44]

That too can backfire. When people become so crazed about booking a class or securing a front-row seat because fitness is their new sense of purpose, they'll resort to bad behavior. They'll pay off the front desk (in money or in "personal favors") and harass employees to secure what they believe they must have. Building such a cult brand can also lead to elitism and fanaticism. You run the risk of replicating everything that soiled certain sects of organized religion: bribery, arrogance, and abuse of power. You run the risk of *bad* religion.

In the early years, the media found the SoulCycle fandom rather amusing. As one member described "groupies" to the *New York Times:* "If [the instructor] said they could go to the pharmacy with her, they would be thrilled . . . Anything to be close to her."[45] But some clients became obsessed with fitness instructors to the point of treating them to holiday vacations, cash bonuses, and fancy meals. Several went so far as to romantically pursue them.

SoulCycle contributed to the idolatrous excesses: "Our riders should want to be you or fuck you," was one master instructor's advice to trainees.[46] It worked: Some women bullied other riders they believed to be competing for a beloved instructor's attention. Jealousy ran amok, with women vying like *Bachelorette* contestants for a chance to chat up their teacher after class. Some even verbally assaulted fellow riders whom they deemed unworthy of the front row. "I watched grown women cry," an ex-employee told *Vox*. One popular instructor sent nude photos of himself to riders, which were then shared among other riders. "That became problematic because people's spouses were complaining, and then it caused a lot of infighting with riders as well," a former employee told *Business Insider*.

Others had their confidence shot if they weren't invited to drinks after class or freaked out if the instructor didn't acknowledge them in class. There's an account of one woman, like some sort of unsanitary mafia, sneaking a used tampon into a fellow rider's purse as punishment for riding on the podium with a star instructor. Call it tribalism, pettiness, or desperation— but a wellness community can devolve into something not unlike a (very expensive) religious cult.

Tampon-bombing is the rare occurrence, the offbeat turned fitness apocrypha. Despite a fall in popularity, die-hard SoulCycle customers will continue to go, enjoying a calorie-burning catharsis (or more likely just buy a Peloton instead). As the spiritual landscape continues to expand beyond organized religion, we start to see that faith isn't disappearing, it's evolving. New players will find ways to reimagine what women sorely feel they're missing. At the same time, we need to accept that selling something bigger, more "meaningful," is just how business is done these days. Every brand shooting for cult status knows it needs to stand for something larger than itself.

But what happens when you buy in to the gospel and are left holding the bag?

Testing Deconstructed Faith in
Troubled Waters

In early 2020, my father passed away. He had been sick for several years, but his death occurred suddenly. Or at least it *felt* sudden. Even those who anticipate a passing feel gobsmacked by having their loved ones taken away. There is no real way to "prepare" for such an event. It unmoors and devastates and shocks no matter the warning signs.

My father was my hero. Gentle, curious, and soft-spoken, he was a physician and academic heavyweight who devoted his life to the sciences and Judaic history. He was remarkably down-to-earth, preferring to discuss science fiction novels or recount impressive football strategy moves. On Sabbath afternoons, when we refrained from watching TV or driving anywhere, we'd play games of chess to pass the time. Then, as soon as the Sabbath ended, we'd jump into the car to head to the movies. After that, we'd go out for ice cream or frozen yogurt, and he'd insist on either a waffle cone or a root beer float.

My dad was earnest and nerdy, in all the best ways. He quoted *Star Wars* as much as he did the physicist Richard Feynman. When I was twelve, my father gave me a copy of *"Surely You're Joking, Mr. Feynman!,"* filled to the brim with witty and brilliant observations. One that has stayed with me is "The first principle is that you must not fool yourself—and you are the easiest person to fool."[47]

After his death, I was devastated. Insomnia returned, as did the anxiety. But I did find solace in joining my family in abiding by Jewish rituals that seemed bizarre on paper but made sense in practice. As soon as the nursing staff announced my father's departure, we tore a piece of our garments—signifying the tear in one's heart—which we then wore throughout the week. We kept shiva, the structured seven-day mourning period in which friends and community members console the immediate family during waking hours. It's nearly all day, every day, for an entire week. Shiva also has its own laws: our family covered up mirrors and abstained from cosmetics, serving as a break from caring about how we looked.

On the last day of shiva, it's customary for observers to walk around the block, marking the end of intense mourning and the need to move on—to reengage with society. These were powerful, helpful traditions.

When I returned from my parents' home, I felt adrift. Basic household tasks and routine errands felt overwhelming. Talking to friends about standard fare—politics, new restaurants, celebrity gossip—infuriated me. I was out of sorts. The first week back, friends visited to express their condolences, and it was all appreciated, but my mourning didn't subside after seven days. I'll say I'm not sure our society is well equipped to handle lingering grief. We seem to expect everyone to buck up and mourn a loss all too quickly, to be back in the office by Monday.

Self-care went only so far. To be honest, I needed consoling. I needed support. I needed a way to express and make sense of my grief. Mainstays like The Class or SoulCycle were unappealing because I didn't want generalized pep talks for what was a very specific, sensitive process. There wasn't anything they could offer at that moment, not in terms of rituals nor counseling. It was outside their purview.

Of course, none of my fitness instructors were going to show up with a casserole. Nor was there any program in place to support milestones or crises. Unlike religion, gyms have not had centuries to perfect communal outreach and manage difficult life transitions. Although I instinctively knew it was ridiculous to even suppose your local gym could help in such times, I started to wonder: What was I investing in? Not just the gyms, but everything? In centering career success, a toned body, and nonstop consumption, what was I getting in return?

Surprisingly, the strongest support came from what I had veered from the most in years prior: my synagogue. Though I wasn't a member and generally showed up only on holidays, the community came out in full force: The staff sent an email out to all the other members. The rabbi invited me to participate in rituals that acknowledged the passage of time, such as saying the kaddish, a communal mourner's prayer, week after week with others who had also lost loved ones. Community members asked me to share memories of my father, then invited me to group meals. They showed continued support far beyond what I had anticipated.

Obviously, thriving humanist churches and grief support groups exist. I am in no way suggesting religion has a monopoly on ritualistic activities and community. Not in the slightest. But my gym as a grief outlet felt absurd: *I'm not working on my body during a crisis.* It was the first crack in the armor of my otherwise complete devotion to my wellness regime.

I wasn't necessarily committing to going to synagogue every day moving forward or chucking my gym memberships. But I began contemplating the energy I devoted to my "healthy" lifestyle, which absorbed more and more time, energy, and money. I enjoyed working out and eating well, and would continue to do so, but doubts were creeping in about what exactly I was consuming in those Sunday morning workouts. Despite the quasi-liturgical platitudes in classes, I couldn't help but shake the feeling that this was all still an exercise in perfecting the physique and not too much else, thereby confirming that what mattered most was . . . my body.

I had bought in to my gym's gospel of community. It served a purpose, but it hadn't turned out to be what I wanted or needed when I reached the spiritual milestone of parental loss. The promise of gym as church had led me somewhere though. It led me to this book. Now more than ever, I felt the need to investigate why I was so preoccupied with these elements of my life—and how much of what I was being sold was true, and how much was simply what I wanted to hear or believe.

Chapter 5

A Plea to Be Heard

A smorgasbord for the curious, a blur of theater and wellness, the Goop conference could just as easily have been called the Alternative Health Convention. Six hundred well-groomed women paid between $500 to $1,500 for a full day of healthy eating, toxin-free pampering, and guilt-free Gwyneth gawking. Inside a Century City warehouse that resembled a luxury jet hangar, guests learned the importance of gut bacteria, how our minds manifest sickness in the body, and the use of poisonous frog venom as a healing agent. They sipped "brain-boosting" Bulletproof coffee as IVs dripped vitamin B_{12} into their bloodstreams. The younger ones analyzed their futures with a crystal-wielding shaman. Others had their "auras read."

Goop founder Gwyneth Paltrow brought along her celebrity pals. They were, as she attested, friends she "constantly" swapped healers' phone numbers with: the actress Cameron Diaz, the designer Nicole Richie, and the supermodel Miranda Kerr. The latter was eager to share her most recent discovery: leech therapy, in which creepy crawlers suck on one's face and the collected blood is then smeared back on the skin. "Health is wealth," Kerr told the crowd.

To be fair, not all Goop fans take Paltrow seriously. To them, she and her lifestyle site are more entertainment than a solid news source. For them, knowing that some of the health information Goop promotes raises more than a few questions is part of the fun; part of "the journey," as Gwyneth might say.[1] They welcome the $135 coffee enema kit and vaginal steaming (reportedly to "cleanse" the uterus) with Pilates-toned open arms.

In some ways, Goop isn't all that different from the traveling salesmen of the nineteenth century, who turned medical road shows into popular venues of entertainment. Brandishing magical elixirs and opium-laced concoctions, the salesmen knew the psychology of persuasion; they recognized a gap that could easily be filled with tonics, a bit of empathy, and mesmerizing onstage antics.[2] And the audience had no issues with that. Plenty knew the Rattlesnake King straddled the line between health and sensationalism. To them, seeing the snake oil show was their version of dinner and movie. Santa Monica's finest aren't any different: they take their colonics with a dash of skepticism.

The conference alternated from informational and empowering to kooky and downright pseudoscientific—but above all, it was highly entertaining. Women reclined on chaise longues in the branded outdoor picnic area, making friends and swapping notes on meditation practices and sneaker styles. While I got an "organic manicure" (a manicure with "nontoxic" nail polish), I spoke to a woman in her late twenties who had spent the last hour taking in the parade of fashion.

"Aren't they all just wearing yoga leggings?" I asked.

"Yes," she responded, "but the *best* yoga leggings."

Naturally, the longest lines led to the checkout counters in a scene that can best be described as self-improvement Black Friday. Goop fans might have been eager to learn about the latest health fad, but their consumerist tendencies drive the site's ad and product revenue. Starting at 9:30 a.m., participants crowded numerous indoor shops, each one dedicated to a different sector, such as athleisure, beauty, and home. And of course, all the panelists hawked their own books and supplement lines. No wonder the company is believed to be valued at over $250 million.

But Paltrow remains the biggest attraction. Inside, as participants crowded into their auditorium seats, the founder took the stage, her designer paisley dress brushing the floor. "Why do we all not feel well?" she asked the audience. "And what can we do about it?" A good question, and one the actress turned leader purports to solve, one diet cleanse at a time.

Looking around the hall crammed with Louis Vuitton handbags, I did not doubt that the audience had access to doctors and specialists, if not some of the finest health care in the country. No one there *looked* sick. No one acted sick. A Black beauty stylist working at a touch-up station—one of only a handful of women of color in the room—remarked, "They look fine to me."

And yet they were there, spending hundreds if not thousands of dollars on health advice from an actress who had no medical credentials. No schooling. And certainly no mainstream acceptance. The very same actress who, when confronted by the late-night TV host Jimmy Kimmel about Goop's more bizarre suggestions, admitted, "I don't know what the fuck we talk about!" As long as Paltrow provides hand holding, Goop fans don't question an adult woman who once declared she was on an eight-day goat-milk cleanse—a diet that medical experts have concluded offers no benefits save for "more flatulence."

So, if it isn't mainstream acceptance or the backing of scientific studies, what *has* become so very seductive about Goop? How has Paltrow been able to so effectively crawl into her patrons' ears?

Part of the answer lies in the fast-growing field of alternative health. Goop is part of a larger and flourishing ecosystem: 30 percent of Americans now use alternative medicine, with women more accepting of it.[3] Some turn to alternative treatments as a complementary add-on, though many fully adopt them instead of Western medicine. Women, or more accurately, *dissatisfied* women lead this movement.

Women are stepping outside their doctor's office, searching for something. And Gwyneth's fattened golden goose is happy to lay vaginal jade eggs for them. But what precisely is inspiring this mass conversion?

Dismissed and Disillusioned: A Frustrating Patient Experience

The crisis of faith in modern medicine starts long before someone buys a ticket to the Goop show.

The inefficient and, at times, mind-bogglingly frustrating patient experience starts with sorting premiums, deductibles, hidden fees, and a maze of coverage limitations. (And that's for those fortunate enough to even have medical insurance.) In the U.S., the consumer faces a cat-and-mouse chase of referrals and sign-offs to see specialists or get approval for a treatment. Long wait times and onerous paperwork can make a simple procedure seem like applying for a mortgage. Who has the time? Amidst work, parenting, household chores, and little to no time off, medical appointments only add to an already hectic schedule.

And it doesn't end with just nabbing an appointment. So many times, I've gone in for a routine checkup, then weeks later received separate surprise bills for blood work, lab testing, etc. In my thirties, medical bills have been sent to collection agencies not because I didn't have the money, but because *I couldn't keep track* of all the various individual bills.

Then there are the experiences that leave women's faith in the system badly shaken.

Jacquelyn Clemmons from Baltimore, Maryland, is one such woman. In 2003, the friendly and no-nonsense Queens, New York, native was two months into her first pregnancy when she visited a local doctor for help with a persistent yeast infection. Her mother was a physician, so she had full confidence in the doctor's capabilities—what she called "a healthy respect" for the experts. But the appointment proved less than assuring. The doctor and personnel spent only a few minutes chatting with Clemmons, then quickly penned a prescription. "They didn't touch me, they didn't really look at me," Clemmons told me. "They kind of sat at their desk and then wrote the script. I felt dismissed."

Clemmons says she looked up the medicine prescribed, Metronidazole, only to discover it was linked to an increased risk of miscarriage, which she was not made aware of.

The questionable treatment didn't end there. While pregnant with her second child, she experienced severe abdominal pain and back-to-back contractions and sought hospital treatment. The staff assumed Clemmons was overreacting because she didn't seem like she was "in enough pain." They sent her home.

Clemmons returned, demanding attention. This time she came with a plan. Clemmons turned to her partner and said, "I'm going to have to fake it because they're not believing me. So don't look at me crazy." She then proceeded to scream and wail at full volume. The Oscar-worthy performance did the trick. Staff discovered Clemmons was dehydrated and experiencing preterm labor, thereby endangering her unborn child. Afterward, Clemmons was placed on three months of bed rest.

As Clemmons recounts, pulling theatrics "is nutty to do on any day, but when you're experiencing contractions and you just want to be comfortable, it's even crazier."

Then came the third pregnancy. Clemmons said she was subjected to a forceful cervix check and dealt with an anesthesiologist who attempted to administer an epidural while half the lights were out. Terrified and angry, her perception of medical care shifted. She explains, "I felt like I could no longer just safely walk into a doctor's office, trust what they're telling me, and walk out without harm being done to myself or my child." Clemmons soon found herself asking "a million questions about everything, and not taking anyone else's word about anything that I needed." She decided to independently seek solutions, including natural remedies or changes in diet to alleviate ailments. "From then on, I was just going to do my own due diligence," she says. "If it was something that I could do, I was going to do it before I decided to involve a doctor."

These experiences inspired Clemmons to become a doula. She founded her practice, De La Luz Wellness, to be an advocate and pillar of support for women who also felt disregarded by medical personnel. Incorporating wellness modalities such as traditional herbal medicine, Reiki energy treatments, breath work, and relaxation techniques, Clemmons mostly serves Black and Indigenous women who come to her with the same goal: "I don't want to die."* These women distrust hospitals, and that alone is enough to make them opt for an at-home birth. "They get very tense and very afraid because they've had other hospital traumas and they don't want that reaction to come up subconsciously while they're giving birth," explains Clemmons. "There's this tension that builds, you automatically go on the fence. You walk in there already knowing you're going to face a fight."

Clemmons tallied multiple transgressions before throwing in the towel, but sometimes all it takes is one bad experience to taint one's entire view. Whether it was a physician, therapist, or health expert, if someone hurt or dismissed you at your *most vulnerable time*—which is generally when we interact with medical providers—you will need to get over that experience. Some might need to break away for a while. But others, especially when it pertains to trauma, might vow never to return.

Clemmons is Black, part of a segment of the American population that has historically not experienced the same level of "care" as other patients. (More on this later.) Surely wealthy white women aren't in the same boat. Affluent individuals presumably live a far different existence, for which the adage "see your doctor early and often" still holds considerable weight. Blessed with health insurance and access to top docs, they must have a better go at the whole medical appointment game. *Right?*

Unquestionably, wealth helps. *A lot.*

But wealth doesn't necessarily protect you from everything. Having

---

* In the United States, Black and American Indian women are two to three times more likely to die from pregnancy-related causes than white women, according to the CDC.

legitimate concerns dismissed by a physician is a problem that cuts across race and income.

In 2019, the actress Selma Blair appeared on *Good Morning America* to share what had been a silent struggle: an agony-inducing medical experience that spanned years. At just forty-six years old, thin and clutching a cane, the *Legally Blonde* star leaned on host Robin Roberts as they walked on the balcony of her Cape Cod–style L.A. home. Sitting down indoors, Roberts asked her a simple question: "How are you doing?"

Blair, sporting a chic blond bob, shocked viewers with her answer. It wasn't what she said, but how she answered. Through broken and stuttering speech, Blair struggled to respond. Nobody had known that the Hollywood star had become so sick. She persevered through the interview, which covered years of attempting to convince doctors that something was wrong with her body. Blair said she was besieged with pain and bizarre symptoms like blurred vision, extreme exhaustion, and numbness in her leg. Sometimes she had trouble walking, experiencing a sense of vertigo. She started falling.

The single mother would become so fatigued that she'd need to pull over and take a nap while driving her son to school. She'd truly feared how she was going to get by from day to day while taking care of her child. "I was ashamed, and I was doing the best I could, and I was a great mother, but it was killing me," she explained.[4] Thinking she might have Parkinson's disease, Blair reached out to actor Michael J. Fox, who was diagnosed with the neurodegenerative disorder in 1991. "I said, 'I don't know who to tell, but I am dropping things. I'm doing strange things.'"

Doctors didn't take her seriously. "Single mother, you're exhausted, financial burden, blah, blah, blah," she recalled. They blamed it on postpartum depression or a hormonal imbalance. One said she was simply being "dramatic."[5] None of these doctors offered further significant testing, even as symptoms worsened. The unrelenting strain became so unbearable that Blair turned to self-medicating the old-fashioned way. "I was drinking. I was in pain," she told Roberts. "I wasn't always drinking, but there were times when I couldn't take it."[6]

Finally, after years of pleading with doctors, Blair's condition was ultimately diagnosed as an aggressive form of multiple sclerosis—a chronic autoimmune disease that affects the nervous system. When Blair received the diagnosis, she cried. They weren't tears of sadness, but of relief at finally being acknowledged. She thought, *Oh, good, I'll be able to do something*.

The actress's story struck a nerve with women across the country, many of whom showered the frail star with gratitude on social media and offered their own medical mishaps and battles with chronic conditions. "My symptoms were chalked up to stress," wrote one woman in solidarity. "[My doctor] said I was having a panic attack!" shared another. Like Blair, they described doctors who denied their pain and brushed off medical inquiries. They felt they had to prove their case. Doubling over in agony, they were told to "suck it up" or simply accept that "this is part of being a woman." Others were told to go see a psychotherapist, implying that their pain was purely psychological. Some were offered the most patronizing advice of all: "Just have a glass of wine."

It would seem that average American women and Hollywood celebrities are united by their medical experiences. (Stars: they're gaslit just like us!) It's quite telling that Real Housewife Yolanda Hadid titled her memoir about Lyme Disease with a simple request: *Believe Me*.

When some women describe a medical condition, their doctors tell them they're exaggerating or overreacting. If they dare express emotion (as opposed to the more stoic male stereotype), it is used against them as evidence of the "hysterical woman." Although if they are *too* stoic, doctors will still not believe them; a lose-lose scenario if there ever was one. Worse, practitioners dismiss symptoms as a by-product of the patients' own failings: Higher-weight individuals report being told it's their own fault. Even younger patients face prejudice, as doctors just can't believe a twentysomething-year-old could have a serious health condition. In one chronic pain treatment survey of twenty-four hundred women, 90 percent said they felt the healthcare system discriminated against female patients.[7]

The list of dismissed or misdiagnosed chronic conditions runs as long as a CVS receipt. Women suffering from fibromyalgia—a chronic condition that causes fatigue, pain, and tenderness in the body—usually see several doctors before they receive a proper diagnosis. Same for vulvodynia, a chronic burning and soreness in the vulva that affects roughly 16 percent of women at some point during their lifetime. Of those who seek treatment, 60 percent consult three or more doctors, many of whom can't provide a diagnosis. The condition is often misdiagnosed.[8] Some vulvodynia patients deal with constant pain across months and even years, at times so severe that they cannot sit, let alone have sex or use tampons.

Endometriosis is another chronic condition that often gets ignored. It occurs when tissue that generally lines the inside of the uterus develops outside it, and can be marked by intense pain in the lower back and pelvis, nausea, fatigue, cramping, and infertility. Those living with endometriosis have been shown to have a 52 percent greater risk of heart attack (in comparison to women without the condition).[9] The painful disorder affects an estimated 190 million worldwide—one in ten reproductive-aged women. These women are often handed birth control (which manages some symptoms) and sent on their way.

Samantha Bee, host of the TBS talk show *Full Frontal*, best immortalized the issue in the public eye when she likened endometriosis flare-ups in the body to the horror slasher flick *Saw*. Bee asked the audience to imagine all their furniture thrown onto their front lawn, only for the police to say, "That's life. Wanna take the pill?" She further declared, "One in ten women suffer from endometriosis and it's just one of the many painful, debilitating lady diseases that get treated with birth control and a shrug."[10]

And it's not just male doctors—women experience subpar treatment from both genders. One study found that emergency room doctors were less likely to prescribe painkillers to women for acute abdominal pain.[11] And statistically, women received far less aggressive treatment for heart disease than men, even though heart disease is the leading cause of death for women in the United States. This cardiology gender gap is called "Yentl syndrome," a reference to Barbra Streisand's iconic role as an aspiring Talmud student who disguises herself as a boy to enter a yeshiva. In medicine, this term connotes underdiagnosis and undertreatment, implying that women's symptoms need to be more like men's to receive adequate care.

Meanwhile, male patients undergoing coronary artery bypass graft surgery receive more opioids and pain medication than female patients. Women, however, are given *more sedatives*.[12]

Disillusioned and fed up with a system they feel doesn't believe them, a growing number of women have taken it upon themselves to course correct their own medical care.

But the problem of not being heard starts with a medical structure that disinvests in meaningful physician-patient relationships even as it invests in bureaucracy and speed. For many women, traditional Western medicine seems built to make a buck, not to significantly care for their needs.

Just Tired of It All:
Hurried and Impersonal Care

Fortunately, not every woman has a horror story or a traumatic history with medicine. But too many harbor a general dissatisfaction that opens the window for more alluring competitors to breeze in.[†] And this has a massive impact because they're the stakeholders: women serve as the "chief medical officer" in their households, accounting for 80 percent of healthcare decisions for their families.

When I have gone in for a routine checkup, the experience has often been less than inspiring. Modern gynecology is best described as awkward. Convention forces me and so many women to strip down and don

---

[†] Women generally interact more with the medical industry than men, and starting from a younger age (gynecology, etc.). As such, they might accrue more complaints.

an embarrassing, paper-thin cloth gown, all while shivering like a hairless cat, and lie on a clinical examination table. The physician asks perhaps one question before crudely inserting tools, making patients feel more like a lab specimen than a human. Little is done to make us feel safe, comfortable, or welcomed. A quarter of women who skip their yearly OB-GYN appointments give this simple reason: they hate going.[13]

Let's put it this way: I have seen at least six gynecologists over the last twenty years and cannot remember most of their names. But I know the names, hobbies, and favorite musical artists of nearly all of my hairstylists.

Maybe that's a problem.

Surprisingly, the only time I found medical personnel willing to take the time to get to know me was at the NBC News onsite medical station, the inspiration for Chris Parnell's Dr. Spaceman on the TV comedy *30 Rock*. But that was likely because the staff were as lonely as the Maytag repairman—no one was ever there, since most NBC employees didn't want their employer knowing their private medical issues. (As a Loehmann's shopper, I valued a good deal and convenience over privacy.) I almost felt I was doing them a favor. Nurses would invite me to take a nap if I had a headache, listen to my fear of bedbugs, and ask how I was managing stress. I'd swing by to thank them following a recovery, and they'd offer me a hug along with free Tylenol packets for my purse.

But that's not the norm. The current clinic model produces a hurried appointment, leaving little time for a well-intentioned doctor to meaningfully engage with the patient—a system that can be demoralizing for both parties. A 2018 study in conjunction with the Mayo Clinic monitored conversations in doctors' offices, only to find that most patients were afforded eleven seconds to explain the reason for their visit before being interrupted.[14] The average length of a primary care office visit runs 17.4 minutes.[15] The system incentivizes productivity; some doctors are paid according to how many patients they see, not by the quality of health outcomes. Physicians see an average of twenty patients per day.[16]

With all too often lackluster impersonal care, diminishing allegiance to the medical system is understandable. A study by Harvard confirmed that although the United States spends nearly twice as much as other countries on health care, it has poorer health outcomes.

And that's just the general population. Minorities are more likely to face discriminatory healthcare practices, which feeds into a general apprehension of medicine.

One study published in the *American Journal of Public Health* found that among Black patients, physicians were more likely to dominate conversations. Patients feel less involved in decision making and then less receptive to the doctors' guidance.[17] Results from a 2017 survey conducted by NPR, the Robert Wood Johnson Foundation, and the Harvard T.H. Chan School of Public Health showed that a third of Black patients felt discriminated against at a doctor's office or health clinic, while nearly a quarter avoided medical care all together lest they suffer the same treatment.[18]

In 2017, ProPublica and NPR jointly collected over 200 stories from Black mothers, and "the feeling of being devalued and disrespected by medical providers was a constant theme."[19] Likewise, some women I've spoken to insist they were pressured into hurried and unnecessary cesarean sections to limit a lengthy labor or to accommodate a doctor's shift.

"I am not a person who believes Western medicine is totally unuseful, and I'm also not going to say that traditional medicine or alternative healing is unnecessary. There's a balance," clarifies Clemmons, who longs for the days when family doctors took the time to know individuals. "There is a level of connection, compassion, and tailor-fit care [missing from institutionalized medical care]. Someone has to take time to ask you questions, discuss your background and body composition . . . It's so personal and so detailed. And I think that's what is attracting women to wellness."

Many doctors are equally unsatisfied with how care is currently managed. Do they want to rush clients out the door? Do they want to spend precious time dealing with multiple insurance companies? They didn't break their backs throughout medical school and exhausting residencies to treat humans like factory inventory. Neither do they want to star in their own version of *The Office*, filling out piles of administrative paperwork. As the physician Dr. Danielle Ofri writes in *What Doctors Feel*, doctors spend over 60 percent of their time documenting ailments, reviewing records, and communicating with staff. "For physicians, this 'indirect care' is perceived as time they are spending on patients' cases, but for patients, this indirect care is invisible. Patients are aware only of the time they actually see their doctor, and it feels like almost nothing . . . the patients, rightly, feel shortchanged."[20]

It's not necessarily the doctors. It's the system. Too many physicians are overwhelmed—working long, stressful hours—and beholden to the current healthcare model. Some research suggests patients feel more satisfied and better adhere to treatment compliance when cared for by empathetic doctors, but for that to happen, we need a system that lets doctors flourish. Instead, 47 percent of physicians report burnout, which naturally affects their patience, empathy, and quality of care.[21]

Of course, doctors also have their own legitimate gripes about patients, including the frustration that comes with doling out guidance that's ignored: *stop smoking, exercise, eat your vegetables* . . . When patients repeatedly refuse to take responsibility for their health, doctors—who are human too—can feel as if they're living in their own *Groundhog Day* in which their empathy is constantly tested.

Still, some patients take issue with the outcome of such visits, which often end with a prescription. Although most symptoms—say, a cough or rash—will mend themselves in time, doctors and patients succumb to the "do something" psychology in which a specific remedy must be provided at the end of a consultation.[22] Nearly half of the U.S. population took a prescription drug in the last month.

Once lost, it's tricky to regain trust, especially in an age of ever-proliferating information. Constant access to the Internet pushes people to believe they can self-diagnose, while conflicting media reports erode faith in one consistently reliable source of medical information. Much of the general public is likely to encounter misleading information on social media because sensationalized headlines perform better. They're *juicier*. False stories prey on emotions like fear, disgust, or shock, and people are more likely to share what moves them—for example, an emotional anecdote.

In 2019, a bipartisan network of scientists examined the one hundred most popular health articles of the previous year; specifically, those with the highest number of social media engagement. Of the top ten shared articles, they found that three-quarters were either misleading or included some false information. Only three were considered "highly credible." Some lacked context on the issue, exaggerated the harms of a potential threat, or overstated research findings. Others, it seemed, had a skewed agenda.[23]

With doubt seeping in at multiple points, U.S. women are looking to try something different. Many women have had less than stellar doctor appointments. Or perhaps they're convinced they alone can self-diagnose and treat an ailment, MacGyvering their way to better health. The question is: What is the alternative?

Roaming to Alternative Health Pastures

In 2018, the journalist Sarah Graham founded *Hysterical Women*, a blog documenting personal accounts of biases in women's health care from the UK, the United States, and Canada. Female patients write in with complaints covering the spectrum: reproductive health, chronic illnesses, and disabilities. Graham found the consensus to be *Hysterical until proven otherwise*. According to testimonials, doctors accused patients of seeking attention, imagining symptoms, or attempting to acquire drugs. Often, women were reluctant to push back or challenge a doctor's authority because they were raised to trust and obey them. Some reported they were taken more seriously only when a male partner accompanied them to an appointment, like some sort of medical chaperone.

Plenty didn't get what they needed. So they pursued alternative self-care methods, including acupuncture, marijuana, and dietary changes—

not necessarily as cures, but as complementary treatments to minimize symptoms. Many joined patient advocacy groups or online communities to share knowledge and to find peer support. "People are looking for alternatives outside of medicine, even if that's just about sort of managing day-to-day life," Graham told me, noting a prevailing sense of desperation. "There is definitely a sense of people being willing to try just about anything."

I meet women all the time who want nothing to do with Western medicine, which they call "sick care" rather than health care. They believe the system isn't all that invested in solving "root causes" (a trope used to slam doctors; mainstream medicine addresses both causes and symptoms, though there's certainly room for improvement). The system doesn't incentivize preventive medicine, they'll say, so it's no wonder people are unable to stave off chronic illness.

Alternative health is presented as a proactive approach—trying to prevent ailments in the first place, as opposed to traditional Western medicine's reactive approach. Wellness advocates promise partnership over "patientship," heralding ways to fine-tune the machine so it doesn't break down as often, which is why seemingly fit and healthy women attend a Goop conference. That's the point; they want to stay healthy. Or more like: *what they believe* is healthy. And they'll work damn hard—or spend lavishly—pursuing it.

Western medicine's approach is simply too myopic, these women say. Hospitals and physicians are ideal for acute problems like heart attacks or broken bones, while alternative medicine is preferable for chronic conditions. Eastern medicine or "natural" remedies appeal to those who say they want more personalized, less potentially harsh methods. They only need to turn on their TV to see how prescription painkillers like opioids have harmed millions of Americans.

More and more often, women are asking, What else is out there? Is there some other way besides pharmaceuticals? And how can I manage symptoms on my own?

Take Naomi, a marketing executive and mom of two preschoolers in

Brooklyn, New York. She was diagnosed with rheumatoid arthritis and ulcerative colitis, an inflammatory bowel disease. Pharmaceuticals prescribed by her gastroenterologist failed to manage the symptoms; Naomi was besieged by fatigue, rectal bleeding, and abdominal cramps.

Naomi decided to visit a holistic doctor, who told her three things acted like "shards of glass" in her digestive system: gluten, dairy, and sugar. He told Naomi she must never consume them again. "That diet was the first thing that ever really helped my symptoms," she recalls. When Naomi went back to her gastroenterologist for a routine colonoscopy, she mentioned her newfound strategy only to receive a heavy dose of skepticism. The doctor stated it wouldn't work, even though it seemingly was working. "I said, 'I have stomach issues all the time. How can you look me in the face and actually tell me that the things I'm [eating] are not affecting the pain that I'm feeling?'"

In the following years, Naomi began researching alternative methods of self-care, becoming more and more entrenched in the wellness world. Now she pretty much avoids traditional Western medicine, save for surgical needs. Her health regimen incorporates whole, gluten-free foods and fresh juices, which she says helped heal her gut. When she last got sick, she went straight to an energy healer. "You have to just take [your health] into your own hands," declares Naomi.

In self-preservation, the sick and vulnerable might avoid what let them down in the past, then invest their faith in promising cures. If they find the system isn't addressing their concerns, they'll find new sources to meet their needs.

Flashback: When Americans Succumbed to "Puke Doctors"

Samuel Thomson faced the court, a sea of serious faces stretched along the wooden pews. It was winter 1809 in Massachusetts. The mood was solemn, the cold air filled with tension. Among those in attendance were Thomson's lawyers and an array of witnesses who at one point had been his patients. Thomson knew the press would turn the court case into a media circus, as this was no slight accusation. Thomson was on trial for murder.[24]

Thomson was famous for his botanical treatments and purging techniques, which he sold to licensed administrators across the country. He believed that sickness stemmed from an internal temperature imbalance, that all an ailing body needed was a restoration of heat and a release of toxins in the stomach and bowels. To that end, he employed steam baths, oral purgatives, and enemas laced with cayenne pepper. His licensed operators were soon dubbed the "puke doctors."

Thomson had prescribed one patient the emetic herb *Lobelia inflata*, also known as Indian tobacco. The patient was forced to puke daily, to the point that he lay in perpetual sweat. He died within one week. At one point, Thomson's lawyer dangled Indian tobacco in front of the courtroom. The lawyer then abruptly swallowed it whole, drawing gasps from the audience. He claimed he felt just fine and in fact could easily consume three times the amount without ill effects. The press ate it up like a page-turning thriller.[25]

Thomson was ultimately acquitted, but that didn't satisfy him. He saw the trial as the product of a power-hungry, corrupt medical establishment attempting to quash alternative medicine. At that time, who had access to information—and how it was wielded—was shifting. The "anti-establishment" President Andrew Jackson, who campaigned on a populist platform, celebrated the average citizen who relied on nothing more than grit and intuitive wisdom. The idea of rugged self-reliance permeated more than just D.C. politics; it became a siren song for the Everyman to revolt against what was seen as a two-tiered system of health care, making do with herbal remedies while access to doctors was reserved for the privileged few. Playing up a common perceived enemy, as always, bolstered support and galvanized communities. Medicine—both access and quality—became fuel for class conflict.

For Thomson, it was also personal. As a young man, he bore witness to the rudimentary medical care administered to his mother, who suffered from the measles. By prescribing mercury and opium, the doctors "galloped her out of the world in about nine weeks," he reported.[26]

By the 1830s, the Thomsonians had grown into a sizable movement, and botanic physicians came to be seen as on par with medical doctors. The ordinary people applying this new democratic approach sometimes obtained better results than those who were bled by doctors. Reportedly, 2 million Americans—more than a tenth of the population—adopted the Thomsonian system, which stressed a key motto: "To make every man his own physician."

Thomson wasn't alone in taking on the medical establishment. Americans soon embraced a hodgepodge of alternative healthcare methods, everything from magnetic healing to homeopathy. For better or worse, medical care was no longer concentrated in the hands of a select few.

Give Me Your Tired, Your Sick, Your Dissatisfied Masses

Those who flock to Paltrow's altar take comfort in believing that the Oscar winner (or more likely, her team of employees) is playing lab rat for them, although it's unclear whether any of these rituals in any way make her, per the mission, healthier. But that doesn't matter, for Goop provides a seductive fantasy of health and beauty. There's a strain in American culture that leads us to believe we can have or do anything as long as we put in enough effort. We live by the prevailing creed of personal control over one's environment—the very same creed that propelled man to the moon. Our go-getter mentality, bred by a Puritan work ethic and a belief in American exceptionalism, made us hard workers but also big dreamers. This unique mix finds its way into our leaders, our markets, and our health landscape. High expectations coupled with rugged individualism push health seekers to greener, more holistic pastures.

Goop also lends women a much-needed ear. It caters to a population longing to hear three simple but powerful words: *I believe you*. After years of feeling minimized and discredited, women gravitate toward those who validate their pain, who take them seriously.

Gwyneth Paltrow embraces this disillusioned group, filling a vacuum in which no empathetic or aspirational brand captured the market. Goop publishes pieces on Lyme disease, fibromyalgia, and other chronic conditions. Paltrow and her publication share alternative treatments, such as biomagnetic therapy (to balance the body's pH levels) or bee venom (which involves live bee stings to supposedly treat inflammation). For patients whose doctors offer nothing more than a shrug, these kinds of alternatives feel like manna from heaven. Just buying her pricey wares makes them feel cared for and comforted.

That's because navigating a chronic condition isn't just extremely aggravating and painful. It's lonesome too. Many women describe how friends and family are quick to offer a helping hand at the start: casseroles, babysitting, pharmacy runs. But when they fail to improve—over weeks, months, even years—the attention wears thin. Meal delivery tapers off, the visits more seldom. It's not that people don't care, rather they just don't quite know how to react to someone who isn't getting better. We're not accustomed nor equipped to manage medical failure, even on a social level. (We Americans are far more comfortable with success stories; we want to hear of triumph, of overcoming the hurdles!) The long-suffering know there are only so many times they can reach out for help before they're considered a "burden" or labeled *that* person who is "still" sick. In this regard, digital patient communities and websites provide crucial emotional support.

Even those with minor chronic ailments seek solutions and support. With that mindset, Goop launched its most ambitious product—a collection of supplements to address women's everyday health issues. The cleverly named Why Am I So Effing Tired? pill to "help re-balance an overtaxed system" was created because Paltrow found herself feeling sleepy all the time. She joins a big club: fatigue is the most common complaint for 10 to 20 percent of primary care visits.[27]

The pills, $90 for a monthly pack, were also designed for people suffering from "adrenal fatigue," a theory suggesting that overworked adrenal glands might not produce enough cortisol. Western medicine doesn't officially recognize this malady (which is not to be confused with myalgic encephalomyelitis, also known as ME/CFS or chronic fatigue syndrome). The Mayo Clinic describes adrenal fatigue as a lay term given to a collection of nonspecific symptoms, like body aches, fatigue, and nervousness, but one without an accepted medical diagnosis. Goop's Dr. Alejandro Junger, in comparison, likens it to an "epidemic."[28]

Adrenal fatigue is a new, invented term for feeling tired or stressed. It's possible that one's adrenal function is shot, but it's generally not a primary problem with one's adrenal gland, doctors I interviewed tell me. But as soon as it was *suggested*, consumers were convinced they had it. Before hearing the term, they might have assumed feeling sleepy sometimes was just a marker of modern life. Now they were self-diagnosing and buying Goop vitamins in bulk. It then becomes socially contagious, with friends suddenly discussing the "condition." And this is where Goop and unproven remedies can become potentially harmful. Some buyers might be ignoring actual symptoms with actual solutions. Their sleepiness could be the result of real medical conditions, including immune disorders, a thyroid condition, or depression.

Goop's supplement line sold $100,000 worth of product on its first day. (Even though you can buy the supplements' equivalents for half the price at your local GNC.) If women feel more understood by Gwyneth Paltrow than their own doctor, there's a problem with medicine.

Many of Goop's quasimedical suggestions lack solid scientific evidence. Moreover, their health advice always seems to converge to one end point: Buy more stuff. And not just any stuff, *expensive* stuff. At their conference, I noticed a $42 "transformational" flower essence oil—also called "vibrational" medicine—to combat a wide assortment of ailments: social anxiety, self-consciousness, self-criticism, and the "tendency to isolate." (What, it doesn't also cure my Netflix addiction? Align my bowel movements to my horoscope?) Is this science? Probably not. Is it great salesmanship? Definitely.

This hasn't gone unnoticed. In 2018, Goop agreed to pay $145,000 in civil penalties after an investigation by a task force of prosecutors from ten California counties claimed its product advertisements lacked reliable scientific evidence. Consumers who bought their jade vaginal egg, marketed for "hormonal balance," were entitled to a full refund. A year earlier, the advertising watchdog group Truth in Advertising filed a complaint with two California district attorneys against Goop after it found more than fifty instances in which Goop claimed it could treat, cure, prevent, or reduce the risk of developing a number of ailments.[29]

Goop was on a roll at that time. Their signature perfume claimed its collection of ingredients "improves memory," "treats colds," and "works as an antibiotic." Then there were Goop's $120 wearable energy healing stickers, which generated as much media scrutiny as Ben Affleck's back tattoo. These stickers reportedly "rebalance the energy frequency in our bodies" and were said to be made of the same conductive carbon material NASA used in space suits to monitor an astronaut's vitals. Not only did NASA deny the existence of the material, but a former NASA chief scientist went so far as to respond, "Wow. What a load of BS this is."[30]

Goop products and content now often include a convenient disclaimer: "This article is not, nor is it intended to be, a substitute for professional medical advice, diagnosis, or treatment, and should never be relied upon for specific medical advice."

Goop as a company does not shy away from controversy and has defended its practices. The brand said it anticipates questions surrounding its content but takes issue with attacks on its methods, reframing them as an attack on women's empowerment (and thereby appealing to consumers' feminist leanings). "We always welcome conversation. That's at the core of what we're trying to do," read an open letter Goop published in 2017. "Being dismissive—of discourse, of questions from patients, of practices that women might find empowering or healing, of daring to poke at a long-held belief—seems like the most dangerous practice of all."

Goop's strategy is to put edgy wellness ideas out into the world and let readers make up their minds about them. In a way, the company absolves itself of any responsibility because their role is to simply introduce new ideas—not to ensure their efficacy. It's a brilliant business model—the possibilities are endless.

While there is a glimmer of logic to Goop's openness to new treatments, the issue is that many of their products are not put through any kind of rigorous medical evaluation process. And without an approval process that involves rigorous testing and standards, their claims of benefits are just that: claims, not medical advice.

But Goop is not the whole of alternative medicine, and it would be unjust to presume as much. There are plenty of other players in town who don't resort to steam-cleaning their private parts. So, one might ask, what about all the other alternative healers and clinics exploring new treatments? What if they know something mainstream medicine doesn't?

The Gray Zone: The Space Between Medicine and "Something Else"

When it comes to poorly understood or chronic conditions, a gray area does exist between evidence-based medicine and unorthodox treatments. I tread lightly here—appreciating mainstream medicine while fully accepting its current limitations—because physicians have yet to truly figure out some of these debilitating conditions that leave women in agony.

Many conditions go undiagnosed or misdiagnosed, especially ailments that don't show up on blood tests.[31] That does not invalidate mainstream medicine, rather it reminds us that medical mysteries still exist. Also, it doesn't necessarily follow that alternative practitioners *do* have the answers. Some alternative medicine practices have little, mixed, or no scientific backing. Homeopathy, for example, is based on the philosophy of "like cures like"—that a condition can be treated with an ultra-diluted ingredient that has similar symptom effects. So an allergy remedy, by this logic, might contain onion because it too causes irritated eyes and a runny nose. This "similar" symptom concept goes against basic scientific principles. Besides, ingredients are generally so diluted that it'd be hard to label them an active ingredient. Homeopaths argue that dilution increases potency, while scientists counter that they're diluted to the point of being negligible.

Homeopathy (which is often conflated with herbal remedies) hasn't been proven to significantly affect specific diseases or symptoms even after thousands of papers.[32] In this regard, we need to separate interventions that have been *disproven* from interventions that are *unproven*.[33]

As for patients, their suffering should be taken seriously. While people can certainly convince themselves of symptoms or illnesses, we should not be quick to assume "it's all your head."

Doctors I interviewed say we aren't always equipped to deal with complex chronic conditions, particularly those that lack clear causes and treatments. Part of this has to do with how we think about medicine. We generally think of acute infectious diseases, in which there's this *one thing* that causes a disease, and if you take an antibiotic it all goes away. That's the gold standard: a simple cause-effect-treatment paradigm. "That is actually the exception, not the rule," explains Dr. Adam Gaffney, a critical care physician and assistant professor at Harvard Medical School. "A lot of our symptoms have not one cause, but a multitude of causes."

Many chronic conditions need more than one intervention, and conditions can manifest very differently in each individual. This is especially true for some contested chronic illnesses—those that some doctors debate are even real. ME/CFS, for example, is marked by extreme fatigue and severe body aches over a long period of time. It's a brutal condition that can leave some patients with dizziness and intense brain fog and others unable to get out of bed. Uniform cookie-cutter treatments just won't cut it.

What you hear from women with chronic conditions, many of them living with agonizing pain and fed up with what little medicine has to offer, is defeat: *Doctors aren't going to save me. It's up to me.*

It might be up to them because doctors generally abide by the philosophy "First, do no harm." That mentality can translate to "do nothing" if they don't have treatments they believe are guaranteed to work when it comes to patients with a certain constellation of symptoms. There are always trade-offs with any intervention, so doctors balance risk versus benefit. But if someone is desperate, they might be willing to take more risk—provided there's *some* scientific plausibility to the treatment in question. Given what we know about the human body, chemistry, and biology, does this intervention make sense?[34] Their best bet is to find a doctor who fits their threshold of risk-taking if they are open to experimenting with treatments that have less evidence behind them. Ideally, that doctor could interpret the available data and safely see what works for them.[35]

Those doctors exist but are rare. Inevitably, this puts desperate patients in a sleuth-like position where they search for under-the-radar therapies within patient support communities. Throughout my research, I have spoken to women who experiment with (and swear by) unconventional treatments few Western doctors would endorse: water cures, laser therapy, mold avoidance, mixing of pharmaceuticals, and the like. Some will be money-sucking bunk, some will nary move the needle, and some might actually help. A portion might be dangerous (certain interventions carry real risk of harm). But patients will say the best they can hope for is to lean on that which has the most data—or, more likely, anecdotal success stories—to manage symptoms.

Anecdotes are a fine place to begin the process, but personal tales of recovery are subject to all kinds of biases and misleading contributing factors. Anecdotal "data" is not reliable. Thousands of people who attest to something can very well be wrong. (Exhibit A: flat-earthers.) At first glance, it may look like a strong grouping of evidence, but because the data was collected in a nonscientific way, it can leave out pivotal information.

Anecdotes are powerful and potentially misleading. Too often, especially in alternative medicine, we only hear the success stories. We rarely hear about the person who depended on energy healing, then got sicker, and ultimately died. They're not here to warn us. *Dead men tell no tales.*[36]

It's also at times difficult to measure the efficacy of any one treatment. This goes for both mainstream and alternative medicine. Generally, common medical conditions improve on their own, whether or not a patient took something, so intervention is hard to judge. It's very easy to assume causation when it's in fact correlation or placebo. If you take an herbal supplement at the height of a flu and then you start feeling better the next day, you might think it was the pill's doing. In reality, it was just the passage of time; in the normal course of things you were going to improve regardless.

Likewise, when patients go for an energy healing appointment, it might be the calming spa environment that relieves pain and stress or reduces tension headaches. It could be the act of something touching you or even the practitioner's personal attention and reassurance. In one study, participants who received a sham acupuncture (placebo) treatment said they experienced a 43 percent reduction of headache frequency.[37] Some might also believe a treatment works because they've invested time and money, in the same way I'm "certain" my pricey Estée Lauder serum dissolves wrinkles.

For these reasons, alternative medicine flourishes: people believe whatever they're taking or doing is what's aiding their recovery.

But alternative medicine isn't completely harmless, much in the same way mainstream medicine isn't. One element in mainstream medicine's favor is that—when practiced correctly—doctors evaluate the best body of evidence and weigh it against risks before recommending a particular intervention. Not always so with its competitors: "Sometimes alternative medicine gets a bit of a pass in the risk assessment department because it's seen as being 'natural,'" explains Jonathan Jarry, a biological scientist and science communicator with the McGill Office for Science and Society. "So it's seen as having only potential benefits and no real risks."

But there are risks: of side effects, physical harm, and just wasted time or money. There are cases of people who got liver damage from Chinese herbal medicine. On rare occasions, acupuncture has resulted in a punctured lung.[38]

Of course, most alternative remedies are not actively dangerous. But here's another issue: they potentially replace actual science-backed interventions and rob consumers of real therapeutic opportunities. It's sort of like how believing in flying carpets is harmless, but if you're stranded on a desert island and you wave off a rescue boat to wait for Aladdin's mode of transport, you've got a problem.

Alternative medicine can induce a rejection of traditional medicine, potentially leading down a slippery slope of conspiracy thinking or overconfidence in alternative methods. A 2018 observational study published in the medical journal *JAMA Oncology* found that cancer patients who depended on complementary medicine (herbs, vitamins, homeopathy, and other alternative therapies) were more likely to refuse conventional cancer treatment such as chemotherapy or surgery and therefore had a twofold higher risk of dying than those who never sought complementary care.[39]

Once you start questioning medicine, researchers warn, you might just take it too far. Steve Jobs shunned what might have been timely and lifesaving cancer surgery in lieu of alternative therapies and a strict vegetable diet. (Jobs had a rare form of pancreatic cancer, a neuroendocrine tumor, which is less lethal than the more common forms of pancreatic cancer.) He died at age fifty-six. His biographer, Walter Isaacson, reported that he later regretted his rejection of orthodox medical treatment.[40]

There are those opting for a more hybrid approach when it comes to medical innovation. Dr. Lucinda Bateman is the founder and medical director of the Bateman Horne Center, a medical center devoted to ME/

CFS and fibromyalgia. She was inspired to dedicate her career to these conditions after her older sister became sick with ME/CFS. Dr. Bateman has gathered other doctors and specialists to come up with expert recommendations that could be used in the absence of a large evidence base.

As a physician, Dr. Bateman readily admits it's "heresy" to criticize the high standards of evidence-based medicine, but "the concept that everything has to be evidence-based before it can be taught is a problem because when you have something new that you're discovering, it takes a while to build an evidence base." COVID-19, for example, helped us understand we can't wait to initiate care. Yes, double-blind, randomized, controlled trials are ideal, but when a crisis hits, we don't always have that luxury. "In order to have more rapid progress, we've had to let down our standards in the United States about what constitutes good evidence."

While Dr. Bateman recommends working with a physician, she fully understands that that isn't always a possibility. To that end, she advises: Buyer beware. "There's lots of good education online, but don't go hook, line and sinker, especially after someone is making a lot of money from selling products," she says, singling out supplements, for one. "As soon as people are earning their living by selling these [pills and products], then all credibility goes out the window as far as I'm concerned."

The Alternative MD Will See You Now

Mainstream doctors don't have all the answers, but it doesn't follow that then *anything* goes. All science is evolving, though there are stark differences between pseudoscience and that which is supported by evidence.

The commercialized wellness space can lend itself to predatory practices by those who seek to profit from the needs of the struggling. Uncredentialed influencers assert themselves as legitimate substitutes. They push pricey placebos masquerading as supplements, sham "detox" diets, and unsubstantiated IV vitamin injections. If you were to believe the marketing hype on cannabidiol (also known as CBD), you'd think the cannabis extract could cure cancer *and* solve the Middle East conflict; while CBD shows promise, cure-all claims are supported by little conclusive evidence and lack sufficient clinical trials. The Federal Trade Commission has pursued companies like HempMe CBD—which sells oils, creams, and gummies—for what they say were misleading claims regarding AIDS, autism, bipolar disease, cancer, depression, epilepsy, and seizures.[41]

It can be hard to judge "other" treatments when the marketing, branding, and presentation are just so good. A great example is the hot new trend of an alternative medicine MD or a functional medicine practitioner.

These are primary care doctors trained in a variety of alternative medicine modalities. Functional medicine says it treats the patient "as a whole" using herbal remedies, acupuncture, and other unorthodox methods along with lifestyle changes, but it doesn't necessarily shun pharmaceuticals if necessary. "The best of both worlds" is how it's described: bridging wellness and medicine. These practitioners are available for lengthy, in-depth appointments at sleek new clinics that feel more like fancy spas. Patients are welcomed into a beautiful space boasting lots of natural light, potted plants, stocked kombucha, and a comfy hotelesque lounge.

Upper-middle-class women in their thirties and forties, many dealing with chronic conditions, flock to these coastal clinics. Some clients likely saw functional medicine billboards sprouting up around L.A., preaching "You deserve a better doctor." These are women, as one clinic founder told me, who just can't get a doctor to "investigate" their medical issues. Here they will not be rushed out in seventeen minutes. They get more like a full hour.

These alternative clinics are attractive because they advocate preventive lifestyle habits that no one would argue with: eat more vegetables, exercise, get proper sleep. In many cases, they do help people by holding them accountable to these modifications. But they sometimes add on treatments with little or any rigorous evidence, such as detoxes and hefty supplement regimens. It's a mixed bag: a bunch of great recommendations combined with what sometimes amounts to pricey pseudoscience and unnecessary lab tests.

What's wrong with endless rounds of fancy-sounding tests? Well, it insinuates that conventional doctors are keeping essential information from you ("Why doesn't my doctor check XYZ?") while encouraging a preoccupation with details that might not lead to anything worthwhile, especially since some functional medicine tests are considered bogus by mainstream medicine.

Science communicators liken overtesting to conspiracy thinkers who fixate on teensy details as if they're holy grails. Too often, these details prove to be nothing more than red herrings. Unnecessary lab tests without a specific reason aren't recommended because the more tests you order, the more likely you are to get a false positive result *because tests aren't perfect*[42] (as anyone who has taken a COVID-19 test knows). The likelihood of an "abnormality" is high. This results in heightened anxiety, then more pricey tests, and then more supplements.

Many functional medicine clinics lambaste conventional doctors' relationship with pharmaceuticals even though they often follow the same format with supplements.

Part of this fixation with testing lies at the intersection of the quantified-self movement and the "do something" medical mentality. Dr. David Scales, a sociologist, physician, and assistant professor of medicine at Weill Cornell Medical College, also observes a psychological component: "[Wellness seekers] tend to be uncertainty avoidant people. There is the thought that more data is better, more data is going to provide more certainty." Usually these are people who believe the worst thing possible would be to "miss" something, without realizing that overdiagnosis (and overmedicating) pose their own risks.

Regardless, functional medicine's messaging is effective because it positions alternative care as empowering and anti-authoritarian even if it too can be plagued by exploitative practices. Or, more simply, this messaging and marketing is a heck of a lot better than that of mainstream medicine. Functional medicine clinics look like spas, and they understand women's pain points. They know exactly what we want to hear: that we are unique and therefore require tailor-made treatment, that Western doctors aren't listening to us, and that medical care can be enjoyable.[43]

It's hard to understate how much women want a better relationship with their physician—the primary reason they go to these clinics. Patients want more time to talk. They want doctors to help them retool their lifestyle and better emphasize preventive medicine. Many women are not getting this from traditional medicine. If we only look at treatments strictly from a medical perspective and not a psychological one, medicine will continue to lose patients. The experience *does* matter.

• • •

The hard left turn to alternative health has been galvanized by the dissatisfaction women have experienced in their doctor's offices. None of this, however, should undermine an appreciation for medicine and great strides in scientific discoveries. Antibiotics, vaccines, and proven medical methods ensure that most of us reach an age well beyond what any of our ancestors ever dreamed possible. No one should throw the baby out with the rose quartz–filtered bathwater.

And yet a gender bias continues to plague a portion of female patients dealing with a laundry list of mistreatments at the hands of an imperfect system that can ignore, trivialize, or misdiagnose ailments—and then follow with inadequate treatment.

But this phenomenon almost doesn't make sense. Why would those who take the Hippocratic oath purposely ignore women's calls for help? Surely they don't intend to hurt their patients who come to them in tears and desperation.

Undeniably, some harbor discriminatory tendencies, but in light of such a large volume of complaints, a bigger story must be behind it. There's an explanation for why physicians shrug their shoulders and rattle off perfunctory prescriptions. And it goes way back: back to when women were purposely excluded from the halls of medicine solely because of their sex.

Chapter 6

Can't Treat What You Don't Know

Since she first got her period at thirteen years old, Noémie Elhadad, had had constant pain in her legs. It was sometimes so painful she had trouble walking. Then other debilitating symptoms popped up: agonizing pelvic pain, chronic inflammation, and exhaustion. At times it got so bad that she ended up in the hospital only to be told "there's nothing wrong with you."

Doctors eventually diagnosed Elhadad with endometriosis. While validating, the diagnosis didn't do much of anything. "I knew I wasn't making it up, but that was it," Elhadad told me on a call. She underwent various hormone treatments, including being put on artificial menopause, with little success. "There's a lot of uncertainty and a lot of frustration because most treatments don't work," she explained. As Elhadad got older, her health took a nosedive. She was forced to take several leaves of absence from work. In total, she endured seven surgeries.

Elhadad ultimately became a computer scientist and an associate professor of biomedical informatics at Columbia University. Her personal experience inspired her to take action, specifically with what she knows best—data. She realized that what endometriosis needed more than anything was . . .

research. "When I started looking into endometriosis, there was no good quality information in these large data sets and it didn't fit at all what I was experiencing as a patient," Elhadad explained. "I started talking to a lot of support groups and I realized that I'm not the outlier here. *The data is the outlier.* And I knew from my research in other diseases that if you don't have an accurate representation of disease, you're doomed. You're not going to be able to identify what treatments work or what or who is at risk."

In 2016, Elhadad founded the Citizen Endo project, which aggregates female patients' experiences through "the power of crowds." She launched an endometriosis monitoring app called Phendo for women to self-document day-to-day symptoms and treatments, which it couples with existing patient health records. This crowdsourcing platform builds a stronger data set so researchers can better understand how different subpopulations precisely experience the condition.

It's an innovative approach. Already, the research project has collected data from 2 million endometriosis patients—making it the largest collection of endometriosis patient clinical data to date. The hope is that the collected and analyzed data will produce better self-management treatments. "We're using AI to learn what works specifically for you and what doesn't, to the point where I can build a tool that would say, given how you feel right now, it would be best to go for a walk for half an hour rather than rest, for instance," said Elhadad.

Elhadad isn't alone in her mission: she's part of a growing group of women servicing their peers. But the Citizen Endo project also hints at a fundamental piece of the puzzle in the growth of the wellness market, a growth that's often led by women. And that explanation lies in exactly the problem that Elhadad confronted: not just the present-day but the historical failure to develop effective treatment solutions for women.

Keep Out of Medicine: No Girls Allowed

Many issues we experience today have their origins in decisions made long before we agreed that both men and women deserve equal rights. The effort to keep women out of the official practice of medicine extends back to the Middle Ages, when women paid with their lives to administer care. Female healers were labeled as witches, seducers, and heretics for tending to their sisters. "No one does more harm to the Catholic Church than midwives," reads the definitive witch-hunter guide, *Malleus Maleficarum*. Published by Catholic clergymen in 1486, the manual served as the ultimate expression of distrust of females.

As the clergy saw it, the only reasonable way to account for women healers was as testaments of malicious magic. Their herbal concoctions and childbirth techniques became proof of consorting with the devil (as if Satan were, of all things, a doula). A high percentage of women who practiced what we would call medicine were accused and subsequently burned for "practicing witchcraft," though undeniably because they circumvented (and threatened) the Church's authority. Fueled by religious dogma, those in charge successfully pushed women out of care, thereby restricting their role in society.[1]

For centuries, women were sidelined out of medicine until it turned into an elite, male-dominated industry. And once medical schools required college education as a prerequisite for admittance, minorities and lower-income groups also faced exclusion. Maya Dusenbery writes in *Doing Harm: The Truth About How Bad Medicine and Lazy Science Leave Women Dismissed, Misdiagnosed, and Sick*, "The regular doctors had finally gained a legal monopoly over the practice of medicine, and in the process created a profession that was overwhelmingly white, male, and wealthy."[2]

This medical reorganization resulted in a massive loss of valuable health information, tools, and remedies that had been passed from generation to generation. For centuries, midwives and village elders oversaw childbirth; now, this task was outsourced to male doctors. The normal transmission of knowledge about sex or the female body by word of mouth stopped flowing. By the end of the nineteenth century, doctors discovered that 25 percent of young women were unprepared for their first menstruation.[3]

Sometimes doctors did attempt to learn more, but not always in the most ethical ways. *How* many of these doctors perfected their surgical techniques was often just as sinister as how frivolously doctors treated female bodies. Dr. James Marion Sims (1813–1883), considered the father of modern gynecology, practiced ovary operations on enslaved Black women. These women were not anesthetized and were sometimes operated on numerous times.

Medical misogyny no longer involves flaming torches and barbaric research practices. More women are becoming doctors, as they now constitute half of medical school students and more than a third of the U.S. physician workforce.[4] But while women increasingly joined the fold, structural sexism has hummed along through the modern era.

Problems in the Pipeline:
The Gender Health Gap

Here's one of the biggest issues in medicine we still feel today: Females were largely excluded as subjects from clinical research up until a few decades ago, leaving wide gaps in heart disease prevention, cancer treatment, and drug research. More recently, women represented only 19 percent of HIV drug trials and 11 percent of cure trials despite constituting half of the world's cases.[5]

Before the nineties, many researchers scoffed at testing drugs on women because they believed fluctuating female hormones might obscure results or they were worried about reproductive effects. (And, well, it was just easier and cheaper to omit them.) Instead, the standing presumption was that male findings could represent findings for both sexes. Hence the male "norm."

But hormones, immune systems, responses to chemicals, and the stages experienced over a lifetime differ between the sexes, such as female menstruation, pregnancy, and menopause. Women experience conditions differently. They have, for example, a higher tendency to experience migraines, and their migraines are more painful and longer-lasting than those of their male peers.[6] Women also make up 80 percent of autoimmune disease patients.[7]

Women's bodies can and do respond differently to drugs, putting them in greater danger of side effects if they're underrepresented in research. Between 2004 and 2013, women experienced over 2 million drug-related adverse events, in comparison to 1.3 million for men.[8]

To give an example of how this plays out: For years the media reported strange incidents involving women who took the insomnia medication zolpidem (also known as Ambien). Women woke up to a chaotic kitchen with a bizarre hodgepodge of ingredients and pots in disarray. Mysterious packages began arriving—a fire extinguisher, fifteen boxes of decaffeinated tea, used wigs, T. rex erotica—the result of two a.m. online shopping splurges no one could recall. Some were sleepwalking, sleep eating, and even sleep driving in the middle of the night.

A former manager of mine had the scariest story of all. She wrote an email to her boss in the middle of the night signed "I love you!"

It turned out that women process zolpidem at a slower rate than men, so it lingers in their system longer. But without proper research on the biological differences between the sexes, women weren't aware of that effect. In 2013, the FDA finally announced that manufacturers must lower the recommended zolpidem dose for women by nearly *half*.

Speaking of gaps, remember how Samantha Bee said that women receive just birth control pills and a shrug to treat endometriosis? Well, now you may have a better idea why. Women's concerns are dismissed due not just to bias but to a literal lack of knowledge. There's a painful need for more inclusive research.

Granted, doctors aren't handing out hysterectomies like Halloween candy, as they did during the nineteenth-century hysteria craze, but we're sometimes still defaulting to catchall labels instead of thoroughly investigating conditions. Occasionally, doctors dismiss or tell women, "It's exhaustion" or "It's all in your head," because they truly do not know what to make of symptoms. They are sincerely baffled; your body is a Picasso to their realist minds. But at the same time, the issue is almost circular: women are also not progressing on issues because medicine doubles down on the hysteria myth, dismissing telltale signs instead of investigating them.

"Doctors sometimes aren't very good at just saying, 'I don't know. We don't have enough research on this,'" says Sarah Graham, founder of the women's health blog *Hysterical Women*. "For a lot of women, although it doesn't necessarily give you the answer you want, it would still be better than being sent away feeling like you're going mad."

Many endometriosis patients do indeed feel like they're going mad. Endometriosis is one of many underrecognized, underresearched, and underfunded chronic conditions affecting women. It's pretty nuts considering endometriosis is estimated to affect nearly 10 percent of American women of reproductive age—roughly 6 million women.

In 2020, the U.S. House of Representatives doubled funding for endometriosis research, which amounted to just $26 million per year. Kim Kardashian's home is worth more than double that. All in all, that comes out to about $4 per U.S. woman afflicted with endometriosis.

This relates to the flawed outcome: If half of the population isn't properly studied, how can we expect proper diagnoses, let alone effective treatment? Insufficient data influences how all doctors—both male and female—then treat patients.

It's also just counterproductive. Increasing women's health research initiatives would save money in the long run: not as many women would have to quit their jobs or seek as much medical attention. One study commissioned by Women's Health Access Matters—an advocacy organization that aims to increase funding for women's medical issues—ran economic simulations to analyze the potential impact of increasing research investment. Chloe E. Bird, a senior sociologist at the RAND Corporation who co-led the study, predicted a "shockingly high return" on investment.[9]

"What we don't know about these diseases with tremendous impacts on women's health is costing billions," says Bird. For example, doubling the $20 million the NIH spent on coronary artery disease research related to women's health in 2019 to $40 million would yield an ROI of 9,500 percent and add 12,000 years back to the workforce. Doubling the $6 million spent on research for rheumatoid arthritis in women would conservatively deliver an ROI of 174,000 percent, saving $180 million in healthcare costs and adding $10.5 billion to the economy over 30 years.

There has been significant progress: sex as a biological variable is now a key part of the NIH's policy on research. Women now make up nearly half of all participants in NIH-supported clinical trials.[10] Still, that does not yet make up for the years they were excluded from medical research. There are gaps in our knowledge that can be filled with studies that take decades, not a year or two.

"There is a lot more work to do," says Kathryn Schubert, the CEO and president of the Society for Women's Health Research (SWHR). The nonprofit advocates for better representation of women in clinical research at the federal level and within various industries (pharmaceuticals, medical devices, etc.). Schubert says more women have been included in clinical research, although subpopulations of women—more ethnically diverse women, as well as specific groups like pregnant and lactating populations—"have not necessarily been included as we would like."

Schubert understands women's frustration. She too is frustrated, pointing to a telling stat: since 2000, there have been seventy-eight drug trials on erectile dysfunction, compared to fifty on preterm birth.[11] "When we think about the population impact and the return on investment, it's a little lopsided," says Schubert. Why is there such an imbalance in investment? Probably because many of the stakeholders in health care have been and are men. "It's not just about elevating these voices of women, but also making sure that we're getting women into leadership roles and decision-making roles."

A 2019 report found that women make up 30 percent of C-suite teams and 13 percent of CEOs in healthcare leadership. On average, reaching CEO status in the healthcare field takes women three to five years longer than men.[12] That means we're losing out on those who can better advocate for women's health needs.

Silicon Valley can prove just as challenging when it comes to femtech, a term encompassing apps, software, diagnostics, and consumer tech focused on women's health. Femtech start-ups—predominantly founded and led by women—still struggle to secure large-scale institutional funding.[13] I've interviewed roughly two dozen femtech founders across categories—fertility, menopause, chronic conditions—who told me they experience bias in the tech industry despite rah-rah enthusiasm in media outlets.*

One sexual wellness start-up founder told me she would walk into a typical investor pitch meeting, which would be composed of thirty middle-aged men and maybe one woman. She would begin her pitch with "I'm here to talk about vaginas," only to face an uncomfortable, beet-red audience. She went so far as to describe it as "looks of horror." This founder was never able to get a VC or a fund to write a check until she hired a middle-aged man—basically the carbon copy of the easily shocked middle-aged investor—as her CFO. "Literally just having my CFO stand in the room next to me gave me instant credibility with this group," she said, adding that the CFO was indeed qualified and not just VC arm candy. "He looked like them. He talked like them. And that made them [think], 'Okay, this is actually a real business, a real opportunity.'"

If venture capitalists can't personally relate to a health issue, they're less inclined to take interest. This could be why start-ups like Hims—which started by selling erectile dysfunction and men's hair loss pills—snagged $100 million in funding just a year after launch. Meanwhile,

---

* Like any Silicon Valley sector, femtech has its fair share of bunk and overhyped products—not to mention, it's limited in its capability to fix systemic issues—but an increasing number of companies are attempting to address the gender research gap.

menopause start-up founders tell me they still struggle to be taken seriously. Representation influences research and funding, as numerous entrepreneurs in the space attest.

"I've heard the same story over and over of male investors who did not really understand the problem well enough to get excited about a company," says Halle Tecco, an investor and founder emeritus of Rock Health, a seed fund investing in digital health start-ups, who has since co-founded and successfully exited the fertility start-up Natalist.[14] "And the few women and doctors that there are [in this sector] are spread so thin because they're overwhelmed with the amount of opportunity."

Women's digital health had a "banner year" in 2018. The subsector collectively stood at $650 million in funding across dozens of companies. That might sound like a lot, but Juul raised the exact same amount in one funding round that very same year. Basically, just one company (an e-cigarette maker, no less) was able to raise as much as an entire category devoted to women's health solutions. It's apples to oranges, no doubt, but it gives an idea of the money flowing in Silicon Valley.

This divergence could be because reportedly only 13 percent of venture capitalists are women,[15] meaning far more femtech founders continue to encounter blushing audiences. Having women on board makes a sizable impact: women VCs invest in twice as many female-founded companies than their male counterparts.[16] (It would be safe to presume that most traditional investors aren't dying to learn about vaginas.)

And yet there's much consumer interest in this field: women are 75 percent more likely to use digital health tools—e.g., pregnancy-focused apps or health management trackers—than men.[17] So not only can health tech make a sizable difference in research and treating women's issues, but women *want* it.

Femtech founders tell me that investors often ask the same question of their company's goal: Why hasn't this been done before? It could be because women shied away from freely discussing intimate issues, thereby reinforcing its hidden status. That tendency is changing as more open discussions erode the stigmas. But maybe they also avoided discussing these issues because they knew no one wanted to hear about them.

A "Shattered" Trust: Scandals, Controversies, and Lawsuits

A lack of research is more detrimental than just the paltry solutions it leads to. It can cause real, lasting harm. Many women are wary of medical institutions as a result of horrific episodes in healthcare history that stemmed from rushed, undertested research.

In the last two decades, more than a hundred thousand lawsuits have been filed against the makers of transvaginal mesh (a netlike implant used to treat pelvic organ prolapse) and midurethral mesh sling (a narrow strip of mesh positioned under the urethra to treat stress urinary incontinence—the loss of bladder control when sneezing, laughing, and coughing).[†]

Marketed as an easy and safe solution for patients dealing with weakened vaginal walls, millions of transvaginal mesh implants have been administered worldwide since the nineties. But some doctors weren't properly trained in optimal insertion techniques or on what could go wrong, says Dr. Maude Carmel, an associate professor in the department of urology at the University of Texas Southwestern Medical Center.

While many women were successfully treated, it's been estimated that between 5 and 15 percent of mesh patients[18] suffered complications, including bleeding, infections, severe cramps, nerve damage, and organ injuries.[19] Poorly installed mesh resulted in erosion, making patients feel like the implant sliced into their vagina, bladder, urethra, and bowel. Suddenly these women couldn't walk or sit without debilitating pain. New brides stared at a lifetime of painful sex. Moms deserted their jobs due to chronic complications. One marathon runner found herself crawling to the bathroom.

[†] Mesh slings and transvaginal mesh use the same plastic material, polypropylene, but they differ in their applications, how they're anchored, and the way they are placed.

Consider Kath Sansom, whose friends called her "the Ritalin kid" for her inability to sit still. "Too much energy," they said. Super active in her forties, the photographer and journalist boxed twice a week, swam most days, and went mountain biking on weekends. Sansom had experienced a little bit of incontinence after having her second daughter, which was embarrassing but didn't truly inhibit her lifestyle.

In 2015, Sansom's surgeon said the condition was simple to fix. The physician sold her on an "amazing" procedure which took only twenty minutes and had a "really quick" recovery. "Perfect for a career woman like you," her doctor told her. She was training to cycle up Snowdon—the highest mountain in Wales—right before her mesh surgery.

But immediately following the procedure, Sansom experienced an extreme reaction to the foreign material and all-over pain in the lower half of her body. The plastic mesh pressed on nerves and muscles, instigating excruciating pain—a feeling like being cut with a cheese wire. Despite being promised seven days for recovery, the pain intensified as the weeks wore on, causing burning sensations in her groin. Sansom couldn't even walk up a flight of stairs. "It felt like someone had taken a baseball bat and smacked me down the back of my legs all the way down to the bottom of my feet," she recalls through tears. "I would lie in bed at night terrified because I couldn't think of living the rest of my life in this much pain."

Some patients learned that mesh removal isn't always so simple. Their doctors told them that revision surgery is complicated and runs the risk of further damage. As one patient described it, revision surgery is like "trying to remove gum from hair."[20] Thousands of patients never fully regained their health.

Sansom wasn't warned of these risks. Had she known, she would have never agreed to have it implanted. "None of us [patients gave] fully informed consent. If we had been told of all the risks, we would have run out of the room."

Sansom never cycled again, and her boxing days are long over. She can no longer take part in many of the high-octane activities that once gave her so much joy. In addition, she began to experience constant joint aches, making even light outings difficult to endure. The once carefree, energy-filled Sansom no longer exists.

That same year, Sansom launched Sling the Mesh, a digital community support group for women harmed by and recovering from mesh implants. Many of the nearly ten thousand members report chronic complications, and in a site survey, seven out of ten say their sex lives were destroyed. To clarify, they didn't lose their sex drive. Rather, they lost the ability to *have sex* due to intense burning sensations and pain. For some women, the mesh quite literally slices through their vaginal walls and cuts their partner. Of those, a percentage say their doctors show little sympathy, some telling women over fifty they're too old to be having sex anyway. "If it was men losing their sex lives on that scale, you can bet your bottom dollar that operation would have been stopped years ago," says Sansom. "Men would not stand that kind of a risk."

In 2016, the U.S. Food and Drug Administration reclassified surgical mesh products for the transvaginal repair of pelvic organ prolapse (POP) as "high risk" following reports of long-term complications.[21] Three years later, the FDA ordered manufacturers Boston Scientific and Coloplast to halt the distribution and sale of any remaining surgical mesh products for the transvaginal repair of POP, stating that they had "not demonstrated a reasonable assurance of safety and effectiveness for these devices."[22]

In 2021, Boston Scientific agreed to pay $188.7 million to settle claims that it deceptively marketed their transvaginal surgical mesh devices, although the company stated that the settlement was not an admission of misconduct.[23] Subsequent reports[24] alleged that implant manufacturers hustled their products without sufficient testing,[25] reinforcing suspicions that women had been essentially treated like guinea pigs.

How exactly did these products slip through in the United States without the potential complications being made more apparent? Well, medical device companies can simply prove their devices are substantially equivalent to ones already available on the market in a process known as the 510(k) pathway. "If you use that process to have a device approved, you don't need to provide any patient data," says Dr. Carmel. "This is how they got around it." (In 2019, the FDA announced the agency would enforce stricter standards on its medical device program to increase transparency.)[26]

The medical community is split over vaginal mesh in terms of what should and shouldn't be banned.[‡] Pelvic surgery experts I interviewed said it isn't necessarily the transvaginal surgical mesh devices themselves that are problematic, rather their incorrect placement by surgeons. Many were not adequately informed about the risks involved. A surgeon could be just one centimeter off and accidentally hit a nerve.

Still, there are lessons learned from this controversy, including the need to adequately train doctors, to implement stricter regulations, and to listen to female patients.

But while changes are underway, there are still those picking up the pieces.

Today, Sansom relies on alternative therapies to manage lingering aftereffects. For example, her nose began dripping immediately after the procedure, and she believes the ongoing symptom is directly related.[§] Sansom makes a homemade paste with turmeric, known for its anti-inflammatory properties, which she says stops nasal leakage within half an hour. Fellow sufferers say they use cannabis or alcohol to manage their daily pain. "I have no trust in [the medical establishment]," says Sansom, who mourns

---

[‡] Doctors reiterate there is a big difference between the use of mesh for urinary stress incontinence, which is still in wide use, and for that of prolapse surgery, which has more complications.

[§] It is unclear whether it is directly related, as urologists I interviewed expressed skepticism. However, Shlomo Raz, professor of urology and pelvic reconstruction at UCLA School of Medicine, told the *Washington Post* in 2019 that he had seen "lupus-type" complications such as a runny nose disappear when the mesh is removed.

participation in all the sports she'd previously based her life on. "All gone. Absolutely shattered."

Flashback: The Scientist Who Protected Women from One of the Biggest Drug Fiascos

Decades peppered by horrific medical fiascos have at times eroded public trust and enabled peddlers of alternative care. Many women have been left questioning the attention to safety and adequate research precautions. But women have also fought to protect consumers, and they serve as a testament to why their inclusion in medicine is vital.

In the late fifties, one such pharmaceutical tragedy across Europe involved a new drug to combat morning sickness: thalidomide. It was heavily marketed to pregnant women, or, more specifically, to their physicians.

But when taken during the first trimester of pregnancy, thalidomide could cause severe developmental abnormalities. More than ten thousand babies were born with limb malformations and other birth defects including blindness, deafness, and brain damage.[27] The drug, which was not sufficiently tested, was estimated to have also caused just as many miscarriages.[28]

When the drug tried to enter the U.S. market—months before its effects were widely known—a female FDA reviewer and scientist named Dr. Frances Oldham Kelsey demanded more testing. The drug manufacturer behind thalidomide, William S. Merrell Co., complained to Dr. Kelsey's supervisors—calling, sending letters, and even showing up in person to try to rush their application.[29] Dr. Kelsey remained resolute, demanding more research demonstrating the drug's safety and efficacy. "I held my ground," Dr. Kelsey reflected decades later. "I just wouldn't approve it."[30]

Thanks to Dr. Kelsey's steadfastness, thalidomide was never approved in the United States. An estimated 20,000 Americans—600 who were pregnant—did take the drug as part of clinical trials conducted by drugmakers; seventeen cases of congenital deformities were reported, but "that could have been thousands had the FDA not insisted on the evidence of safety required under the law (despite ongoing pressure from the drug's sponsor)."[31]

As *Life* magazine wrote in 1962, "A woman of fortitude and determination had proved that the wheels of progress should occasionally be slowed and examined."[32] That same year, President John F. Kennedy bestowed on Dr. Kelsey the President's Award for Distinguished Federal Civilian Service, the highest honor granted to a civilian in the United States.

The thalidomide crisis pushed Congress to sign legislation empowering the FDA to have more authority over drug testing. In addition, Dr. Kelsey helped compose guidelines that govern clinical trials and which are now used worldwide.

Funny enough, Dr. Kelsey got her professional start in pharmacology because she was mistaken for a man. Dr. Kelsey had applied to be a research assistant in the University of Chicago's pharmacology department. She was offered the position—without an interview—after the hiring manager read her name as "Francis," and assumed she was "Mr. Oldham." Dr. Kelsey, realizing the mistake, asked one of her professors at McGill University what she should do: "When a woman took a job in those days, she was made to feel as if she was depriving a man of the ability to support his wife and child," Dr. Kelsey told the *New York Times*. "But my professor said: 'Don't be stupid. Accept the job, sign your name and put "Miss" in brackets afterward.'"[33]

Insufficient medical knowledge, which leads to misdiagnosis and medical fiascos, is improving, in part due to more women entering medicine, health tech, and research.

Kathryn Schubert of SWHR is optimistic: she points to several wins at the policy level, including increased funding for the Office of Research on Women's Health (ORWH), which coordinates women's health research across the NIH. The National Institute for Child Health and Human Development (NICHD), which handles endometriosis research, discovered "pretty critical scientific breakthroughs" regarding the progression of the condition and treatment options "versus just looking at hysterectomy," says Schubert. "It's hard to see the wins because there is so much work that needs to be done, but it is happening."

Elhadad, meanwhile, has her sights set on more than just endometriosis. She plans to take the Citizen Endo model and apply it to other underrepresented women's health conditions, including polycystic ovary syndrome. She's also working on an organization dedicated to building a community for female-focused medical research. "We're making sure patient voices and women are actually heard."

That's in addition to plenty more research-focused start-ups and biotech companies uniquely focused on women's health. (Digital health start-ups serving women's needs raised $1.3 billion in 2021.)[34] Researchers, for example, are building "smart bras" that are basically heart monitors; they're using medical-grade fabric sensors and machine learning to gather heart health data because heart disease is the leading cause of death for women worldwide. Universities are mining the databases of period tracking apps such as Clue to better understand menstrual cycles' effects on pain, mood, and ovulation. Big ideas are in the pipeline, with plans to tackle everything from nonhormonal birth control to neuroimmune disorders.

Women are also talking more publicly about their health, which helps bring attention to the cause and assists in finding solutions. Postpartum depression is a great example of this: in earlier decades, women weren't necessarily telling friends or their clinicians about the phenomenon, so nobody knew it was an issue, let alone one deserving of research. "People are not always talking about what they're experiencing, and I think that sets us back," says Schubert. "We need to have these open, honest conversations."

Either way, some might feel the growth is not keeping pace with the dissatisfaction and issues inherent in an overburdened medical system. (Not that it's an easy feat: research studies are time-consuming and costly, racking up millions and taking years.) And within that vacuum, alternatives take root. Patients who become tired of trying to change a system that doesn't prioritize them take their business elsewhere. Sadly, desperate women are often mocked or criticized for self-treatment, and doctors roll their eyes at "Dr. WebMD." But these women turn right back around and demand: What other option did I have?

Chapter 7

Nutritionmania:
Why Are We Confused About What We Eat?

You wouldn't think the Kardashian sisters would be the yin and yang of wellness, the light to each other's dark, but let me share my favorite episode of *Keeping Up with the Kardashians*: In 2019, the reality TV stars Kim and Kourtney Kardashian fought over an issue that would have puzzled viewers a decade prior. It was so petty and so emotionally charged—and yet representative of a growing sentiment in American households.

In the back of their chauffeured Range Rover, the siblings argued over what to serve at their kindergarten-age daughters' joint birthday party. And it was getting heated. Name calling, raised voices, and insults ensued. The party theme was Candy Land, but older sister Kourtney—founder of the wellness lifestyle brand Poosh—refused to go along with it. She wanted none of the "nasty" and "gross" gumdrops or lollipops from the iconic board game. There would be no homage to Princess Frostine's Ice Palace, nor a nod to the bountiful Peppermint Forest. This candy-free Candy Land would present nutritious treats instead of sweets. Maybe even some salads.

Kim, who couldn't fathom carrots masquerading as licorice, called her health-conscious sister "insane."

"*It's Candy Land*, Kourtney," emphasized Kim. "It's not going to be healthy." The two went back and forth debating whether or not candy canes had to be, well, literal. An astonished Kim accused her sister of foisting a completely "sugar-free, gluten-free, party-free, fun-free zone" on two innocent six-year-olds. "My kids eat at home really, really healthy. And the one day they want a Candy Land birthday party, and you're saying they can't have sugar?!"[1]

Kourtney disagreed, accusing Kim of hurting the children. "You're dated, you're in the past," Kourtney lectured Kim, claiming food coloring "literally" gives people diseases. "Everyone is going to come to this party and everything is going to be disgusting chemicals?!" *How can you not feel guilty about that?* she asked. Unhealthy food, she added, wasn't what she "stood for."

The disagreement continued for several days, to the point where other family members needed to mediate between the two. And it was real: long-term show fans (such as myself) can tell whether a fight is manufactured or legitimate. In the latter, Kim quickly escalates a heated exchange into threats (or actual instances) of physical violence. At one point during "sugargate," Kim threatened to hit her sister in the face with a piñata.

After refusing to come to a consensus, the sisters decided to break with tradition and settled on separate parties. Though the cousins were inseparable best friends, they were subjected to their mothers' nutritional divide. Kourtney would serve sugar-free organic cotton candy, while Kim displayed mounds of gummy bears, chocolates, and marshmallows. Later, after the episode aired and viewers took sides on social media, Kourtney tweeted, "I am actually shocked that people are so unaware of how harmful certain foods can be."

Perhaps no better issue demonstrates the fading trust in Big Food than that of sugar, which has been dubbed the "new smoking," declared "addictive as cocaine," and gives new meaning to the danger invoked by the *Ghostbusters* Stay Puft Marshmallow Man.* There's no question that too much sugar is an issue in American diets. And as the number of children with obesity has increased tenfold,[3] some parents ponder: How do we best feed our families?

But fear of eating the wrong foods can quickly devolve into confusion, extremism—and judgment. In mommy circles, peers can pour the gasoline: Six out of ten mothers of young kids say they have been criticized about parenting, with over half of those complaints centered on diet and nutrition.[4] Even Reese Witherspoon "incurred the wrath of the food police" when she shared an Instagram photo of glazed cinnamon rolls for her son's breakfast.[5] "Child abuse right there," wrote one critic.

If choosy moms once chose Jif peanut butter, now they must choose only the *right* healthful products to cement their parental reputation.

Cutting out sugar isn't a fad diet, but it's just one of several popular food doctrines, along with vegan, dairy-free, gluten-free, or (Paltrow favorite) "clean" eating. The United States saw a 600 percent increase in veganism between 2014 to 2017,[6] and 30 percent of all Americans now avoid gluten,[7] though only a small percentage actually have Celiac disease or a gluten sensitivity. Cookbook sales grew 21 percent in 2018 partially because consumers were sold on the nutritional superiority of cooking at home versus going out (where presumably unwholesome food awaits).[8]

Anxiety over nutrition has inspired new food commandments, much like the ever-growing list of lifestyle laws dictating exercise and other practices. Food is no longer neutral territory; strict views have polarized our daily consumption. Within specific middle- and upper-middle-class communities, the message has gone from *Try your best* to *Do exactly this*. Talk with the average woman and you will notice a disturbing pattern

---

* While one could certainly have sugar cravings, nutrition experts I interviewed note that sugar is not literally addictive like drugs. In addition, a 2016 study led by University of Cambridge neuroscientists found "little evidence to support sugar addiction in humans."[2]

surrounding what is or isn't "healthy," what supplements you should take, how many meals to eat per day, the need for organic . . . Americans are, quite frankly, a nutritional mess.

"There's so much information about food being thrown at you, it's hard to know what to believe and what really works," writes bestselling author and blogger Vani Hari. "As a reader of this blog, you're on the right path. I'm showing you how to become the smartest consumers out there."[9]

Vani Hari, who goes by the moniker Food Babe, has built an entire empire lambasting ultra-processed food while waging war against Big Food. A charismatic brunette with an inviting smile, Hari is perfectly put together: slim, hair styled in loose waves, unfussy makeup, like one of those cool moms from a Nickelodeon show in designer skinny jeans and a moto jacket. But unlike a Nickelodeon mom, Hari will not offer you a Pillsbury cookie: in fact, this food safety champion won't invite you to enjoy much of any conventional snacks. To her, "refined sugar is the devil." She tells fans to avoid artificial dyes at birthday parties. She warned that Kellogg's waffles are a "disaster for children's immune system." She lobbied Starbucks to stop using Class IV caramel coloring in pumpkin spice lattes.

Her other big beef? That those pumpkin spice lattes contain "absolutely no real pumpkin."[10]

Hari is not a nutritionist, food scientist, or toxicologist, yet she became a leading health blogger, activist, and one of *Time* magazine's "Most Influential People on the Internet." The former management consultant was revered and feared for demonizing common ingredients found in *everything*: preservatives, additives, GMOs, and added sugars, all of which she says carry great health risks. In criticizing food companies, she goes hard: "Big Food is deliberately confusing us," she tweeted. "They don't want us to know how to eat right." There's not much love for regulatory oversight either, for that matter: "The FDA is asleep at the wheel and the Food Industry is in charge."

She's right about one thing: it's a bit odd just how confused we are about a basic biological function (though who is entirely to blame is a bit more complicated). At first glance it seems surprising. After all, weren't those laminated United States Department of Agriculture (USDA) food pyramids posted in every classroom—telling us to eat our vegetables and fruits like good healthy soldiers—the quintessential guides to healthful eating? What happened?

Piling on the Plate: Corporate Greed Further Confuses Matters

The iconic food pyramid has played the villain as much as the hero when it comes to clarifying eating recommendations. The nutrition guidelines reshuffled mandates on categories like fats and oils. A failure to define serving sizes or distinguish between types of fat, let alone between minimally processed grains and refined ones (not all carbs are created equal), opened the doors to mass confusion.[†]

Surprisingly, the pyramid was built on the architecture of a widely adopted (though contested) food theory. In the 1950s, a physiologist named Ancel Keys proposed that heart disease was linked to high-fat diets and high cholesterol levels. To prove it, he studied seven countries, including Greece, Italy, Japan, and Finland. Great travel destinations, no doubt, but the world is bigger than just a half dozen countries. Regardless, the infamous Seven Countries Study's findings prioritized carbohydrates, discouraged saturated fats, and oversimplified the issue of cholesterol. Eggs were out, cereal was in.

Despite conflicting evidence, it took off.[11] Research circles and the media—which were both looking for solutions to the heart disease epidemic—pushed the theory. The government then adopted it for their first dietary guidelines. In 1980, the USDA advised Americans to cut back on red meat, eggs, and dairy products and pile on carbohydrates like pasta, rice, bread, and cereal instead, among other recommendations. The position

---

[†] In 2011, the USDA introduced MyPlate, which emphasized a more holistic approach to nutrition.

was solidified into nutritional dogma, then rolled out across companies, schools, agencies, and the media, but not with the clearest communication. The guidelines were often misinterpreted.[12]

The established viewpoint claimed that if you reduced fat, you would automatically reduce calories because fat is higher in calories than carbohydrates. There was just one problem: once fats were removed from foods, the result was less appetizing. The only way to make the now textureless morsel tasty was to *add sugar*. Food manufacturers quickly swapped one ingredient for another and capitalized on the health lingo of the day. Suddenly grocery stores were filled with rebranded "low-fat" but sugar-packed snacks, granola bars, and yogurt. That led to what's been dubbed "the SnackWell effect," which refers to the psychological tendency to eat more of a food marketed as low-fat.

Based on this logic, Americans became fearful of butter and cheese but embraced "fat-free" muffins. From 1971 to 2000, American women increased their carbohydrate intake by nearly 25 percent, as fat became enemy number one.[13] What started as a fight against heart disease ended as a surrender to carb overconsumption.

The ongoing battle between sugar versus fat was further complicated by sugar lobbyists and biased researchers, who weren't very helpful at preventing this nutrition misunderstanding. In the 1960s, sugar producers paid Harvard scientists to discredit anti-sugar science and downplay its role in heart disease.[14] Instead, these researchers (whose pre-existing work, to be fair, already supported these findings) pointed the finger at fat. However, studies show both fat *and* sugar can contribute to heart disease.

Today, the average American consumes almost 150 pounds of total sugar in one year (the equivalent of six full cups a week). Of that, 66 pounds are added sugar.[15] Why? Because it's in everything. Sugar is in pasta sauce, bread, even salad dressing. It's virtually inescapable. While other factors contributed to our nutritional issues, it's fair to say that poorly constructed messaging surrounding the food pyramid ought to shoulder a portion of the blame.

Incorrect guidance wasn't the only thing leading Americans further astray from the nutritionally sound path. The situation was compounded by pressure placed on food companies to maximize profits, as Wall Street changed the way it evaluated corporations. Long, slow returns on investment gave way to the shareholder value model, forcing corporations to provide higher, more immediate returns on investment. Companies, under intense pressure, were forced to look for ways to sell more; growth became the focus. Gordon Gekko seized the dinner table.‡

Cheap and easily accessible highly processed food took off. Some ultra-processed-food manufacturers also followed what's been dubbed the "potato chip marketing equation," selling 90 percent of their products to 10 percent of their customers, many of whom were low-income. They decided that spending marketing dollars going after an existing customer and selling them on increased consumption was more lucrative than targeting new ones.[16] Essentially, they're persuading current clientele to buy not one bag of chips per month, but one bag of chips *per day*.

Lay's potato chips slogan "Bet you can't eat just one!" is therefore actually quite literal. You can't eat one not only because ad dollars ask you to eat more but also because the product is chemically engineered to be as delicious as possible. Food chemists craft ultra-processed foods to appeal to our biggest cravings—added sugar, salt, and fats—which light up our brains' reward centers like a Vegas slot machine, researchers suggest.[17]

As more food was produced and marketed, portion sizes got bigger. Calories in the food supply increased, and people started eating more. The

---

‡ Many twentieth-century food trends have roots that go further back in American history, touching upon technological advancement and agricultural policies. Food historian Sarah Wassberg Johnson says that after WWII, food companies expanded on defense-funded nutrition and chemical research to increase their bottom lines. Then, in the seventies, new government policies allowed food corporations to cheaply purchase commodity crops like corn and soy, which incentivized using them as additives.

Big Gulp trumped the soda can. Fast-food chains rolled out supersized meals. Restaurants introduced all-you-can-eat buffets. And even standard foods were reworked. The average bagel went from three inches in diameter (140 calories) twenty years ago to six inches in diameter (350 calories) today.[18] "We used to eat less, end of story," Marion Nestle, a consumer advocate and the author of *Food Politics*, told me.

The industrial food revolution and fast-food dependency clearly affected eating habits. A modern American consumes more than 3,600 calories each day, a 24 percent increase from 1961, in part because highly processed foods and snacks make up to 60 percent of their diet.[19] Just 7 percent of American adults meet the daily recommendation for fiber (because fiber is found in foods like beans and lentils).[20]

Granted, not all processed food is bad for you. Processed foods lie within a spectrum. Some foods are lightly processed to prevent spoilage or boost mineral content, like canned vegetables, whereas others are ultra-processed and packed with sugars, salt, and additives. But the latter is usually far tastier and hence more popular.

It should be noted that the 1980 dietary guidelines advised minimizing added sugars, advice that Americans ignored.[21] In all fairness, how could nutritionists compete against Big Food's billion-dollar marketing budgets? Our childhoods are marked by McDonald's Happy Meals and Pop-Tarts advertised on television. We can't recall too many cartoon characters shilling for vegetables (except maybe the Green Giant, but he was drowned out by the party-loving Kool-Aid Man). Even today, more than 80 percent of food advertising—nearly $14 billion—promotes fast food, soda, energy drinks, chips, and candy.[22]

As enticing as it may be to squarely blame the original faulty science, our modern food environment—cheap, processed food available at every turn, from the gas station to ubiquitous food vending machines—does need to be considered. We never stood a chance. In time, we all started to realize it.

Growing Distrust of "Big Food":
The Personal Becomes Political

Awareness of issues with processed food took off in the sixties, when the growing natural food movement—think hippies, communes, and food co-ops—confronted the mainstream food industry for its greasy grip on consumers. Young baby boomers voiced their dissent through what they ate, wore, and believed. By revolutionizing their private life, the conscientious rebel would also transform "the system." Rejecting the mass-produced hamburger was, in its own way, a radicalized act. And so brown rice wasn't just brown rice—the sticky grain was an act of defiance.

Healthier eating produced a new kind of discernment that motivated reformers to rally against agribusiness *and* their parents' kitchen. And "unlike sporadic anti-war protests, dietary rightness could be lived 365 days a year, three times a day."[23]

It was more than just disgust at McDonald's beef patties. Food politics were part and parcel of a larger shift in societal attitudes toward mass industry. People were fearful of nuclear war, toxic waste, and environmental issues and saw many issues reflective of industrial failings. Corporate manufacturers proved they couldn't always prevent damaging ingredients from seeping into a hamburger. Tainted, contaminated, or misrepresented food sparked skepticism then and continues today.

Meanwhile, media exposés reinforced suspicions that government agencies aren't fully invested in nutrition but are smoking cigarettes in bed with food lobbyists. Reports confirmed the USDA is under constant pressure from meat and dairy groups.[24] The USDA is obligated to promote food commodities, thereby facing intense opposition whenever it wants to recommend a decrease in any food group in dietary guidelines. At a Senate hearing, former Illinois Republican senator Peter Fitzgerald characterized this blatant conflict of interest, "like putting the fox in charge of the hen house."[25]

Even the health associations and leading nutritionists no longer carry the weight they once did, in part due to their participation in paid endorsements or studies sponsored by bigwigs like Coca-Cola. In 1988, the American Heart Association (AHA) raised money for research efforts by selling a "heart-healthy" label to food companies eager to capitalize on better-for-you marketing. A product only needed to meet a specific requirement for levels of saturated fat, cholesterol, and sodium. By labeling single foods as "heart-healthy," it "distorted basic principles of good nutrition which depend on overall dietary patterns," writes Marion Nestle in *Food Politics*.[26] Many sugar-laden cereals boasted the AHA seal of approval. Shoppers scanned the grocery aisle and wondered, *How the hell is Trix healthful?*

Then there are the food scandals. Here is just a sample from recent global headlines: Chicken from some major fast-food chains might contain only 50 percent chicken DNA.[27] Mars recalled chocolate bars in fifty-five countries over "fears that customers could choke on pieces of plastic."[28] Consumer Reports found that 97 percent of chicken breasts sold in retail stores contained potentially harmful bacteria (often the result of fecal matter contamination).

Though rare, such debacles seep into the American psyche. In one 2020 survey of five hundred consumers, less than half said they trusted the overall food industry. Instead, 77 percent of respondents said cooking in their kitchens was the best course of action.[29] And when health-conscious consumers shop, they're pickier; almost half considered whether a product was processed before heading to the cash register, according to a Nielsen report.[30]

Women not only learned not to take the word of Big Food on what to eat, they started having nutrition meltdowns like never before, spinning a revolving door of restrictive food rules. Which led to even more confusion. When it comes to nutritional guidelines, harsh restrictions like Kourtney Kardashian's "healthy Candy Land" rule for her kids are extremely clear. But are all the restrictions deserved? Or accurate?

Flashback: Yearning for Nutritional Nirvana

In a Depression-era ad for Post Bran Flakes, a young girl named Sally is mercilessly mocked by schoolmates for her dismal report card. Turning to her mother, she finds little refuge. "Sally Lennox! I'm ashamed of this report card. What will your father say?" the mother lectures the child.

But not so fast, the reader learns. The mother is the villain here. The problem was not caused because young Sally didn't study. Instead, the selfish mother is to blame. For you see, it turns out the poor grades were the result of constipation . . . from not eating enough cereal. "Maybe you have a little girl like Sally," the ad reads, laying the guilt on thick, "and perhaps like Sally's mother, you have been unjust to her."[31]

Starting in the 1920s, national government campaigns coupled with women's magazine articles stressed a very specific nutrition mandate, reinforcing the idea that fortified foods (products with added nutrients) were "necessary" for a normal healthy life. Some brand campaigns relied on scare tactics, like Grape-Nuts cereal, which suggested that a cereal-poor diet puts children at risk of "unfortunate personality traits" like shyness and self-pity.[32] In time, nutrition was imbued with a sense of morality and elitism, claiming to ensure good nerves, composure, energy, beauty, and steadfastness. Health, essentially, secured one's future prospects.

This messaging reached deep into women's maternal core, causing utmost anxiety and thereby frantic obedience. No mother would refuse Grape-Nuts, lest her child turned into Eeyore.

Taking aim at children's success was a calculated action. Advertisers were "fascinated" by a growing competitive struggle—specifically, how it played out with parents dissatisfied with their own ambitions. Brands discovered that parents could be pushed to pass their anxieties and quashed aspirations onto their children. In effect, the next generation was coerced into actualizing their parents' disappearing dreams and pummeled into competitive one-upmanship.[33]

This collective guidance led to a nerve-racking quest for nutritional perfection in the fifties, equating a morning bowl of cereal to extra tutoring. Vitamins were synonymous with health, even though consumers knew very little about food chemistry. Women were told to put their faith in experts and nutrition gurus, for fear of gambling with the family's fragile health, as Catherine Price documents in her book *Vitamania*. "Americans of both genders embraced the notion that careful homemakers had a responsibility to ensure that their families—through food and, later, supplements—had enough of each," writes Price. "How much was enough, though? Nobody knew."[34]

Organic or Bust: How Concerned Should We Be About Produce?

While shoppers rack their brains over what to eat, many seem to be certain about one thing: they want their whole foods to be organic. Despite the extra cost and often reduced shelf life, in certain circles, organic is the new given. Sales of organic foods more than doubled between 1994 and 2014.[35] I too favored organic for several years. It sounded right. Why wouldn't I want the "healthier" option?

The problem is that organic is a description that seemingly confuses the consumer as much as it supposedly clarifies what should or shouldn't be on their dinner plate. Is organic the same as "natural"? Does it mean GMO-free? It turns out that 23 percent of consumers think "local" is synonymous with organic.[36] (It's not.)

Not to mention that the health benefits of organic are—and I know this might come as a shock—nowhere near as proven as most consumers would like to think.

Many women I've interviewed switched to pricier organic after reading the Environmental Working Group's "Dirty Dozen" list, a shopper's guide to produce that purportedly contains high levels of pesticide residue and therefore should be avoided. Every year, the EWG announces which misbehaving fruits and vegetables made the naughty list, prompting mainstream media outlets to publish which conventionally grown produce is "in" or "out." It's ubiquitous to the point where we don't even question it.

In 2021, the EWG warned that "imazalil, a fungicide that can change hormone levels and is classified by the Environmental Protection Agency as a likely human carcinogen, was detected on nearly 90 percent of citrus."[37] This was all very scary-sounding! Who wants evil chemicals lounging on their fruit?

The thing is, organic farms *also* use pesticides and fungicides to ward off pests and fungal disease. They're less discussed because they're "organic." Organic means derived more from natural substances than synthetic. But "natural," as we have learned, doesn't necessarily always mean better. Organic farms generally try to minimize pesticide use, and some of their pesticides are gentler than synthetic ones, but they can sometimes be less effective, leading organic farms to use much more of the organic pesticides in order to achieve the same results.

As for conventional pesticides, the science might not overwhelmingly support a reason to switch for *health* reasons. I'm focusing on the health benefits here, understanding full well that people choose organic produce for other substantial reasons, including animal welfare and planetary concerns.

Carl K. Winter is a toxicology expert and professor emeritus at the University of California, Davis, Department of Food Science and Technology who specializes in pesticides. He says researchers have consistent data demonstrating that the very tiny presence of pesticide residues on most conventional foods is far too low to constitute a health threat. Winter investigated the EWG's 2010 Dirty Dozen list, homing in on the specific exposure to the ten most frequently detected pesticides on each discouraged fruit and vegetable. His researchers concluded that typical exposures to chemicals on those particular foods were at "infinitesimal" levels. "For most pesticides, if we were to feed consumers ten thousand times more pesticides in their diet than they're getting, those levels *still* wouldn't be of health concern," explains Winter. "It's the amount of a chemical, not its presence or absence, that determines the potential for harm."

The EWG's imazalil claim—the one that warned about fungicide on citrus plotting against us? Their interpretation is partially based on extremely high doses.[38] A 150-pound adult could consume more than eight thousand conventionally grown nectarines *in one day* without any ill effects even if they contained the highest pesticide residue recorded by the USDA. Scientists criticize the EWG for scaring consumers with "deceptive" sensationalized warnings that distort the science.[39] Several scientists told me the same thing: the organization blows things out of proportion. Mind you, the EWG is not merely inflating the danger to the size of a birthday balloon; they're inflating it to the size of a Goodyear blimp.

Toxicologists I spoke to attack the EWG's Dirty Dozen for what they deem a dubious, arbitrary methodology that ignores the basic pillars of toxicology. The three principles of risk assessment—toxicity of the individual pesticides, consumption rates of these foods, and actual levels of pesticide residues detected on foods—don't seem to have been taken into consideration. The EWG (which, again, is partially funded by the organic industry, including Organic Valley, Stonyfield Farms, and more) readily states as much if you dig into their website: "The Shopper's Guide does not incorporate risk assessment into the calculations. All pesticides are weighted equally, and we do not factor in the levels deemed acceptable by the EPA."

Now, studies have found that organic produce does indeed have a lower presence of pesticide residue. That could be because organic farms use pesticides after exhausting nonchemical methods, including crop rotation, among other reasons. But does that mean it's much "safer" to consume than conventional veggies? Not necessarily. There's no doubt that most pesticides, both synthetic and organic, are potentially dangerous, especially for farm workers exposed to high doses in a work environment. The issue I'm discussing here, however, is whether the level of pesticide *residue* in regular produce—after it's been rinsed—should be of concern.

The FDA announced that nearly 99 percent of foods sampled and monitored in 2019 showed pesticide residue levels "well below" Environmental Protection Agency (EPA) safety standards, while 42 percent had no detectable residue levels at all. According to the FDA, results confirmed that residues "do not pose a concern for public health."[40] This is not to say that there isn't room for improvement in FDA regulations, just that experts agree it's inaccurate to label conventional produce as "unsafe."

Okay, but what about the nutrition factor? More than three-quarters of consumers who buy organic are "looking for healthier foods."[41]

There's not enough information to meaningfully conclude how organic foods benefit overall health. To start, observational studies following eating populations are quite difficult to decipher because, for example, if one cohort ate organic and were less likely to develop cancers, was it due to the food consumed? Organic eaters usually have access to better health care, exercise more, and suffer less stress than those without the means to afford such food. So how do you prove causation and not correlation?

Food consumption studies are also extremely difficult (and often fundamentally flawed) because they're short-term and not controlled: they're generally self-reported. Unless you keep thousands of people cooped up in a lab for years, it's hard to determine whether they're actually eating what they say they're eating. That is, if they can even remember what they ate.

We do have research, although scientists are mixed on the inconclusive evidence. A 2012 Stanford University meta-analysis study of 237 existing studies (basically, a study of studies) compared organic to non-organic counterparts, only to conclude that, overall, they "showed no evidence of differences in nutrition-related health outcomes."[42]

Other studies suggest higher levels of nutrients in certain organics.

A 2014 meta-analysis study based on 343 previously published studies[§] found that organic produce contains a 17 percent higher concentration of antioxidants than conventional crops.[43] Published in the *British Journal of Nutrition*, it was reportedly intended as a scientific reply to the 2012 Stanford study. But while antioxidants are associated with health benefits, they are not synonymous with it, especially since there's a wide range of antioxidants. As one of the lead researchers told the *New York Times*, "We are not making health claims based on this study, because we can't . . . [the study] doesn't tell you anything about how much of a health impact switching to organic food could have."[44]

The researchers also found that organically grown crops produced lower levels of proteins and fiber than conventional produce.

The question remains: Are there *significant* health differences between organic and conventional? There is a strong general consensus among nutritional science experts I spoke to: that consuming organic food has no considerable health benefit. Even the USDA pauses before staking a claim to benefits. The *Washington Post* asked Miles McEvoy, the former chief of the National Organic Program at the USDA, a very simple question: Are consumers right to think that organic food is safer and healthier? McEvoy was evasive, replying, "The question is not relevant."[45]

The organic industry is betting on consumers conflating farming standards with supposed health benefits. More specifically, they're counting on moms worried about properly feeding their children and made fearful of overhyped pesticide risk (more on that in chapter 12).[46] As far back as 2001, General Mills—having acquired organic lines such as Small Planet Foods—was quite forthcoming about their tactics. In a *New York Times*

[§] The 2014 study included studies that the 2012 Stanford study excluded. Critics argue that this does not necessarily mean that the 2014 one had more robust or more critical data, but rather that it potentially included weaker studies that didn't meet the Stanford team's criteria. The 2014 study also received partial funding from Sheepdrove Trust, which supports organic farming research, while the Stanford University study had no external funding from a farming group.

piece by Michael Pollan, General Mills marketing executive R. Brooks Gekler acknowledged that Small Planet Foods targets "health seekers" even though he doesn't know if organic is healthier. "At first, I thought the inability to make hard-hitting health claims—for organic—was a hurdle," Gekler offered. "But the reality is, all you have to say is 'organic'—you don't need to provide any more information."[47]

What Gekler meant is that brands don't need to actively mislead shoppers. At this point, consumers fill in the blanks with their assumptions all on their own.

We might assume certain things about organic because there's a lot baked (so to speak) into our views of food. When NPR ran a report on the Stanford study, they got so many complaints ("prompted a powerful reaction," is how they put it) that they had to run another segment just to address the backlash. In an attempt to calm down listeners, they interviewed NPR's social science correspondent Shankar Vedantam, who is also the host and creator of the *Hidden Brain* podcast. He said something that applies to many of the things we buy or do: strong emotional values are tied up with organic food. It has come to represent so many other things—anti-industrialization, good parenting, nature, spirituality—that might not have anything to do with these studies' findings.[48] "There are these tensions between what we want organic to be at a psychological level, and what it actually does at a practical level," says Vedantam. "And the science is very good at telling us at the practical level what's going on. But sometimes, that could feel like the science is attacking our values."[49]

Normal nectarines aren't keeping nutritionists up at night (at least the ones I spoke to). What does worry them is far more practical: organic's scare tactics could make people more fearful of consuming conventional produce and may lead them to consume less produce overall. Indeed, here's what sometimes happens with some lower-income shoppers: nervous and confused[50] about pesticides—and too cash-strapped to afford organic— they end up skipping the produce aisle altogether. A small 2016 study of five hundred low-income shoppers' habits indicated that some planned to consume fewer fruits and vegetables after being alerted of pesticide residue concerns such as the crudely named Dirty Dozen.[51][¶] As the *Washington Post* speculated, the EWG "may be doing more harm than good."[52]

Because of our current nutrition discourse, those without the means or time to devote to an all-encompassing clean/organic/"superfood" lifestyle believe healthy living remains unattainable. This is especially true for those who do not have access to fresh organic food, or the time to prepare it.[**] The price of organic food varies from 5 to 100 percent more expensive, though on average, it hovers around 47 percent pricier than conventional alternatives, according to a Consumer Reports study. (Granted, organic produce is becoming more affordable and on rare occasions, it's actually cheaper than conventional produce.)

In one Facebook group for natural parenting, a moderator asked moms who eat 90 to 100 percent organic to share how much they spend each week. Quite a few were forthcoming about the challenges of trying to live their best Goop life:

"Ugh, I want to eat like that but I just cannot afford it!"

"I want to do better for my family food-wise, but geez, the prices are crazy!"

"We don't buy all organic because of this . . . We can't afford it. So we do half and half. The kids' stuff is mostly organic and then we eat the cheap gonna-give-you-heart-disease stuff."

[¶] The 2016 study did receive partial funding from the Alliance for Food and Farming, a nonprofit which represents both organic and conventional farmers. Though the AFF states it was uninvolved in the study nor made aware of the study findings until after the paper was peer reviewed, some could still interpret the findings as inevitably benefitting their members.

[**] Sylvia Klinger, a registered dietitian and the founder of Hispanic Food Communications, has witnessed decreased consumption of conventional fruits and vegetables within lower-income Hispanic communities. "I see the fear," she told me, noting that they can't afford organic alternatives. "We forget that almost half of the U.S. population is financially struggling."

"It's almost like supermarket shaming," says Winter of the two-tiered class of produce shopping. "We've got enough stress in our lives right now. We don't need to invent additional ways." Already, lower-income individuals consume fewer vegetables than higher-income groups.[53] Given that 90 percent of Americans fail to eat the recommended intake of produce, the food toxicologist shares only one piece of advice: "Just eat your fruits and vegetables if you're really concerned about health and don't worry so much about whether they're organic or conventional."

Health is obviously not the sole reason consumers choose organic produce. Organic can also taste better or fresher to some people. And taste is not to be discounted; for certain individuals, more delicious produce inspires them to eat more of it. Consumers are also influenced by production values, zeroing in on farmworker safety or environmental reasons. (The latter are also debated.)[54] These are legitimate, important concerns that aren't raised half as much as the health claims.

Although, if you're buying organic from Whole Foods—owned by Amazon, which generates millions of pounds of plastic waste per year—to "help the environment" . . . you might want to reconsider your patronage.[55] You're probably better off buying from regional producers (whether their food is organic or not).

Answering the question, *What produce should we buy?* is complicated. You're measuring a host of issues spanning environmental, financial, nutritional, and farmworker safety that go well beyond the conventional versus organic binary. I am in no way advocating against organic or suggesting it doesn't have merit. I am simply questioning a marketing-led narrative that has been so ingrained in our culture even though the science is more complex than advertised. Should we be made fearful about consuming "toxic," i.e., regular, produce when the evidence suggests otherwise?

Meanwhile, you'll notice that conventional produce is increasingly resorting to its own marketing tactics. It's why you might spot an apple with a sticker reading, "100% fresh!" or "All natural," hoping to compete against organic's seductive branding.[††] We've turned our supermarkets into a screaming match of flashy good-for-you labels. Everyone is pressuring us into nutritional choices. There's a lot of conflicting information out there—information from what should be trusted sources that just continues to proliferate.

Wait, What's Healthy Today?

Sifting through breaking news from nutritional researchers can prove just as challenging as navigating food labels. From a young age, Americans witness an ever-changing nutritional landscape that treats food like some sort of Whac-A-Mole game. One day avocados have too much fat, the next they're the crown jewel of any worthy millenial's toast. Red wine might be heart-healthy, but maybe it just correlates to a Mediterranean diet. Depending on the weather, red meat is a good source of protein or will usher in a cancer apocalypse.

This dietary nitpicking inspired the parody publication *The Onion* to opine, "Eggs Good for You This Week" but they "may be unhealthy again as soon as next Monday."

Having worked as a producer at NBC News for seven years, I can assure you that no one in the newsroom is afforded the time to sit back and consider what all this information cumulatively does to the audience. Many news organizations suffer from a lack of resources and staffing, forcing journalists to hammer out pieces at breakneck speed. Junior reporters grab viral items from social media or newswire offerings based on attention-grabbing headlines or top audience interests. I vividly recall laughing when some provocative food study would come across a newswire service vehemently contradicting a previous one. "Those perform well," an editor would chime in, pushing me to publish.

Journalists don't want to crank out a sludge of meaningless and contradictory stories, but they're forced to when clicks reign supreme. It's a lot

---

[††] In some instances, "all natural" does mean organic, as the farmer does abide by organic practices but hasn't completed the lengthy and costly certification process.

like a factory farm in that if you ever saw how the media sausage is made, you'd likely put your fork down.

But this trend has been going on for a long time, and across media. Listening to the radio or reading a magazine without being bombarded with the latest nutrition discovery or a debate on keto vs. paleo is near impossible. We're subjected to a constant tug of war over what we should and should not consume, with experts duking it out under sensationalized headlines.

At the Goop conference, I listened to panelists who depicted one's refrigerator as a nutritional minefield. According to one Goop expert, certain fruits, vegetables, and beans are reportedly harmful to the body because they contain "toxic" plant proteins called lectins, which supposedly do not want to be eaten. Lectins are apparently plants' clever answer to predators (that is, us) and cause inflammatory reactions that result in extra pounds and serious health conditions, such as "leaky gut syndrome." This panelist had written a book about how plants are quite literally trying to kill us with poisons, essentially likening the produce section to *Little Shop of Horrors*. Lentils, edamame, and eggplant are some of the many forbidden foods that over time will make you "very, very sick." And tomatoes—watch out, they're inciting "chemical warfare in our bodies."

After this talk, women were discharged into a food hall featuring twenty booths from L.A.'s top health restaurants. It was a cornucopia of bountiful vegetables, spruced-up fruits, and berry chia pudding cups— Willy Wonka's factory for Erewhon devotees. Alas, all the ingredients they were *just* warned about awaited them. Tomatoes! Edamame! All the big no-nos! What hell hath Gwyneth wrought?

Some attendees wondered aloud: "Should we, as we just learned, not eat?" Another sighed audibly to her pals, "Wait, what's safe here?"

A relentless torrent of food rules doesn't simplify women's lives but clutters their minds, drains their wallets, and confuses them to the point of paralysis. Roughly 80 percent of all Americans wrestle with conflicting nutrition information, and of those, nearly 60 percent admit that it makes them doubt their choices.[56] They stand in the grocery aisle pondering: Which frozen entree will do the least amount of damage? (Those who counter with "get out of the frozen aisle!" should keep in mind that many working women might not have the time or resources to cook from scratch.)

The conflicting information compounds "nutritional schizophrenia," a new-findings ping-pong that propelled the *Washington Post* to declare even back in 1984, "Nothing lasts. No assertion has a shelf life of more than 11 months."[57] There's no consistently reliable source of information. No definition of healthy is fully agreed upon. Depending on whom you talk to or even what culture you belong to, a variety of different definitions exist.

If people feel like they can't rely on magazines or soup cans, they'll latch on to strong leaders who do seem worthy of our trust. Or those that, at the very least, cut through the crap and just tell us what to do already.

Taking Definitive Direction from Overnight Gurus

Food Babe blogger Vani Hari has an enticing story and stark before-and-after photos to go with it. She tells the tale of a busy working adult too time-strapped to eat anything but takeout and junk food until her typical American diet—"candy addict, drank soda, never ate green vegetables"—landed her in the hospital. She then spent "thousands of hours" researching chemical production in popular items and changing her diet.[58] Hari learned how to cook, ditched processed food, went organic, and says she eventually saw health issues like eczema clear up. She also lost thirty pounds.

Hari credits the changes in her diet for the transformation. She's become an advocate for investigating what's in your food and detecting "the lies we've been fed about the food we eat."

She proclaims she's no longer duped "by big business marketing tactics" or confused by complicated labels. Offering similar salvation to fans, Hari tells them precisely what to avoid, calling out specific brand products and entire ingredient categories. Like Beautycounter, she's also on a mission for more transparency, placing pressure on conglomerates like Anheuser-Busch to divulge or remove what she considers hazard-ous ingredients. Through online activism (namely, mom-fueled petitions), Food Babe tries to get the "bad" stuff off shelves.

Hari has amassed more than a million Facebook followers, also known as the "Food Babe army." She built this legion by hitting moms where it hurts: their children. In 2015, Hari led a petition for Kraft Foods to ditch "dangerous" artificial food dyes in its iconic macaroni and cheese. These additives, she wrote, were "contaminated with known carcinogens," caused an increase in hyperactivity in children, and were linked to long-term health problems such as asthma. After the petition garnered 360,000 signatures, Kraft begrudgingly obliged. Hari comes across as a health-conscious David taking on the Big Food Goliath, a crusade that's catnip for moms.

Even those of us without kids started paying attention when Hari began making the rounds on morning news shows and cable TV stations like CNN. The activist grew to be the face of *women who care about food*.

Hari, like many successful influencers, understands the obvious: Out-rage works. Fear sells. Here are just a few of the headlines that led her lifestyle website over the past several years:

Is This Weedkiller in Your Favorite Hummus Brand?
Do You Eat Beaver Butt?
Don't Poison Santa!
Does Kale Destroy Your Thyroid?
Sparkling Water Contaminated with Chemicals Linked to Eczema,
Immune Suppression, Cancer, and Birth Defects
Are You Getting Conned by Cheap & Toxic Chocolate?

The point isn't to convey a nuanced scientific argument. It's to tap into the public's fear of "chemicals." Or as she once told ABC News, "When you look at the ingredients [in food products], if you can't spell it or pro-nounce it, you probably shouldn't eat it."[59]

Most famously, Hari started a petition against Subway to remove the chemical azodicarbonamide—which is used to condition and whiten dough during the baking process—from its bread. Hari warned it was linked to a who's who of health issues: respiratory issues, allergies, asthma, tumor development, and cancer. She then dubbed azodicarbonamide the "yoga mat chemical" because it's something that is also found in rubbery objects. "North Americans deserve to truly eat fresh—not yoga mats," she railed.

Calling it a "yoga mat chemical" leaves the impression that we're munching on gym products, which is presumably what Hari intended. But chemicals can have multiple uses across industries, and that in no way invalidates their safety—in the same way that we don't stop drinking water just because it's also found in dish soap. It's an irrelevant fact, but as soon as readers saw that exaggerated association, it was hard to undo. Then the media ran with the "yoga mat chemical" line because, well, it makes a darn good clicky headline.

Hari painted a vivid scene of just how "dangerous" this chemical is, citing a 2001 incident in which an overturned truck carrying azodicarbonamide prompted city officials to issue a hazardous materials alert and evacuate nearby residents. "Many of the people on the scene complained of burning eyes and skin irritation as a result," she wrote. First of all, this was a large spill, and therefore heavy exposure to a raw chemical, which is not comparable to the minuscule amounts found in food production. Furthermore, Hari conflated the chemical's use in products with aerosolized exposure. Those accident bystanders and factory workers who might be subject to direct airborne exposure are at risk when raw azodicarbonamide is *inhaled*. That has no bearing on its physical use in bread baking. You could launch the same attack on flour: that too is a respiratory irritant that can cause lung damage.[60]

The tiny, nearly negligible amount of azodicarbonamide used in the processing of bread does not pose a health risk, according to scientists I interviewed. I'm not insisting on a need for azodicarbonamide, but what's problematic is how influencers present these facts and terrify the average

American. This is why Hari is controversial: though she might be well-intentioned and justifiably mistrustful of the food industry, her calculations miss the mark, devolving into nothing more than worry porn.

Hari claims many common ingredients will "destroy your gut" and cause a host of health problems. If, as she suggests, American pantries can increase risk of cancer, reproductive problems, and thyroid dysfunction, then the onus is on her to prove that. As it stands, the "worrisome" ingredients she cites are generally heavily tested and proven safe in their intended use.

And it's not just food that Hari goes after: she had also previously lambasted the flu vaccine as "a bunch of toxic chemicals and additives that lead to several types of cancers and Alzheimer disease over time"—an accusation without adequate substantiation.[61]

Hari is one of many influencers targeting "toxic" grocery carts with not always proven claims. With the death of the expert and nutrition information descending into chaos, wellness gurus and cookbook authors swooped in, sticking their flags in the ground to claim authority. Problem is, a lot of the information they offer is skewed.

Hari has defended her extreme views by arguing that moderation never leads to change. (Or fortune, one might argue.) "People chastise me for being too simplistic," she told the *Atlantic*, "but it's like, okay, how are you getting through to people?"[62]

Food rules give us order. Like Karl Lagerfeld committing to starched white shirts and fingerless gloves, taking out whole food groups or abolishing sugar (but, oddly, permitting monk fruit or agave, sugars by another name) offers simplicity in what's become a complicated nutritional mess. You can devote precious brain cells to anything but your dinner plate. Having someone else figure it all out for you provides a mirage of safety, as does the ease of tuning out whatever debatable information comes down the six o'clock news pipeline.

But there may be another motive at play in telling people exactly what they need. Like plenty of other bloggers, Food Babe makes money with affiliate marketing. When Hari recommends "clean" or organic brands, she gets a cut of the sales. As for products for which she professes not to have found a suitable alternative elsewhere—such as snack bars or deodorants—she offers replacements from her own organic brand, Truvani, made "with ingredients that you can trust."

Her biggest line is that of supplements meant to round out what is supposedly our crappy diet. She sells turmeric tablets to "support" healthy joints and weight loss; plant-based pills to "support" immune health; and ashwagandha that "supports" brain health, among other supplements and powders.

You sure see the word "support" an awful lot in wellness branding, but never the words "treat," "cure," or "fix." There's a reason for that (and it's not because influencers don't have a thesaurus). "Support" is vague enough for them to promise you something without really guaranteeing anything. It's a clever marketing term that helps brands evade full responsibility, because how can one define support? What measurements could one use for that? The same goes for ambiguous terms like "ease," "stimulate," "boost," or "promote," which do not specifically claim to prevent or treat a health condition.

Sneaky terminology is one of many issues plaguing the behemoth that is the supplement industry, which feeds on those who believe they're at a loss with just a sensible diet alone. So many supplements either hint to an edge on average health, or they invent reasons for people to assume they are, on their own, not healthy *enough*. The more we're marketed to, the more we believe we're "not well."

"There's a Pill for That"

Paving the road to nutrition with supplements has generated big business not just for the likes of influencers such as Vani Hari, but for the industry overall. The $50 billion supplement industry went from 4,000 available products in 1994 to 50,000 in 2019. More than 75 percent of all American adult women take a multivitamin or supplement regularly, despite ongoing skepticism from the scientific community.[63]

Now, some people have legitimate nutrient deficiencies and are prescribed very specific supplementation by a health professional, such as during pregnancy (folic acid) or for conditions like osteoporosis (calcium). Vegans might need some extra B_{12}. People certainly have gaps that require supplementation. But that's not the average pill popper.

The general consumer doesn't seem troubled by the fact that many of their over-the-counter vitamins might just be mere placebos or that "energy" pills often owe their effect to stimulants like caffeine—hardly miracle pills. Supplements notoriously lack the more rigorous regulations imposed on pharmaceutical drugs because they don't require FDA approval before being marketed. The FDA does not monitor whether these products work; the agency just flags whether they're safe to consume. Manufacturers can therefore make vague health claims, like "boosts digestive health," that are not well defined and lack accountability.

In a 2018 study published in the *Journal of the American College of Cardiology*, researchers compared clinical trials over five years to determine whether regular vitamin intake protects against cardiovascular disease. In evaluating multivitamins, as well as vitamin C, vitamin D, and calcium supplements (the most common supplements), "none had a significant effect," reported the authors.[64]

Numerous researchers cast doubt on this American morning ritual. A 2019 NIH-funded study analyzed data from nearly thirty thousand U.S. adults over a six-year period. The subject population was generally healthy: they ate a nutritious diet and were physically active. They skewed white, female, and with a higher level of education and income.[65] Researchers concluded that popular dietary supplements—multivitamins, vitamin A, vitamin K, magnesium, zinc—had no measurable benefit and no influence on their mortality. Any nutrient boosts came from food consumption.[66] "It's pretty clear that supplement use has no benefit for the general population," noted Fang Fang Zhang, the study's senior author and an associate professor at the Tufts University School of Nutrition Science and Policy. "Supplements are not a substitute for a healthy balanced diet."[67]

Plenty more studies have investigated whether supplements impact chronic conditions and just overall health. Too many come up short in proving substantial benefits. As Steven Nissen, the chairman of cardiology at the Cleveland Clinic, concluded, "The concept of multivitamins was sold to Americans by an eager nutraceutical industry to generate profits. There was never any scientific data supporting their usage."[68]

Many consumers don't even know what's in them. Due to a lack of sufficient oversight, supplement ingredients are often not accurately reflected on the label. One 2018 study published in the journal *JAMA* analyzed the FDA's tainted supplements database between 2007 and 2016. Researchers found 776 instances in which supplements were tainted with unapproved pharmaceutical ingredients, steroids, or other contaminants. (Some contained sildenafil, the active ingredient found in Viagra.) The FDA issued voluntary recalls for a little under half of them.[69]

Or better yet, a *Quartz* report discovered that Goop supplement ingredients were awfully similar to those sold on Infowars, the far-right website owned by "Sandy Hook is a hoax" conspiracist Alex Jones. They're branded differently—Goop vitamins go by Why Am I so Effing Tired? while Infowars prefers the more aggressive-sounding Brain Force Plus—but both rely on Ayurvedic-heavy ingredients like the medicinal plant herb bacopa. Unfortunately, bacopa doesn't score too high on efficacy: "The science, based on animal studies, shows some preliminary—but contradictory—evidence of improvements to memory and brain function," read the report.[70] "There is minimal support for the claims about epilepsy and anxiety."

The general supplement consumer is bewitched by the marketing because it sounds great: supplements are easy and promise faster results. Taking them sounds better than what's actually necessary: eating nutritious meals and committing to big, concrete lifestyle changes. We are prone to buying what we want to believe, and we want to believe in quick solutions.

But no magic pill can replace a solid diet, stresses Craig Hopp, the deputy director of the division of extramural research at the National Center for Complementary and Integrative Health, part of the NIH. "You can't eat crap and take a multivitamin and expect to be healthy. It just doesn't work that way," says Hopp. Vital stuff like fiber shows up in what we eat, not what we pop out of a bottle. Hopp sees this insta-quick mentality stemming from a pill that does indeed promise fast, revolutionary results: "You took antibiotics and poof, you were better. It was magic. And I think the incredible success of antibiotics really contributed to people thinking that, well, there is a pill for everything."

Dr. Danielle Ofri, an author and a clinical professor of medicine at NYU, views the supplement industry a bit more suspiciously. The physician believes the industry preys upon desperate patients who don't feel as though they have other options. Many supplement companies take advantage of the fact that medicine is complex, ambiguous, and imperfect and that we don't have cures for all chronic illnesses. "It's never that easy in real life," says Dr. Ofri, "so it's hard, as a physician, to explain that our options for your diabetes are actually quite complicated."

Dr. Ofri's clients, mostly women, are typically very suspicious of taking prescription medication, but that initial suspicion drops to zilch when it comes to supplements grabbed off a Whole Foods store shelf. Dr. Ofri tries to explain that you should be suspicious of anything you take, "whether it's from a health food store or that I prescribe. You should ask the same questions, have the same concerns." These patients do their homework, but they either don't know how to interpret research or it gets muddled by effective labels like "clinically proven." That sounds good, but what does that mean? Who conducted the research? (Was it the brand?) Was there a placebo group? Where were the results published in a peer-reviewed journal?

"The vast majority of dietary supplements, if they had to be a hundred percent truthful in their advertising, wouldn't sell anything," says the clinical exercise physiologist and nutritionist Bill Sukala. Terms like "promotes good health," "detox," or "gently cleanses" have no real medical definition, while "clinically proven" is not regulated. They can mean anything and are therefore meaningless.

It's not just supplements. If you, like so many women today, are indeed concerned with the microbiome, you might opt for probiotics, which quadrupled in use between 2007 and 2012 and propelled kombucha into a billion-dollar industry. Most likely you've done so because brands like GT's Kombucha promise to not only "support gut health" but also "rejuvenate, restore, revitalize, recharge, rebuild, regenerate, replenish, regain, rebalance, and renew" your overall well-being. This is part of the growing "better for you" food trend, in which botanical extracts, probiotics, or "immune-boosting" ingredients supposedly greatly improve our health.‡‡

There's some exciting new research on the microbiome, but it's not *there* just yet. Nutrition experts will tell you a probiotic-infused cookie or bottle of kombucha won't do much of anything. A healthy gut needs fiber—fruits, vegetables, and whole grains.

Kombucha lacks scientific evidence for its aggressive claims, thereby receiving a thumbs-down from medical professionals. Even the alternative health scene isn't fully sold on it: celebrity doctor Andrew Weil downplays the hype, concluding, "The sugar and caffeine may be responsible for the energy some consumers claim they feel . . . I do not recommend kombucha, but if you like it, drink it."[71]

Fantastical marketing is not an anomaly, nor is it new. Jamie Lee Curtis told us we'd poop better in those probiotic-endorsing Activia commercials (parodied by Kristen Wiig on *Saturday Night Live* in 2008). Then suddenly the ads disappeared. Ever wonder why? Well, parent company Dannon had to settle charges brought by the Federal Trade Commission for deceptive advertising. The yogurt maker agreed to pay $21 million for advertising that Activia is "clinically proven" to relieve irregularity—claims that it could not substantiate.[72]

---

‡‡ GT's Kombucha's parent company settled a 2016 class action lawsuit that alleged the brand's products contained "misleading statements" regarding kombucha's antioxidant content and ingredients.

Sukala doesn't have too many kind words for the wellness industry's tactics. As he says, "the business is money. The storefront is 'health.'"

Taking Definitive Answers from Inconclusive Ideas

Today, three-quarters of consumers are actively cutting back on sugar,[73] and an increasing number of shoppers say they check the sugar content of food labels before they buy a product.[74] Overall, this new consumer behavior is a good thing. The wellness industry (for all its flaws) encourages individuals to take a closer look at what they pile into their shopping cart. And that fast-food chains, airports, and vending machines now offer more fruits and vegetables is not something to gloss over.

But there is a spectrum of nutrition, and it deserves a bit more moderation than is currently being touted. Food has become an utterly fraught ordeal for the average woman. A *Fear Factor* episode that never ends. If you're to take extreme wellness gurus and fad diets at face value, you cannot consume any sugar, gluten, pesticide residue, dairy, "chemicals," and more. But these kinds of stark restrictions do more harm than good. We don't need thirty lollipops. But one won't kill us. Have that cake on your birthday.

Where we do need to focus more is on the big picture of whether we're meeting our overall nutritional needs. The thing is, we basically already know what to eat. We're aware we should lay off too much processed food and increase our vegetable intake. All these specialty diets and strict rules are essentially debating the minuscule percentage of what could be a *wee* bit better in our diet, but they're overblown. Often they're gateways to some hawked product.

All the conflicting, extreme advice has gotten out of hand, which is why experts increasingly weigh in to redirect the conversation. Trailblazers like the registered dietitian Vanessa Rissetto are expanding access to sound, relatable information. As the co-founder of Culina Health and the director of New York University's Dietetic Internship Program, Rissetto shares budget-friendly recipes and practical tips on her Instagram account, incorporating accessible foods that appeal to underserved communities, including vegetables and boxed macaroni. As she advises, if your culture prizes collard greens or rice with beans, go with collard greens; don't feel pressured to eat kale. "It's not so easy if food is where you connect with people and then someone is telling you that the food that you're eating is 'not right.' And oh, by the way, I don't have the money to make those changes."

A far cry from the hardcore purity tests of certain wellness influencers, Rissetto doesn't stress a restrictive orthodoxy. Instead, she advocates doing the best with one's abilities and resources. Not that it stops online critics from lambasting her over the "gall" to recommend a yogurt cup. "It's just the way that society views things—we want it to be hard," says Rissetto. "We want to feel like we worked harder than everybody else."

We are responsible for what we eat (though certain factors certainly don't make it easy). But the hypermoralized mandate to eat well induces guilt whenever we're simply unable to adhere to such regimens.[75] Most Americans barely get the time to take a proper lunch break away from their desk, yet somehow they're held to Alice Waters–level expectations. America is bending toward a healthier future, though it needs a push in the direction of being less confusing and more widely accessible to other groups. You can bend only so far before you break.

Chapter 8

Crystal-Clear Futures:
A New Take on New Age Spirituality

"Close your eyes and bring to mind one thing you're calling in from [the universe]," instructed Lacy Phillips, a former TV actress and model in her midthirties, now a self-proclaimed manifestation expert. "Boil it down to the essence of this thing that lights up your soul."

Wearing a ruffled white shirt and black gaucho hat, Phillips exuded approachable confidence. Over the next hour, she taught the 250 women assembled before her in a sparsely decorated industrial space the basics of attracting their chief desires—which, for most of them, was a better and more meaningful career. The women in the audience soaked in how to find their one true passion and "pass tests" from the spiritual beyond. These tests can come in the form of subpar job offers or being rear-ended in traffic. But more important, the women learned that increasing their self-worth would draw in love, happiness, and a raise. Phillips's presentation was a live version of the lessons she shares on her content platform To Be Magnetic, which sells on-demand manifestation workshops starting at $68.

"How many of you can raise your hands if you feel that you are deserving of what you want?" asked Phillips at the event. An overwhelming majority of hands shot up, and Phillips motioned as if she was counting them. "That's a really *beautiful* number," she cooed.

Following a lecture on establishing confidence to fish for rewards from the great beyond, Phillips proceeded with a Q&A. Participants stood up and stated their astrology sign before explaining their career dilemmas: Can my energy fuel my start-up's success? How do I attract the right kind of clients? Is a disrespectful work colleague a test from the universe? Is my soul "settling" if I go on a reality TV show? Phillips wasn't surprised by the intensity of their frustrations, noting they were experiencing Mercury retrograde. "You guys should have some shit going down right now," she laughed.

Charismatic, attractive, and personable, Phillips comes across like a cool, more successful older sister. She is one of many female manifestation coaches reinventing the law of attraction—the belief that you attract what you focus on—for a new generation. Phillips spreads the philosophy that self-worth is the law of attraction and that we can manifest anything that's in alignment with "our current state of subconscious worthiness." Basically, you need to reprogram your subconscious—rewiring childhood trauma, fixing damaging perceptions, and the like—to break the mold of limiting beliefs.

Through live events, digital platforms, and podcasts, these teachers present a nondenominational spirituality that promises to work in their favor, like a heavenly personal advocate.

Manifestation holds that there's a tangible connection between the mind and cosmic workings. Spiritual influencers' messages of overcoming personal struggles hold that you need a *belief* in yourself since "the universe has your back." That and with talk of modern-day issues—body image pressures, noncommittal boyfriends, sexist bosses—they're instantly relatable.

Dressed like fashion bloggers, these new leaders speak of "calling in" unseen powers to materialize new homes, jobs, or maybe just that perfect pair of jeans. On the To Be Magnetic website, one happy customer detailed manifesting a discounted white Le Creuset tea kettle. Other leaders skew more ambitious, selling $2,000 money workshops that reportedly draw in tenfold the class fee, thereby offering their own spin on the prosperity gospel. Each influencer has their own tweak on the philosophy and the work required.

Many of the more famous manifestation coaches predominantly preach to a group that has their basic needs met, which inevitably sets the tone for the issues addressed. Although some have scholarship programs, it's hard to imagine these experts delivering their advice to those living in poverty or war-torn countries. There are no Manifesters Without Borders. Followers, mostly women, are drawn to the idea that whatever good energy you put out into the world inevitably comes back to you. When I ask, however, whether the Jews in the Holocaust lacked the right energy to escape Nazi Germany, some seem legitimately stumped. "Huh, I didn't think about that," one college-aged manifester replied.

To be fair, manifestation does not entail only thinking good thoughts; the process involves determination, effort, and "co-creating" with the universe. Followers must put in hard work and make sacrifices to be worthy of divine abundance. Essentially, they have to get their lives in order. And Phillips, for one, does not gloss over trauma, racism, and abuse. Nor does she advocate controlling specific outcomes.* "We're certainly very open about how much work has to be involved in this," says Phillips. "It's not a magic show and your life won't change overnight."

At times though, manifestation could also prove a blame-proof strategy: If you get something you wanted, you manifested it. If you didn't, it just wasn't meant to be. Or maybe you didn't do enough on your end to produce the vision to fruition.

---

* To Be Magnetic's workshops offer a disclaimer stating, "It's important to recognize that there are systems of oppression, injustice, marginalization, and abuse that are out of your control. Understand that you did nothing to negatively attract these situations—it is not your fault. Please know that we are not insinuating that you are attracting negativity or being punished because of these situations or events."

While manifestation might have its shortcomings (to be fair, which faith doesn't?), there's no denying people get real value out of it. Three years ago, a Californian named Heather was brutally attacked and held at gunpoint by a stranger. Overwhelmed by the experience, she rarely left the house for a year. Heather credits Phillips—in addition to a therapist—for empowering her to ultimately lead a more conscious, fulfilling life. In the last few years, she said she's manifested her dream job, house, fiancée, even the exact diamond ring and wedding location she envisioned. Her new role as a senior consultant at a health company pays more, aligns with her values, and permits her to do what she always wanted—work from home.

"I would have taken this job before for less money but I have the confidence now to say no, I deserve more," said Heather, who shared her story during the Q&A portion. She was so compelling that Phillips invited her on stage to co-host the rest of the evening. Later, Heather told me she manifested the stage debut, having pictured herself speaking to the audience. "Things just come naturally now because I'm more magnetic," she mused. "I used to use the word 'lucky' but I don't believe that anymore." Phillips was touched that she gained yet another satisfied customer: "I genuinely believe that everybody is worthy of having what they want."

Phillips treads lightly in her role, readily acknowledging that she is not a religious leader or guru. Instead she calls herself a "mold breaker." Phillips says she reminds her audience, 'I'm shoulder to shoulder with you doing this work."

In the wellness world, manifestation joins a medley of other mystical trends that have grown as popular as detox diets. If New Age services were once a scattered industry of solo practitioners, outdated websites, and 1-800 numbers, modern offerings are light-years beyond the Miss Cleo of the nineties. You can now book an on-demand chat reading with a live astrologer. You don't even need to speak to the seer: just *text* them a zodiacal inquiry.

There's also ambiguous spiritual lingo wherein belief in one's personal power takes on a nearly religious narrative. Social media influencers post nondenominational, ego-boosting affirmations such as "I am magical" and "the universe wants me to have the best," which don't align with any specific philosophy but add up to a holier version of the self-help industry. The messaging encompasses radical approval: each individual is special, powerful, and divine. *We are all Beyoncé!*

Influencers got the memo. Suddenly all the style bloggers, fashion founders, and tech stars—choice vocations of the late aughts—became wellness influencers, imparting their self-worth platitudes and yoga wear ensembles like the Dalai Lamas of pop psychology. With an emphasis on maximizing capabilities (à la Tony Robbins) with a sprinkling of fluid superhuman powers ("cosmic intelligence"), they are life coaches turned prophets. You can't scroll through Instagram without these former fashionistas telling you to "trust in the universe," all the while hawking protein collagen powders. Instead of Fashion Week or SXSW, they're reporting from a retreat in Bali.

It's not entirely surprising that the growth of wellness and the explosion of what were once considered "woo-woo" convictions have gone hand in hand—or that they are so intertwined. There's plenty of research indicating the psychological benefits of believing in a higher power. Spiritual involvement has been shown to help individuals cope with stress and is associated with better mental health functioning (like being more optimistic).[1] But this pillar of wellness has since expanded to better include crystals, tarot palm readings, aura photography, and a zillion astrology apps that divulge what Jupiter has to say about asking your boss for a promotion.

These beliefs and practices are certainly not new (as many were popularized during the counterculture movement of the 1960s). But they have since been tweaked and are available everywhere. Urban Outfitters hawks millennial-pink tarot card decks ("cute AF" reads the top review). Boutique fitness studios sell sage bundles to ward off "toxic energy." Spas offer Reiki healers who can massage the bad juju out of your muscle knots. Women's magazines treat these things like essential components of a healthy life. "We all need to take good care of ourselves," reads an issue of *Cosmopolitan*. "And who understands what you *really* need better than *you*? Well, the stars."

"Mystical services" grew 53 percent between 2005 and 2019 into a $2.2 billion industry. Roughly six in ten American adults believe in at least one New Age belief such as astrology or reincarnation, and 40 percent believe in psychics or that spiritual energy is hiding in physical objects.[2] But exactly what kinds of solutions are the new New Agers seeking? A deeper look at manifestation and crystals reveals a great deal about the precise nature of our current spiritual quests. Unsurprisingly, as with the other areas of wellness, a common thread is the frantic attempt to regain control over that which we fear is no longer in our hands.

Working with the Universe to Set Things Straight

The law of attraction didn't start with Madewell shoppers. The concept dates back to the nineteenth century's New Thought movement, and it has seized American popularity at different points and in various flavors, incorporating health, wealth, personal development, you name it.

In the late 1800s, the spiritual pioneer Mary Baker Eddy founded Christian Science, a religion that combines Christianity with metaphysical healing. Pain and disease were all in the mind, she preached. Correct religious thinking could heal sickness. All that separated the afflicted from a cure were prayers and belief.

Hers was a countercultural movement. One of its precepts was that female intuition was better at tapping into divine power. It was an empowering message in a time when society considered women delicate and prone to illness. Their femininity—traditionally treated as a liability—became a sort of superpower. As a result, women made up a strong percentage of Christian Science adherents and leadership.[3]

The movement also had a darker side. Some believers shunned medical intervention for cancer, appendicitis, mushroom poisoning, contagious diseases, and diphtheria. Parents in the sect denied their children essential medical care. People died.

(Mark Twain penned a tale in which he sought the healing services of a Christian Scientist after falling off a cliff in the Alps and suffering several broken bones. He was, naturally, told his pain was but an illusion. When it came time to settle the bill, Twain noted, "I gave her an imaginary check, and now she is suing me for substantial dollars. It looks inconsistent.")[4]

In time, religious leaders adopted the law of attraction to reimagine a God who badly wanted you to be flush with cash. After the Depression, the author Napoleon Hill used positive thinking to sell a vision of capitalist success with *Think and Grow Rich*. It even trickled down to children's education, with an early-twentieth-century story about a small-time locomotive who willed his way into pulling heavier loads. In 1930, the publisher Platt & Munk released *The Little Engine That Could*, about a character who feverishly repeats "I think I can, I think I can," thereby teaching America's youth the treasured values of optimism and hard work. Yet no one ever stopped to consider whether the little engine should risk stress fractures by biting off more than he could choo.[5]

The law of attraction saw a reemergence in the mid-2000s with Oprah and Hollywood celebrities salivating over *The Secret*. The bestselling spirituality self-help book, which sold more than 30 million copies worldwide, claimed that positive thoughts can draw a bounty of enviable good things because the universe has a currency, and that currency is positive "energy." Then, as always, the offshoots came. In 2010, Marianne Williamson, one of Oprah's spiritual advisers, published a book that melded manifestation, naturally, with fat-trimming: *A Course in Weight Loss: 21 Spiritual Lessons for Surrendering Your Weight Forever* advised that "your perfect weight is coded into the natural patterns of your true self." You just need to accept complete dependence on God. Then you can reconcile "your relationship with Not-Thin You."[6]

Today, Jessie De Lowe, a manifestation coach and co-founder of the lifestyle site How You Glow, likens manifestation to life coaching. The former art therapist implores followers to take responsibility for all the issues in their lives thus far, then adopt healthier habits. "It's not promising someone their life is not going to have challenges—in fact, it's the opposite," explains De Lowe. But if the stick is the taking of responsibility for one's life, the carrot is that doing so will help you gain control of an existence that seems increasingly unmanageable.

The majority of De Lowe's clients are young, female, and college-educated. Though they possess countless advantages, she describes an unsatisfied group gripped by peer competitiveness and unrealistic expectations fueled by social media. They aren't comparing themselves to the millennial next door. They're comparing themselves to start-up founders and the globe-trotting friends clogging their Instagram feed. "They feel inadequate, like they're never where they should be [already]," says De Lowe.

Add an unpredictable job market, rampant employee disengagement, and tales of male-dominated workplaces, and it's no wonder young women find themselves searching for ways to hack the universe. It's an appealing concept for those raised to believe that if they follow certain steps, they could get what they want. They were led to trust in a meritocracy, that good hard work always wins. And that, of course, they were special, as told to them 1,001 times by their parents and kindergarten teachers.

Millennials had a hyperstructured upbringing that gave them a false sense of control, says the clinical psychologist Goali Saedi Bocci, author of *The Millennial Mental Health Toolbox*. Raised on happy Disney endings and American exceptionalism, they struggle with the anxiety of not getting what they were promised. "They grew up with the idea that if you want to get the best grades, you do the extra credit," she told me. Apple-polishing millennials got straight As, went to college, then graduated into a recession and found themselves saddled with student debt. Those who secured good jobs later felt stifled by what they considered meaningless positions or weren't adequately prepared for the mundanity of corporate life.

Workplace stress is particularly painful for a percentage of millennials who define themselves through their employment. "Do what you love and you'll never work a day in your life," they were told (much to their grandparents' confusion, who warned that work was to pay the bills). They were naively brought up to "follow your passion," and they just did that. If Americans once clocked in and out at the office, today you'll hear them speak of their life's "calling" and their job as a "mission." In that sense, their job becomes far more than a job—their heart and soul are poured into it. Work-life balance becomes impossible because the self and work are intertwined.

For those who are not living their calling, it's a different sort of pressure—one in which you're forced to endure hearing about cool start-up jobs while you draft legal documents. And if you failed to succeed, the American creed of meritocracy insinuates that you simply didn't try hard enough—*you weren't passionate enough*—despite a flawed and at times unfair employment market (or the loss of nearly 9 million jobs during the 2007–2009 recession). You believe you have only yourself to blame.

The San Francisco–based psychotherapist Tess Brigham sees midcareer patients trying to make sense as to why they can't afford a down payment or why they're still stuck in middle management. Manifestation dangles the promise of speeding up their career—tangible tactics to improve their chances—but also comfort in that it will all work out. "If you say the universe has a path for me, there's something to hold on to," Brigham told me.

Or, as Joseph Baker, an associate professor of sociology at East Tennessee State University and the editor of the academic journal *Sociology of Religion*, explains, there is a natural human tendency to impute purpose to our experiences, to interpret a larger plan in place. If we can't find that framework of agency, we'll create it ourselves: "What we do find pretty consistently is that when organized religion recedes the paranormal often fills that gap," says Baker.

Manifesters essentially adopt a spiritual version of the growth mindset, the Stanford University psychologist Carol Dweck's theory that one's abilities can be cultivated through effort, dedication, and perseverance.

Dweck's research stresses that brains and talent are not the be-all and end-all, rather that optimistically putting in time and diligence leads to higher achievement. On the flip side, a fixed mindset is a belief that you lack the right traits, leading you to adopt a defeatist attitude that holds you can't influence your future.

From this perspective, manifestation makes sense. Followers simply take a resilient can-do outlook on life—that how you view yourself can determine success. Most psychologists will tell you that you're better off keeping your chin up and taking actionable steps to build the life you want. As one manifester told me, it's about expelling negativity "to get shit done."

Manifestation serves as a mix between self-care and self-help, according to manifestation expert and bestselling author Gabby Bernstein, a former nightlife publicist who now leads $1,999 online courses on clearing psychological blocks to increase magnetism. Bernstein readily admits "it's hip to be spiritual," but she also acknowledges a climate that bred a need for her messaging. "The collective feels out of control. People are traumatized . . . Millennials want a sense of security, but they also have the sense that I can do anything and create my reality. That belief system is actually what makes manifesting work."

Positivity is beneficial, but some manifestation leaders teach their flock to block out the negativity that hampers their pursuit of unrealistic dreams. Simplified versions of manifestation propel the idea that we can all reach our potential to draw in success or riches. But that shouldn't disregard structural, social, and irrefutable challenges. As Steve Salerno argues in his book *SHAM: How the Self-Help Movement Made America Helpless,* all of us can't prosper in the free market. "In any competitive closed system, there must be a loser for every winner. By definition then, self-help cannot work for everyone, and the more competitive the realm, the more this is so. Two wonderfully optimistic women who both desire the same man or the same job cannot both succeed . . . [it] could conceivably help some of us achieve our goals. But not all of us."[7]

The issue of how much we can truly control becomes even more readily apparent as manifesters attempt to conjure up larger gains: a rent-controlled apartment, a bigger bonus, or a romantic partner. In Facebook groups, some are downright frustrated and confused, lamenting unemployment or broken relationships. Some try to manifest better health or to heal diseases.

Nitika Chopra, an affable and upbeat Manhattanite, was besieged by pain when she was in her late twenties. She suffered from multiple chronic conditions that interfered with her work and social life. At times it was head-to-toe psoriasis. Other days it was psoriatic arthritis—a painful inflammation and swelling of the joints. So she turned to those who promised blessed relief from the agony: spiritual influencers.

Chopra started following and buying products from gurus like Deepak Chopra (no relation). She sat in a manifestation expert's living room, soaking up the promise of positive thinking, which she took to believe could cure her medical conditions. At one manifestation meeting, Chopra divulged her excruciating pain, only to be scolded by an instructor who interrupted her with, "I'm going to stop you right there. I need you to take that negative language out of your mind. You are not sick, okay?"

"I was so impressionable," reflects Chopra. "And I was so desperate. I thought, these people are all telling me that if I just believe I'm going to get a check in the mail and I just believe that I'm going to be healthy, then it'll happen." Looking back, she acknowledges how devastating and harmful it was. "It is the definition of gaslighting."

The more Chopra listened to these experts, the sicker she became. Not only were her physical symptoms getting worse, but her mental health was on the decline. "I was constantly trying to fit myself into this world of 'You should just be able to meditate twice a day, you should just be able to say these affirmations . . . And then you should be fixed.'"

Chopra was not "fixed." Soon the pangs of failure started. She believed there was something broken with her thought process. In the ensuing months, Chopra berated herself if she ever felt negative or sad or uncomfortable. "[I'd] think, what's wrong with you? Why can't you just feel positively?" This continued for years, to the point where she avoided medication entirely, hoping to attract a healthier future. All the while, she suffered. Chopra couldn't descend a flight of stairs without debilitating pain. Some nights she would scratch herself so hard her sheets were bloodied.

Chopra's experience shows why manifesting health is a tricky issue that most gurus distance themselves from. (Probably because they're also aware of something called a lawsuit.) Lacy Phillips readily admits she hasn't figured out manifesting a medical recovery: "We can't help you with that." Phillips notes that manifestation teachers have a responsibility to be transparent. "This isn't a cure-all," she says.

It all came to a head for Chopra following the 2016 election. Amid the political chaos and "alternative facts," Chopra decided to take a hard look at everything, including her wellness habits. If it wasn't the truth, it just wasn't gonna fly anymore. She realized that multiple complex factors account for our circumstances, and that thinking can't overcome all of them. Shortly thereafter, manifestation got the boot, kicked right back to the universe's return center.

Chopra ultimately founded Chronicon, a digital community for women with chronic illnesses—like Crohn's disease, fibromyalgia, lupus, or endometriosis—to come together to share their pain without judgment or false promises. Most members have similar stories, having seen far too many doctors who didn't believe their symptoms or gurus selling snake oil. It's not so much "solving" anything for them as it is facilitating friendships. "You can tell us what is going on," Chopra told me. "And we'll be like, 'Yes, girl. I was just dealing with that yesterday. I totally get you. I'm so sorry. I'm here for you.'"

There's no harm in a growth mindset. It's important to believe you can accomplish new tasks. But when that optimism is taken too far—when a growth mindset blinds you to obstacles (including very real medical ones)—problems arise. These new modes of spirituality can at times, if left unchecked, devolve into delusional thinking on steroids.

A Talisman for Healing:
Spiritual Lucky Charms

If manifesters take their ability to influence their lives with the utmost seriousness, crystal collectors have a lighter touch, if not any less of a belief that their practices guarantee positive outcomes.

I investigated the crystal craze for *Fast Company* after noticing that glistening rocks once better associated with covens and Stevie Nicks were flourishing in a massive mainstream business market. Crystals showed up everywhere: at yoga studios, in juice shops, on influencers' social media accounts. In Malibu, some residents hand them out for Halloween. And like any trend worth its (mineral) salt, it hit Hollywood, fortifying a bastion of celebrity acolytes. Gwyneth Paltrow, Victoria Beckham, and Katy Perry publicly swore their allegiance to the stones. Adele even attributed her performance hiccups at the 2016 Grammy Awards to the fact that she'd lost her beloved totems. "I got some new crystals now and everything's been going well," she later assured fans.

I was interested in the financials, but more than anything, I was curious what people got out of crystals. Was it just an artistic appreciation for nature's minerals? Or did they hold more religious weight?

This is how I found myself sitting cross-legged on the floor of Colleen McCann's Venice Beach home. Colleen is Goop's in-house shaman and a self-described "spiritual influencer." Blonde, fashionable, and smiley, the former fashion stylist resembles a young Goldie Hawn. McCann is booked months in advance for her services, for which she charges $100 to $1,500 per session. She sees predominantly young and female clients for garden-variety therapy sessions, and she might perform the occasional crystal-assisted exorcism. ("You never forget your first exorcism," she said.)

But McCann's specialty is using quartz, citrine, and other chunks of minerals for what she calls "intuitive business building." With assistance from the great beyond, she helps CEOs, executives, and Silicon Beach professionals make decisions about their business just by, as she put it, "reading their energy." She weighs in on everything from org charts to investment opportunities to redesigning company logos. "I may close my eyes and say, 'Hey, you're thinking of starting a new division,' and they say, 'How did you know that?'" McCann explained. "Or I'll say, 'I see a girl with red curly hair coming in—that's the girl you need to hire.'"

Her loft was filled with crystals, many of which were organized into parallel lines to my left and right, as if I was stationed in the middle of a spiritual runway. McCann blew on multicolored stones and recited a blessing rooted in shamanism. She then closed her eyes and meditated as she listened to the spirits among us. But before she could foresee whether I'd ever land on a *Forbes* cover, she expressed concern. "What's up with what you're eating?" McCann asked me. "They say there's something weird you're doing every day at a certain time." I confessed to my Sour Patch Kids consumption ritual. McCann nodded as if she and her ghostly helpers were already aware. (To be fair, she had a pretty good chance of predicting that any L.A. woman had an eating issue, so I wasn't blown away.) As part of the $250 package I selected, my healer "prescribed" a few amethysts to control my sugar urges, then wished me luck in resisting my temptation.

My experience might inspire eye rolls and snickers, but for a growing number of consumers, crystals are no joke. McCann's business is lucrative for a very simple reason: she sells solutions, much like the one she sold me to curb my sweet tooth. Whatever your problem is, there's a crystal for that. Her book is called *Crystal Rx*, prescribing rocks to calm, energize, and heal everything from fatigue to a broken heart.

For McCann, the reason for surging crystal popularity is obvious. "What we're doing right now as a people isn't working," she said. Our fraught political climate, work overload, and tech dependency leave people "sad, scared, or nervous." She believes crystals can "help people get back on track." The practice of just sitting down and touching an element that comes from the earth, she said, produces a positive, calming effect.

And for the people building businesses around them, a pleasing *ka-ching* sound.

McCann isn't the only one benefitting from the mining mania. I've reported on newly formed crystal galleries, which are like art galleries, drawing Silicon Valley honchos who buy hundreds of thousands of dollars worth of rare, five-foot-high crystals. One crystal e-commerce business watched business double with $88 "money magnet" bracelets that sold out whenever the financial market dipped. All echoed the same sentiment: Demand increases when people are anxious. Bad news means good business.

When I asked Colleen McCann if crystal therapy is just a case of the placebo effect, she was cagey, replying, "There are many ways to skin a cat."[8] Whatever crystals are or aren't, these tools can be extremely powerful, and not something to be discounted. Women I interviewed say they can have a grounding effect. "It gives me something to focus on when I'm anxious," said one who sleeps with crystals in her bed.

In a period of uncertainty, such spiritual beliefs can provide reassurance. They serve as a coping mechanism, where you can count on something when at the whims of an unfair, chaotic world. This proves both compelling and comforting, not unlike a *TV Guide* to the blessings or misfortune about to unfold. They're also widely available.

People can easily join these belief systems because there's a low barrier to entry, a far cry from in-depth study of a centuries-old book or lengthy conversion processes. No need to understand complex philosophies: to get started, one simply needs to feel ready to "transform" their life, then hop onto YouTube, Instagram, or TikTok, all flooded with twentysomething gurus.

It's hard to tell how many spiritual seekers fully believe in what they're adopting. Some find it fun and exotic, not unlike an interest in style fads. For Gen Z, the more untraditional, the more the social cachet, proving just how anti-establishment you are. That which is foreign and uncommon might seem more appealing than what's available in their backyard.

Once I reported on Summit Series, an invite-only event series dubbed a "young TED meets Burning Man" or "Davos for millennials." This community of start-up founders and successful professionals built their own utopia in the ski resort area of Eden, Utah, drawing entrepreneurs like Netflix CEO Reed Hastings, WeWork co-founder Miguel McKelvey, and others who could afford either to build a home or to pay the $2,000+ weekend attendance fee. It's the type of place where you'll see a Mercedes G-Class parked alongside a giant yurt, where high-powered networking commences during dynamic breath work classes.[9] You meet people who think of themselves as spiritually inclined and "enlightened" capitalists, though they would never use the dreaded C word; they instead say they're vehicles for change, or "creative disruptors."

While I was there for a wellness-themed weekend, talk revolved around "influential astrologers" and manifesting investors. No fewer than three strangers asked what my meditation "practice" entailed. One even opened the conversation with the question, replacing the more traditional "So what do you do?" I responded truthfully: I don't meditate. When I need to recenter myself, I open up a Jewish prayer book and recite the prayers I have repeated since childhood. Sometimes, I'll channel my most treasured intentions when lighting the Sabbath candles on a Friday night. That, I explained, was my version of mindfulness.

One looked at me like I just admitted to marrying my dog. Another nervously chuckled and quickly changed the topic. The third didn't respond for five seconds, carefully weighing his response. "I really don't know what to say to that," he finally offered, slowly removing his Warby Parker sunglasses. "*That's* different."

I had committed a taboo. I had, in their eyes, pledged allegiance to a backward regime, to that which they had so independently rejected. I had veered from the now acceptable answers within wellness groupthink, that which prizes the new and unique and the exotic. There I was expressing, of all things, an acceptance of the traditional—*of religion*. I should have just as soon introduced myself as "basic."

I'm not insinuating that uniqueness is the driving force, just that some truly dislike organized religion. Many people take their newly adopted spirituality quite seriously, including those who plan trips and base life decisions around their horoscope. On Twitter, astrology followers consider the ancient art a useful tool for self-knowledge, "an external thing [to] confirm something you already knew about yourself." Tarot helps individuals tap their intuition and analyze their life path. (Some say it's cheaper than therapy.) For the anxious, astrologers offer solace when life feels too complicated—and a rare occasion when they get sole attention. As one Gen Zer tweeted, "It may not be real but it's comforting. [To] have someone tell me that there's always something positive coming makes me feel okay."

Manifestation, crystals, and a host of other spiritual initiatives require individuals to reflect, to retreat from volatile emotions, and instead focus on their innermost needs. Believers rely on the universe and tarot cards for supernatural guidance or influence—to change the hand life deals them. It sounds a lot like religion, frankly. So why aren't these people turning to more traditional faith when they want some help? Why aren't they just going to church when they want to light up their soul?

Because the big three monotheist traditions, as they'll tell you, just ain't cutting it.

Flashback: When Astrology Went to the White House

It was lightly raining in 1952 when a Southern California housewife named Jeane Dixon entered the historic St. Matthew's Cathedral in Washington, D.C. She prepared to kneel before a statue of the Virgin Mary when suddenly, she was overcome by a vision. Dixon saw the White House in its pristine glory, the majestic white compound across a lush green lawn. The numerals 1960 formed above the building like skywriting. Then slowly, the numbers emitted a dark cloud dripping down "like chocolate frosting on a cake," quickly reaching the bottom before a still man. He was young, tall, light-eyed, and had a head of thick brown hair. A heavenly spirit insinuated that he was a Democrat. And that a violent death awaited him.[10] "God showed it to me," she would later recall.[11]

Four years later, Dixon reportedly told *Parade* magazine that a Democratic president elected in 1960 would be assassinated. The disturbing prediction wasn't taken seriously, but following President Kennedy's assassination, word of Dixon's prophetic prowess spread, catapulting her to national fame. She soon snagged a regular seat inside the very same house she once saw in her visions.

Nicknamed "the seeress of Washington," Dixon carried her crystal ball straight into the oval office. Richard Nixon sought Dixon's advice on future terrorist plots following the 1972 Munich Olympics massacre in which a Palestinian terrorist group kidnapped and killed nine Israeli athletes. White House tapes confirm that Dixon counseled the president on numerous issues, spanning the Panama Canal, nuclear arms talks, and even the Watergate scandal.[12]

Dixon eventually became a household name with a syndicated newspaper astrology column, thus offering an air of legitimacy to her spiritual talent. Her biography, *A Gift of Prophecy*, sold more than 3 million copies. But Dixon wasn't just interested in politics and fame. During the World War II era, she visited Navy hospitals and servicemen parties, counseling Army amputees who had given up on any semblance of normal life. Dixon supplied handicapped veterans with the confidence to keep going, to put faith in better days ahead. She gave them hope.[13]

Dixon got some forecasts right, such as her prediction that a pope would be harmed in the twentieth century and that Oprah, who consulted with her in 1977, would enjoy great success. But many more of her predictions were wrong—among them, that the

Soviets would be the first to put a man on the moon, that World War III would erupt in 1958, and that a cure for cancer would be found by 1967.

Dixon also claimed the world would end by 2020.

Pop culture mostly forgot Dixon, but her name lives on in academic circles. The mathematician John Allen Paulos coined the term "the Jeane Dixon effect," which refers to the psychological tendency to remember successful predictions while ignoring the far more frequent failures—which helps explain the prevalence of paranormal beliefs.[14]

In 1997, Dixon passed away from a cardiac arrest. It is rumored that the last words on her deathbed were "I knew this would happen."

Rise of the "Nones": Seeking Meaning in an Agnostic World

"The spiritual wisdom of the ages is openly accessible as never before, and we are free to craft our own spiritual lives," writes Krista Tippett in her bestselling book, *Becoming Wise: An Inquiry into the Mystery and Art of Living*. The author and host of the popular radio program *On Being* says she has no idea what religion will look like a century from now, "but the evolution of faith will change us all."[15]

Tippett soared to stardom for her spiritual investigative work, calling on listeners to explore the meaning of life during their morning commute. In her radio program and podcast—downloaded more than 350 million times—the gentle, folksy host takes on a soft inquisitiveness that mixes Mr. Rogers with Meredith Vieira, if not the occasional motivation of Oprah. Tippett asks big questions of celebrities, politicians, and thinkers surrounding faith, humanity, and purpose. Her show attempts to answer: What does it mean to be human? How do we want to live? She gets attention. In 2013, President Obama awarded Tippett a National Humanities

Medal for "embracing complexity" through hundreds of conversations about faith.

Tippett started her radio program in the years following 9/11, a period in which she observed a societal pull to explore deeper issues but with few available outlets. The world had changed, and so had everyone's priorities. She is among a long roster of talent ushering in a new realm of spiritual life sparked by the "seekers" of the sixties. Each of them boasts their own specialty: the podcaster Brené Brown stresses vulnerability, the bestselling author Glennon Doyle concentrates on feelings, *The Power of Now* author Eckhart Tolle has a Buddhist-slash-mystical approach, and the onetime presidential candidate Marianne Williamson preaches the power of love.

Though their philosophies differ, all echo an "awakening"—a brave journey of inner work that shapes meaning in a world that increasingly divests from former conventional paths to purpose. For the spiritually aimless, they offer up a spiritual life that transcends labels, rules, or hard distinctions. Living an examined, ethical life, they say, does not require an overarching organization. Values are not restricted to orthodoxy.

Tippett grew up with Southern Baptist parents in Oklahoma. Her grandfather was a Southern Baptist evangelist preacher. But even though she too felt spiritual and graduated from divinity school, she struggled with inflexible, cast-iron religious tenets. How could, she wondered, "every Catholic and Jew, every atheist in China and every northern Baptist in Chicago, for that matter—every non–Southern Baptist—be damned?" In a pluralistic and open society, it didn't sit right.[16]

"We are among the first peoples in human history who do not broadly inherit religious identity as a given, a matter of kin and tribe, like hair color and hometown," writes Tippett, writing in a tone that doesn't sound the alarm so much as open the door. "But the fluidity of this—the possibility of choice that arises, the ability to craft and discern one's own spiritual bearings—is not leading to the decline of spiritual life but its revival."[17]

Tippett's moderate, rational, intellectual doctrine appeals to a growing number of Americans disenchanted with the God of their parents, be it for political or personal reasons. Some women reject organized religion for equity or bodily autonomy reasons. Parents recoil after reading of multiple sexual abuse scandals. Young progressives object to any institution that does not welcome their LGBTQ brethren. Some liberals take issue with what they consider objectionable politics or party affiliations.

Many Gen Xers and millennials never really grew up with a strong faith in the first place. They showed up once a year for services to blankly stare into the distance in boredom. Christmas meant Santa and matching pajamas, with Jesus pushed to the periphery. Hanukkah constituted maybe one night of candle-lighting and an Adam Sandler song, though few could tell you the history of the holiday. For most secularized millennials, their connection to a priest, rabbi, or imam factors only into big milestones like a wedding, thereby equating a religious leader with just another hired vendor. Florist, caterer, pastor . . .

Since 1990, when just 8 percent of Americans said they had no religion, the abandonment of organized faith has accelerated.[†] Four out of ten American millennials now identify as religiously unaffiliated, identifying more with a Harry Potter house than a Catholic saint. Called "nones," they constitute the fastest-growing religious demographic. And they are well represented among highly educated and politically liberal women; according to a Pew Research Center survey, "nones" among women rose by 10 percentage points between 2009 and 2019.[18]

To give an idea of Americans' shifting views—in 1998, a *Wall Street Journal* and NBC News survey asked Americans which values they most valued. The majority cited hard work, patriotism, commitment to religion, and having children. In 2019, the same outlets asked the same question, but got different results: patriotism dropped 9 percentage points, religion was down 12 points, and having kids took a 16-point beating.[19]

Religion lost its stature because people feel free to choose alternatives

---

[†] This is not just a U.S. phenomenon. Individuals are drifting away from organized religion in other countries as well.

that accomplish similar goals. Which is partially why a little less than half of Americans today belong to a church, mosque, or synagogue—down from 70 percent in 1999, according to a 2020 Gallup poll.[20]

Perhaps most telling, the current president of the Harvard Chaplains, Greg Epstein, does not subscribe to any one religion. He doesn't necessarily even look to any higher power. He is a humanist who penned a book titled *Good Without God.* "We don't look to a god for answers," Epstein told the *New York Times.* "We are each other's answers." This tracks with the wide market of spiritual suppliers who forgo a literal God in favor of human connection and emotional satisfaction, like feeling welcomed, happy, appreciated, or nurtured. The sociologist of religion Wade Clark Roof put it best when he wrote, "more and more Americans are making religious decisions on the basis of their feelings."[21]

And yet, however independent we humans believe ourselves to be, we still crave a universal order to the chaos. One of many reasons people historically turned to religion was because it was seemingly in their best interests. When limited by our mortal power, humans—with our imaginative, narrative skills—find creative ways to reassert it. In his book *Religion: What It Is, How It Works, and Why It Matters*, the sociologist and University of Notre Dame professor Christian Smith defines religion as both a belief and a set of practices to connect with superhuman powers that can help people avoid misfortune and garner good things. That's not the sole reason religion finds audiences—people also endeavor to make sense of their lives—but it's one of the strongest.

That's why the overwhelming majority of Americans—90 percent, in fact—are not becoming atheists. Atheism, in our typically optimistic society, feels too final. Too negative. A real Debbie Downer. Americans want to believe in *something.* More than 50 percent believe in God as depicted in the Bible, but 33 percent believe "in another type of higher power or spiritual force," according to a Pew Research Center survey. Maybe it's not King Triton flanked by angels on a bed of clouds, but nearly half of U.S. adults believe that God or some other cosmic puppet master is in charge of what happens to them. Two-thirds think the Almighty goes out of his (or her) way to reward them.[22]

Universally, women are more religious than men.[23] Christian Smith suggests this is because women are more likely to be aware of their vulnerabilities and therefore seek additional resources, including those of the superhuman. Women face more violence, discrimination, and poverty, so they're more inclined to prepare strategies to confront bad situations. It's the same reason why some in lower socioeconomic levels are more religious; they objectively need more help.[24]

Organized religion may no longer hold the same authority, but the quest for spirituality is alive and well—on podcasts if not in SoulCycle studios. As Oprah told Stanford University students in a 2015 graduation speech, "I'm not telling you what to believe or who to believe, or what to call it. But there is no full life, no fulfilled or meaningful, sustainably joyful life without a connection to the spirit. You must have a spiritual practice."[25]

In 2020, "focusing on spiritual growth" made its way into Americans' most popular New Year's resolutions.[26] That focus skyrocketed at the start of the COVID-19 pandemic, since, as always, a crisis awakens religious fervor. One survey found that nearly one-quarter of American adults reported their faith had strengthened amid all that sourdough bread baking. *What did the pandemic mean? Was this God or the universe sending a message? How do you make sense of all the deaths?*

But in much the same way that millennials prefer their tech or sneakers, they want their faith customized—a curated reflection of who they think they are. They mix and match a privatized, pluralistic assembly of traditions, grabbing shamanism here and Buddhism Lite over there, with a touch of cultural Judaism for good measure. Islamic symbols and zodiac charts live side by side in equal coexistence, proving one doesn't need to fully ditch one to latch on to the other. "There's sort of been this liminal in-between position where they're outside of organized religion, but interested in religious and spiritual pursuits," explains the sociology professor Joseph Baker.

Bit by bit, a new generation stitches together an eclectic patchwork of practices that supplies them what they sorely lack in modern American culture: guidance, meaning, and a place to belong in a fractured society. A context to shape their eighty-plus years on this Earth. These are things religion offered, but faced with a deficit, they now need to find new sources to frame their standing in the world. If mankind once fasted on a mountaintop to appeal to a higher power, so too can the modern woman flank herself with crystals to summon good energy before a work presentation. And if not with a spiritual alternative, people might venture out to other tightly held ideologies, finding religious convictions in nationalism, identity-based movements, social justice, or, yes, even health—all of which can offer purpose and structure. America is a deeply religious country. As Smith explains, "if religion goes away, at least in this culture, it's going to have to be substituted with other things."

Is believing in manifestation more or less rational than belief in Jesus? Is meditating the same as saying a prayer? That's not the point. (Honestly, very little of what mankind holds religious contains hard evidence.) The point is that people choose it. They get to redefine their faith in a way that feels far more authentic to them. As one college student told me of her newfound conversion to manifestation and crystals, "I'm on my own: if I don't like something, *I don't have to* practice it."

But in the ongoing quest to nail down the right kind of faith, when do you know that you hit upon the right one? How do you decide what propels self-growth? There's no easy answer. If you discard traditional faiths, you still have to wade through a marketplace of gurus. Some are more honest than others. While Krista Tippett and Brené Brown sincerely aim to forge new paths in spiritual engagement, other influencers are ready to twist faith into something that isn't all that different from what people were fleeing in organized religion. It comes down to the leader in question, and what people are specifically searching for.

Which raises some issues: What if in seeking a solution to their problems people are actually aggravating them?

Spiritual Marketplace: A Deeper Connection
or Self-Oriented Ideology?

In 2018, the trend forecasting group WGSN declared that "spirituality is the new luxury."[27] And it sure was apparent.

Columbia Business School offered a certificate in spiritual entrepreneurship. Instagram saw a rush of "purpose-driven soulpreneurs" (chakra beads on top, Lululemon leggings on the bottom) hawking pricey Tulum vacations. Then Amazon Prime's newsletter started sending monthly shopping horoscopes to its members, aligning specific product suggestions to the stars. This is how I found out that communication is reportedly quite hard for Geminis in April, so they ought to practice giving and taking feedback with . . . an Amazon Alexa.

To put it crudely, there's money in selling *to* your soul. Not that it's anything entirely new: many religions also try to sell you something (whether it blatantly has a visible price tag is another story). The difference is that spiritual wellness, as marketed today, is easily digestible, entertaining, and often dolled up in memes or pastel-hued branding. It sure helps that tarot cards and crystals are instantly Instagrammable. (A communion wafer, meanwhile, leaves a bit to be desired in the aesthetics department.) Better yet: it promises super-fast results.

Products like crystal facial rollers are now sold at Anthropologie. These $28 rose quartz beauty accessories claim to encourage "a renewed sense of self," help "aid in the detoxification of your body," and promote a sense of "connection to the universe." That such products lack clear clinical evidence doesn't mean we should completely discard them as spiritual tools, though retailers should not suggest health benefits. (A conflation between spiritual well-being and health crosses the line. By claiming physical health benefits, we therefore put the wellness bar quite low—at the unscientific level.)

Tarot card sets and crystals are just a few of many spiritual objects sold at popular retailers. Urban Outfitters sold smudge kits (a sacred Native

American practice), while Sephora planned a $42 "starter witch kit." But the idea of purchasing and picking only what you want from different faiths, like some sort of spiritual Sizzler buffet, can also be a way to avoid pricklier issues like a faith's controversial beliefs and instead select just the fun, self-serving parts. Very few seem to pick the more communal aspects, like service, charity, and responsibility. Or it divorces an ancient tradition from its larger context or wisdom to pulverize it down to . . . athletic yoga.

The new wellness marketplace caters to self-oriented spirituality. On Instagram, spiritual influencers encourage people to "celebrate" themselves and seek a never-ending journey of self-love with few calls for humility or consideration of others. These posts contradict themselves in that they stress constant self-work, then proclaim we're perfect as we are. "Never apologize for who you are," they impart, but then demand, "become the best version of yourself." Remarkably, for all of the influencers' talk of empowerment, they encourage you to rely on them, because repeat business pays the bills. Workshops, crystal kits, and horoscope subscriptions are codependency with a price point.

Worse, these spiritual concepts can serve as a hall pass to do whatever the hell you want because self-love is your actual God. Inconsiderate behavior like flakiness is excused in the name of "listening to intuition." Harsh feedback becomes "releasing bad energy." "Don't feel guilty for doing what's best for you," reads an Instagram post posing as spiritual advice. "Dismiss what no longer serves your soul," advises another. College professors tell me of students who manipulate the zodiac like a mental health diagnosis. How can they be expected to accept criticism on their essays when they're a Pisces, known for being sensitive? *This is who I am*, they argue.

Modern spirituality has been a refuge for those alienated by organized religion, most notably those ostracized by it and even individuals who lack the money to participate in certain religious lifestyles. But these belief systems also have their blind spots: self-exploration can devolve into self-centeredness if left unchecked. Conversations revolve around how some life force is always sending signs—in dreams, through Netflix algorithm recommendations, or via Bumble flirtations. The universe, as Regina George would say, is obsessed with these people. And nothing is more important than their needs. That's what it sometimes comes down to: self-love, self-compassion, self-improvement. *The self.*

Also, as the famed social scientist Robert Putnam wrote, privatized religion might feel more psychologically fulfilling "but it embodies less social capital." As people surf from practice to practice, they might be less committed to a specific community and less inclined to be meaningfully involved over long periods of time. That's likely because new denominations have been "directed inward rather than outward."[28]

Not to mention, when everyone has their own mix of practices that shape them, "it's very rare that you get a fullness of experience—of community—because everything is somewhat itemized or bite-sized," says Casper ter Kuile, a Harvard Divinity School fellow and the author of *The Power of Ritual*. That might have unintended effects. "I think that's what contributes to this sense of cosmic loneliness—that sense that nothing fits completely, like something is always missing."

Wellness—*real* wellness—emphasizes communal well-being and social support (not to mention, reasonable expectations about the future) to thrive. But as religious tradition eroded, so did its focus on communal unity, replaced with striving for capitalist success and emotional soothing. We seem far more focused on *feeling* good, seeking acceptance, and dwelling on our innermost lives.

If you are only concerned for yourself, is there room left for others?

Too often, one might choose self-serving spirituality because that's human nature. If deciding between a practice that demands real self-examination, communal sacrifice, intellectual study, and giving back or one that lets you hustle your way to prosperity, you might just choose the latter. You are busy, stressed, and overwhelmed as it is anyway. Why not pick that which suits your immediate needs?

Again, it's not that traditional religions are exempt from similar issues. They too can breed egotistical characters or self-centered behavior.

But spirituality alternatives that focus on success, consumerism, and narcissism create their own meaning crisis. Now some turn to belief systems that seem to fixate on those exact things, in an almost circular cycle of pressure. Or we lean in to a spirituality-lite that argues everything we need stems from me, myself, and I: scribble in your gratitude journal, concentrate on manifesting, squeeze your crystals . . . they all are done alone, in the privacy of one's home.

When a family member dies, crystals do not offer a communal ritual, nor does manifestation soothe collective grief or solidify memorial rites. Belief is one part of the equation. But we can't just prioritize the self, because that puts us back where we started: unwell.

Chapter 9

You're Not Working Hard Enough

Gasping for air, I struggled to keep up with a fast succession of push-ups. This was after what felt like an eternity of jumping jacks. I took a five-second rest, which quickly drew the attention of the instructor. Dressed in a branded sweatshirt and sweatpants, he approached me with a booming voice.

"This isn't SoulCycle!" he shouted, as I insecurely tugged at my leggings. "Get working!"

At CONBODY, a prison yard–themed boutique gym run by ex-convicts in New York, there is no rest for the weary. In this intense cardio class, I, and my fellow gym rats, worked diligently using only our body weight, just like prisoners do. It was all part of the theme: In the basement-level space, mugshot printouts of celebrities—O. J. Simpson, Zsa Zsa Gabor, and three of Lindsay Lohan—lined the entrance hall. At the end of the hall, a metal gate featured a graphic of barbed wire. Further in, a cement wall fenced in the check-in desk. CONBODY offers an "inmate experience" for young professionals intrigued by prison. Their clients watched *Orange Is the New Black* or *Prison Break* and are, by the gym founder's account, curious what lockup feels like.[1]

The trends only got tougher. I've also tried out trampoline cardio, aquacycling (like SoulCycle but in waist-deep water), and super cold HIIT workouts stationed in giant bespoke walk-in refrigerators. By early 2020, I found myself in a Tribeca fitness studio that specialized in electrical muscle stimulation (EMS). I took a high-impact cardio class where I had to wear a powersuit, much like a wet suit, that emitted electric shocks to cause involuntary muscle contractions. Throughout the workout, an instructor would press a button that sent electrical currents through my body, paralyzing me in my tracks as I tried to complete a burpee. Each time I was zapped, it felt as if I had suffered a heart attack.

I thought, *This has all gotten insane.* I'm getting nearly electrocuted or literally pretending to be so fit as to survive prison life. I can't work this hard. The Physical Activity Guidelines for Americans recommend at least 150 minutes a week of moderate aerobic activity (brisk walking, pushing a lawn mower) or 75 minutes of vigorous aerobic activity (running, swimming laps), with two days of muscle-strengthening activities (lifting weights, power yoga).

When did we decide that the average Joe needs to exercise like an American Gladiator? Why does it feel like everything requires so much effort? Or perhaps the better question is: Why do we feel the need to work so hard?

"Crush" Your Workouts:
Hard Labor for Hard Abs

Fitness is important, yet it's become increasingly demanding and performative. Among the trendiest of boutique studios across the country, you'll find Rise Nation, which is pure stair climbing. Crunch Gym launched a class called X-Treme Firefighters Workout to train students as if they were first responders and firefighters (the goal is to become strong enough to carry an unconscious human being out of a burning building). Big cities are home to plenty of popularized boot camps that employ former marines who force paying customers to endure "punishing" exercises like barbed wire crawls. These are all workouts in which we're told to "torch," "burn," or "crush," as though we're gripped in the clutches of war.

The trendiest of fitness regimens, it seems, run on good old American fuel: hard, hard work. When Peloton's internal marketing documents were leaked in 2019, we learned that to differentiate itself from other fitness brands, Peloton suggested that the brand isn't for everyone. It's for the ambitious, those who put in the effort to achieve greatness. "[We're] not a party on a bike," read the materials.[2]

To be sure, there's a market for this. For many, the appeal of a tough workout goes beyond body sculpture. They're attracted to the intensity and the need for endurance—*the sacrifice*. Call it achievement, transformation, or mental resilience, but the discomfort and perseverance required to vanquish "weakness" offer a real high. Some say this paves the path to self-actualization. Others say pain is character-building—a metaphor for overcoming life's many obstacles. And a few will readily acknowledge it as a tool for spiritual awakening.

This is not to suggest there isn't value in becoming strong. Acquiring strength is valuable for obvious reasons: A woman might feel more confident, attractive, and capable. She might feel powerful. She might draw on her physical strength to accomplish more tasks at home or feel more at ease in the boardroom. And that's all great.

But the perception of popularized fitness trends can backfire if it intimidates the average person. "Super high-intensity workouts inadvertently shame people into thinking that if they're not doing high intensity, beat-your-body-up workouts, then you're not really working out and you're wasting your time," says Carrie Myers Smith, a fitness industry expert and the author of *Squeezing Your Size 14 Self into a Size 6 World*. Experts instead offer the most commonsense advice: just go with what feels good to you. If people find walking boring or CrossFit too strenuous, they should find whatever will motivate them, be it tennis, jogging, or dancing in the dark to Robyn. "It's unfortunate that as a society, we seem to feel that more is better, including with exercise," says Heather Hausenblas, a professor of kinesiology at Jacksonville University and the co-author of *The Truth About Exercise Addiction*. "As a society, we really have a warped image of what health is."

If the greater fitness industry isn't pushing strenuous workouts, then they're promoting the idea of optimal fitness—that you need to squeeze every last bit of sweat out of a class. Time is a scarce resource to be managed, and is best handled by fitness trackers or health apps to track "progress" and log weekly "streaks." We keep score of our commitment to our bodies, tinkering with sleep stats and steps taken, guaranteeing we don't fall off the given path. We're besotted with data. By engaging in constant external monitoring, we surrender our own assessment. We let the machines judge, control, and optimize our actions.

HIIT workout franchise Orangetheory, for example, uses heart rate monitors to track your anaerobic threshold during cardio classes. Creator and co-founder Ellen Latham incorporated the idea after speaking with fitness enthusiasts who believed they were underperforming in comparison to those around them. Latham wanted to emphasize individual progress—backed by data. "I'm very much into the belief of competing against yourself," she told me, "specifically your last best self."[3] The goal, therefore, is to strive for *the next best you.*

Goals are great, there's no arguing that. Yet the quest for one-upmanship can taint our view of fitness, or worse. Lee, a mother of one in her late thirties, started running in her early twenties. Her mission, like that of many young women, was, as she describes it, to meet "the fitness standard." She worried that a few extra pounds would jeopardize her ability to achieve the American dream. "I [thought] if I look like that, I will be happy. I'll meet a man, I'll get married and I'll have all the things that I want to have and that society tells me I should have," she explained.

In 2013, Lee bought a Fitbit. At the start, tracking the data was fun. Lee could analyze her runs and daily calorie intake, using the numbers to push herself further. But the new gizmo didn't aid her runs as much as pinpoint all the ways she was falling short. Lee began to obsess over her stats. She punished herself if she underperformed or didn't hit new goals. Lee started planning her meals the night before, calculating exactly how much she would burn off with any given cardio exercise. "So I have to go for a forty-minute run and this is my only food for the day and I can't deviate from that because if I do then I'm probably gonna gain a pound and that's going to make me slower," she reasoned. If her then boyfriend asked her to go out for a meal, she would panic because she would need to schedule an activity to precisely cancel out the calories. "It's rearranging your life to fit with your [fitness] plan."

In time, exercise no longer served as a stress outlet, rather as a nerve-racking chore—an obligation. "It took all the joy away," reflects Lee. The situation came to a head when her fertility shut down due to overexercising and doctors warned her she was headed for a health crisis. In 2018, she finally recognized that she was suffering from fitness OCD, and Lee deserted her Fitbit. "That's when I started to dig into the actual damage that I'd done," she says, "years of depriving myself."

A quarter of American women use fitness trackers. Many indeed find them motivating. But for all the buzz, about half of users will tire of their shiny new tech toy and shove it into a drawer within six months.[4] Some stick with it, though some research isn't all that encouraging. One 2016 study found that while quantifying our every move might increase health consumers' tendency to engage in an activity, it can also simultaneously reduce how much we actually enjoy that activity. "This occurs because measurement can undermine intrinsic motivation," reads the study. "By drawing attention to output, measurement can make enjoyable activities feel more like work, which reduces their enjoyment."[5]

Top-tier gyms, meanwhile, offer a suite of coaches, treatments, and services meant to remedy any issue that might be standing in the way of achieving Halle Berry's body. In 2018, Equinox announced the debut of "sleep coaching," where personal trainers solely focus on improving snooze habits to benefit exercise performance. While sleep coaching isn't anything new, it's often used by professional athletes.

Now it is being rolled out to the general consumer to help them reach their "potential."

Perhaps Gwyneth Paltrow explained this endless quest for self-improvement best when she exclaimed on her Netflix series, *The Goop Lab*, "It's all laddering up to one thing: optimization of self. We're here one time, one life. How can we milk the shit out of this?" And hence we need fitness trainers, gadgets, and strenuous workouts to reach this magically hidden but tappable perfection. Our enhanced self is all there, simmering under the surface, just waiting for us to unlock it.

Flashback: Productivity Through Pumping Iron

In mid-nineteenth-century England, a movement dubbed "muscular Christianity" propelled believers to pump iron in the name of heaven. At a time of a "crisis in masculinity," society sought to uphold man's supposed God-given nature in an overcivilized world. Exercise was performed in the service of a higher power: it was a way to build character, avoid immoral pursuits, and ultimately "protect the weak." Physical prowess not only exemplified a commitment to God, it also made you more useful in service to others. Like a missionary He-Man.

The Protestant work ethic heavily influenced the popularity of fitness. As industrialization quickened, emerging middle and bourgeois classes found themselves with far more leisure time at their disposal. The idea of free time was so novel that they needed to find a purpose for it. Sports and outdoor activities were therefore encouraged as a means for righteous self-improvement, rather than pure amusement, which they deemed lazy and wasteful.

Up until that time, physical discipline—be it fasting or abstinence—was more or less delegated to the clergy. With this new era, the merger of sport and religiosity was touted to the masses as an expression of piety and servitude. This ethos evolved into team sports supported by local churches. Momentum hit a tipping point with the introduction of the first Young Men's Christian Association (YMCA) in London circa 1844, followed by New York City in 1869.

But such an emphasis on strength inherently maligned any form of perceived weakness, insinuating that the less fit were less than devoted to their creator. As one American pastor at the time wrote, "He who neglects his body, who calumniates his body, who misuses it, who allows it to grow up puny, frail, sickly, misshapen, homely, commits a sin against the Giver of the body . . . Round shoulders and narrow chests are states of criminality. The dyspepsia is heresy. The headache is infidelity. It is as truly a man's moral duty to have a good digestion, and sweet breath, and strong arms, and stalwart legs, and an erect bearing, as it is to read his Bible, or say his prayers, or love his neighbor as himself."[6]

You can hear echoes of this sentiment a century later in James Fixx's 1977 manifesto, *The Complete Book of Running*. The jogging enthusiast detailed the need for mastery over ourselves: how exercise cultivates qualities such as "will power, the ability to apply effort during extreme fatigue, and the acceptance of pain." Running takes work, and maybe we *need* more work, he proposed. "Too many of us live under-disciplined lives," wrote Fixx. "By giving us something to struggle for and against, running provides an antidote to slackness."[7]

The Fitfluencer Effect

From the nineteenth century to today, the fitness industry—like the diet industry—has glommed on to wellness to sell us an aesthetic ideal.

Publications like *Shape* and *Women's Health* publish piece after piece promoting how to "drop two sizes" or achieve a "bikini body." They imply that body modification in pursuit of the beauty ideal is the ultimate goal of getting active. Models' and celebrities' bodies are airbrushed to a flawless degree, projecting a surreal and sensual fantasy that consumes the reader. As one former *Women's Health* editor told me, these magazines simply continue a long, complicated legacy of women's aspirational (read: unrealistic) beauty standards because "that's what people want," whether they admit it or not. If magazines won't deliver it, then Instagram or TikTok will. In fact, social media does deliver it—and better—which is why they've stolen the mantle from declining traditional outlets.

Social media networks have exploded with imagery of people working out, via brands but also just peers bragging how they beat their last record. (Far rarer are people posting about being too tired to exercise and resigning themselves to the couch.) On Instagram, the hashtag #fitness has been used nearly 500 million times, which is separate from the 230 million #gym posts. At the top of the heap, often generating those hashtags, are the social media fitness stars—also known as "fitfluencers." The Tracy Flicks of exercise sell us on peak physicality: that hot, ripped body with zero percent body fat and chiseled abs. The most recognizable of this group is Kayla Itsines, "the Internet's undisputed workout queen," a fitness app founder with 14 million Instagram followers.

Just how big is fitfluencers' reach? *Forbes* reported that the top ten combined have an audience of more than a hundred million people—and that was back in 2017. Fitfluencers are only gaining more traction online, with some able to earn up to $30,000 per Instagram post. Fitfluencing has evolved into a real industry: Equinox partnered with Hollywood agency William Morris Endeavor to launch a fitness talent management practice to develop personal brands and score large-scale sponsorship deals.

Most fitfluencers aren't exactly pushing health, even if they look like it. "Be healthy" or "get strong," fitfluencers parrot, understanding full well that "fit" has replaced the space once afforded to "thin." They wear little clothing, ensuring that fans see perfectly sculpted body parts, as they stress workout plans that are more linked to fat reduction and visual appearance than cardiovascular health.

One study of Instagram, Facebook, Twitter, and Tumblr found that "fitspiration" imagery overindexes thin, toned women. These women were far more likely than men to be under twenty-five, have their full body on display, "and to have their buttocks emphasized."[8] Other researchers discovered that while fitspiration posts were "less extreme" than thinspiration (imagery encouraging thinness), there were no differences "with regard to sexual suggestiveness, appearance comparison, and messages encouraging restrictive eating."[9]

During the COVID-19 pandemic, a number of fitfluencers doubled down on the importance of a challenging daily exercise regimen, beating the drum that fans had better start sweating before they couldn't pull up their sweatpants. Suddenly women had to contend with pangs of personal inadequacy while dealing with stay-at-home orders. They feared their peers would emerge from isolation "as the body beautiful" while they barely found the time to shower.

Is this fitspiration or more like fitpressure?

Even athleisure upholds a specific body type. Some women feel that the uniform of women's fitness—the ubiquitous leggings and sports bra—mostly flatters the svelte and toned. *Who else can wear skintight spandex and flash their midsection?* Meanwhile, activewear brand marketing doesn't rely on realistic imagery of an average-sized woman, save for a few images every so often. Bigger-sized models have entered the fold, but they're still a minority that feels more like tokenism. Instead, we're treated to a medley of beautiful twentysomethings—flat bellies and all—that we, in turn, expect in our local gym.

What this all means is that today we are saddled with two equally unrealistic depictions of the female body: lean fitfluencers and perfectly curvy celebrities such as Kim Kardashian. One shows up on your television screen, the other in your Instagram feed. In a way we have triple pressure riding on women today—we need to be thin, curvy, *and* toned. The goal is a big butt, a teensy waist, and feminine musculature. It almost makes you yearn for the days when we simply needed to starve ourselves.

It's discouraging and relatively new, says Steven Loy, an exercise physiologist at the kinesiology department at Cal State Northridge. "Twenty years ago, a thin body was what was being pushed, but you didn't see the muscle. Now you see the same thin body, but it's got muscles that you can see." So basically, society added new bells and whistles to the unachievable ideal. "They've raised the bar on you." One health expert I spoke to reported a steady stream of young gym-goers with the same exact lower back pain, an ailment that usually afflicts an older segment of the population. The culprit? Too many booty-building exercises were performed with poor form.

Fitfluencers would have you believe that a rock-hard body (and booty) is just a matter of scheduling in a daily workout, of "committing to yourself." The audience is not privy to the amount of work that goes on beyond the iPhone screen, where fitfluencers spend hours every day exercising. Not to mention, imagery might be airbrushed and the influencer's poses manipulated to enhance their best angles. In comparison to traditional media, fitfluencers fuel more feelings of inadequacy because these individuals are not supermodels or Hollywood stars; they play up being real, "average" people, which then makes you feel worse for not rising to their bench-pressing level. It *looks* achievable. But fitfluencers fail to disclose that bodies react differently to specific exercises: genetic diversity cannot guarantee exact results.

On the surface level, #fitspo might seem like progress: Why shouldn't we promote fitness? It's healthy! But an onslaught of aesthetic fitness imagery isn't motivating the average American to get moving. On the contrary, it's intimidating them to the point of quitting before even starting. Carrie Myers Smith hears from self-conscious women who believe they need to lose weight and firm up *before* joining a gym. "We're not inspiring [the majority of] people to be fit," she told me. "We're just continuing to support the ones that already are fit, and shaming the ones that aren't." By 2020, 56 percent of Americans experienced this "gymtimidation," according to a Mindbody survey.[10]

The ones opting out of an unwinnable race aren't wrong. The likelihood that anyone can achieve influencers' level of fitness without time, money, and good genes is slim to none. The right kind of body is the product of the right classes, the right clothes, the right sneakers . . . the right effort. Our flesh is thereby an expensive project we must funnel more and more money into, forever iterating on Frankenstein's buff monster.

Aesthetic fitness doesn't necessarily equal health. Being fit looks like many different things. "The images that people are bombarded with are these hyperfit individuals, which I would tend to argue may not even be that healthy at the end of the day," says Heather Hausenblas. "Individuals internalize that and say 'that's what I need to look like to be healthy and to be fit.'"

You don't have to push it to the limits to be within health's reach. But there's no pride in gentleness, right? As with clean eating, extreme fitness yields extreme results—and maybe some respect. That's because moderation isn't prized in our culture.

Likewise, why do fitfluencers harp on rigid aesthetic ideals when science allows for far more body diversity? Because social media incentivizes it. Algorithms reward posts that garner the most likes (or controversy, for that matter), not those that align with medical advice. If someone wants to grow their following so that they can snag partnerships or get invited to live in a TikTok mansion, then they'll follow suit. "[It's] a vicious cycle, because when you're promoting content, the stuff that performs the best is usually the least factual stuff or the terms that aren't scientifically correct," Charlee Atkins, founder of the fitness lifestyle brand Le Sweat, told *Well+Good*.[11] "What sells is 'toning,' 'lengthening,' 'burn,' 'booty'—all of these words that didn't have definitions until the fitness industry created them . . . And so those of us who are in the fitness industry and promoting our products, for us to reach a larger market we're almost forced to also use those terms."

The algorithms don't do any wonders for women's self-esteem. In 2021, a leaked internal research report revealed that Facebook was made aware that Instagram (which it acquired in 2012) is harmful to girls' body image. The company was warned that 32 percent of girls said Instagram worsened their insecurities, blaming the photo sharing app for increased anxiety and depression. As one eighteen-year-old told the *Wall Street Journal*, "When I went on Instagram, all I saw were images of chiseled bodies, perfect abs and women doing 100 burpees in 10 minutes." Facebook, according to the report, made "minimal efforts" to address these mental health issues.

One study, though very small, further analyzed social media effects on young women. After twenty university students viewed fitspiration for one to four hours a day, they experienced greater body dissatisfaction and their self-confidence plummeted. These same individuals, however, had also spent years, like all of us, consuming advertising and traditional media. What was the difference, then? Fitspiration was potentially more potent because "perhaps women do not process fitspiration images *as critically* as they do thin-ideal images, or perhaps adding tone and strength to thinness cumulates to provide women with more ways in which to feel inadequate."[12]

While men also face pressures brought forth by a shirtless Chris Hemsworth, it's far more acute with women. Unsurprisingly, researchers found that women are more inclined to exercise for weight loss and toning, whereas men are more inclined to do it for enjoyment.[13]

Women are far more targeted in body culture, in part due to how gender intersects with social identity—and how it's both constructed and enforced, explains the *Body of Truth* author Harriet Brown. Traditionally, men's social power and reputation stemmed from the things they did, whereas women were typically prized for how they appeared. "It's deeply, deeply baked into our culture," says Brown. "I don't think it's possible to be a woman in this culture and not feel these things . . . We still seem to believe that so much of our value comes from how we look, how thin we are, and how sexy we are, whereas men have a lot of other avenues."

In recent decades, social standings have shifted, but the blueprint remains intact. A 2017 Pew Research Center poll found that society differs over what it values in men versus women. The top traits revered in men were honesty and morality, followed by professional success. For women, it was physical attractiveness, followed by empathy and being nurturing.[14] Women are told from multiple touchpoints that their body matters, that their physical attributes determine their success.

You can't blame them when they simply give in.

Productivity Tentacles Grow Longer and Stronger

It's not just our fitness we need to crush. Nowadays, you also need to leisure better.

Vacations have shifted in recent years. Burned-out Americans popularized wellness travel, one of the leading trends in the hospitality sector. Vacationers seek getaways filled with fitness classes, yoga, surfing, and guided meditation—in that order. They're not as interested in getting wasted in Vegas. (Although even Vegas is looking to reinvent itself as a wellness destination.) "When you have such little time off, you really can't afford to come back from a vacation where you drank too much, stayed up all night, and ate really horrible food," explained Beth McGroarty, the director of research at the Global Wellness Institute. "You can't afford coming back feeling worse than you did when you left."[15]

One poll found that 40 percent of millennials reported they'd rather go on a fitness retreat with their favorite instructor than attend a five-star relaxation resort.[16] I am guilty of this. I will sign up for a surf camp or stay in a fitness-class-focused hotel before ever staying in a regular resort. I just can't let that precious time go to "waste." Heaven forbid I sit by the pool and order a steady stream of grilled cheese sandwiches, which is what I actually want to do.

Like me, women might also fear gaining weight on vacation, aware that one too many midday margaritas might undo all the pre-trip starvation endured to fit into that bikini. As the writer and eating disorder survivor Gina Susanna recounted, to prepare for memorable (that is, Instagrammable) moments, "We need to make sure we are thin enough to enjoy them."[17] Susanna had heard from women who were "terrified" of going on vacations because they feared being surrounded by unhealthful foods or without exercise access. "I was just so sick of the constant diet culture voices telling me I needed to 'look perfect' to enjoy myself," she wrote.

Now, some people truly relax by exercising, and the idea of spending hours moving the body excites them, especially if they never get to be active during their sedentary day-to-day life. For them, hiking for six to eight hours a day is fun. They enjoy the exhaustion—"the good kind"—and clarity that comes from the end of an active day outdoors. Rigorous activities in nature are the ultimate reset for them.

But others feel that their vacations or any free moments require efficiency—a subtle pressure to always be *improving*. They need to maximize their time, no matter the occasion. Bodily obligations are not afforded a PTO reprieve. In an interview for *The Cut*, the Boulder-based physical therapist Nicole Haas said that an urgency to stay in shape on vacation is leading to an increase in injuries. One persistent client of hers blew out her back by attempting crunches in a compact hotel room, among other bad decisions: "I had someone do a thousand squats on that one hotel chair. Well, now your knee hurts! And I'm like, *Seriously?*"[18]

We also just respect hard effort more. There's a hierarchy of relaxation activities, and certain ones get pushed to the top. For Fiona, a full-time elementary school teacher and married mom of two, exercising guarantees a short period of time when no one bothers her. It's a mini-escape built into the workday. She wakes up an hour before the rest of her family to slip down to the basement and engage in a streaming cardio class. Fiona notices a massive difference in her mood if she doesn't get this one sacred hour: a missed class unleashes the Irritable Hulk. "It's definitely 'me time,'" says Fiona. Everyone knows that should they rise early, they can't ask for a snack or help in finding a misplaced sweater when she's working out. "I don't have any other time when I'm alone," she sighs.

In some ways, self-care offers a cover for whatever a woman needs to do to feel sane. For example, if a wife tells her husband to watch the kids because she needs to apply a facial mask, he might roll his eyes. If, however, she changes her terminology, saying she needs to "engage in self-care," she has invoked mental health, and therefore the activity is fully sanctioned. It's much the same way men might train for a marathon "for charity." As some men admitted to Jason Kelly in his book *Sweat Equity*, it's an acceptable way to escape familial obligations. "When you're riding your bike for five hours on a Saturday, it's harder for anyone to argue with you when you say you're helping cure cancer."[19]

Fiona concedes that less active hobbies, like reading, don't quite pan out in her household. To start, "you don't look as productive to other people," thereby inviting family members to interrupt whatever novel she's engrossed in. Although she can't fully blame those around her: she too will interrupt her reading to do some light cleaning. She just cannot convince herself that being immobile earns the same kind of deference as breaking an early morning sweat. Reading just doesn't feel worthwhile *enough*. She was raised to be a high achiever who never slacks off or "takes it easy." So why would her relaxation efforts be any different?

If you listen carefully to American media or scroll your Instagram feed, you will notice a hustle culture that dictates you should always be doing *something* even when that something should potentially be nothing. (Or, as Peloton's Ally Love puts it: "Hustle never sleeps!") We just can't stop indulging our inner high-achiever. The productivity mandate stares down on you in every aspect of your life, requiring you to be more mindful with your kids, get more fit, or become more Zen. It's easy to feel lazy if you're not actively "bettering" yourself at all times. So much so that 54 percent of women feel guilty when they need to take a break or rest.[20]

There's an actual term for this feeling, where you can't ever fully relax because you feel pressured to be productive: "Sunday neurosis." Believed to have been coined by Hungarian psychoanalyst (and friend of Freud) Sándor Ferenczi, it refers to the anxiety we feel when we attempt to be idle instead of, say, training for a marathon. It's the restlessness that comes with being free of structure, duty, and work. Freedom might just feel like emptiness. Or guilt.

Workaholism pervades everything, including, oddly, fashion. Take the famous athleisure brand Outdoor Voices, which popularized over-priced color-blocked workout attire. The company's motto is "doing things," pushing the idea that it's better to be doing things than not doing things—and somehow, these things should be done in $88 leggings. Outdoor Voices floods social media with this doctrine, encouraging young women to photograph themselves hiking, exercising, or buying smoothies with the hashtag #doingthings, thereby communicating, "Look at me! I invest in my health!" Fans' attire, therefore, is not best suited for sitting on the couch watching TikTok. Outdoor Voices shoppers are doers; *they're more active than the rest*. To date, more than 225,000 images include this productivity hashtag.

Fitness culture is also everywhere. Employers build onsite gyms to inspire healthier habits (or, more likely, to lower rising healthcare costs and boost productivity). Gyms are popping up where you least expect them, even inside the supermarket. Orangetheory, the fastest-growing fitness franchise, partnered with the Iowa-based grocery retailer Hy-Vee. ShopRite opened a fitness studio in New Jersey that offers yoga and Zumba classes. Some Whole Foods stores offer a range of workout classes on their premises. CVS Health is testing "health hubs" where customers take a yoga class as they wait for pharmacy refills.[21] There is no escape. Our culture will remind you at every single turn that you should be in the gym.

It's great to have so many opportunities to get moving, don't get me wrong. But it's starting to feel like perseverance and efficiency have invaded our personal lives: hard work, sacrifice, effort . . . these are what get our engine going in our overly ambitious, goal-oriented society. Here's the thing about productivity: it's always a means toward an end goal. It's in service of something you want—or need.

Perhaps we feel compelled to constantly improve our bodies because we know full well what health (or more likely the appearance of health) signifies in our culture. We know we need to effectively compete in a cut-throat market. It seems practical: If you are up against dozens of women for a job, a partner—heck, any opportunity—in our society, you might consider anything that gives you a leg up. And that toned body might very well suggest that you are *self-disciplined, hard-working, and fully in control*, as it's come to mean. It's a survival mechanism to some degree because society upholds the body as a representation of ability.

We live in a culture that preaches you alone are responsible for your success, and that ethos spreads to more than just our career. Such a culture creates a lot of pressure, if not body-shaming. It's also indicative of healthism—a concept connoting a moralized view of health that stresses the responsibility of the individual ("lifestyle choices"). This belief system holds that it's your fault if you fall ill or embody what society considers unhealthy, like being bigger bodied. By this logic, certain people are better than others, with those falling behind likely "deserving" of whatever comes their way (despite extenuating circumstances like budget, access, ability, or genetics). So no wonder we're trying to ensure that we never fail: No one wants to be the deviant. No one wants to be judged.

It sounds like we're working so hard to be perfect.

Although, no matter how hard one tries—you can squat, down-dog, and stage beautifully positioned acai bowls on Instagram all you want—it won't ever be good enough. Unattainability is the leading tenet of perfection. More than anything, perfectionism says a lot about what we crave—it is, at the end of the day, an anxious need for control over our lives.

Girl, Get Happy!

"Six things mentally strong people do," read Gwyneth Paltrow's Instagram post. In bullet point format, the black-and-white text laid out precisely what constitutes the psychologically blessed: They don't waste time feeling sorry for themselves, they "welcome" challenges, and they don't exert energy on that which they can't control. Most important, "they stay happy."

It wasn't long before a mob of women flooded the Goop guru's comments section with critiques of such reductionist advice. "Real life adversities can be incredibly difficult to overcome," wrote one follower. Others noted that though Paltrow had good intentions, the post minimized human adversity and ignored mental health issues. One angry woman wrote, "Feelings buried alive never die." Another simply demanded, "You need to take this down."

What Paltrow was really saying was this: *You should work to make your brain right.* Society constantly emits this kind of low-frequency messaging, but it's turned up high in wellness culture. Herbal supplements allude to fixing your gut *and* your brain. Svelte social media influencers pose with functional beverages as they babble on about their inner peace, beckoning followers to follow their lead. Framed by idyllic backdrops, they promote "quieting the mind" and "choosing" to commit to contentment, repeating that sheer determination cures all ills. They ask us to overcome mental hurdles through gratitude or to imagine a laugh track scoring daily challenges.

It's talking heads and celebrities but also average moms who repeatedly talk of calming themselves into states of bliss. It's everyone on Instagram only uploading their highlight reel without proper disclaimers: these are filtered, calculated depictions. We're led to believe that positive emotions are all under our own control, that happiness is but a "choice." Never mind that many other cultures view happiness as a collective goal, a social endeavor that connects you with other people. Instead, we are asked to shoulder this lonesome burden in a *Truman Show* facade of mental health. And yet Americans are the unhappiest they've been in fifty years: only 14 percent of adults say they're "very happy."[22]

Emma Anderson, a psychologist and senior lecturer at the University of Brighton, has researched the gendered nature of self-help and finds several similarities to the current self-care discourse. Much like how self-help books bang the drum on how we are flawed and can always strive to be "better," wellness posits that we are forever improvable. If historically women were expected to be demure, modest, and subservient, today they're held to idealized femininity dictating constant positivity and resilience. Though self-help and wellness are quite different, "they have a similar impact in disallowing other ways of being—disallowing anger, for example," says Anderson. "'If I can just try to be more positive, practice gratitude, and be more mindful.' These are all aimed at a kind of quiet, pacifying state of mind."

Unsurprisingly, being commanded to be happy often sparks the opposite reaction. Journalist Ada Calhoun, the author of *Why We Can't Sleep: Women's New Midlife Crisis*, spoke to hundreds of women across the country, and nearly all echoed the same sentiment: they are stressed and continually on edge, they are socially obligated to be calm, cool, collected, and they should always be giving and never demanding. "It's the equivalent of being told to smile by somebody who is catcalling you on the street," says Calhoun. "For a lot of women I talked to, it's making them very, very angry."

These expectations soon permeate how we express ourselves. Stacey Rosenfeld, a psychologist and the author of *Does Every Woman Have an Eating Disorder?*, finds that her female patients are socialized to suppress their negative emotions. We're conditioned from a young age to be polite, agreeable, patient, serene, giving—a new anvil of ideals dropped on our head at every stage of life. "And so being angry doesn't really fall into the expectations set forward for girls and for women," says Rosenfeld. Our bad moods and (often justified) anger are simply personae non gratae. Basically: Put that shit away. You are expected to hide your dissatisfaction and instead figure out a way to lessen it for those around you.

Negative emotions are crucial to feeling better. A 2017 American

Psychological Association research study found that people are much happier when they are given the freedom to express their emotions, even when those emotions are resentment, anger, or despair. Yes, we can practice gratitude—which has shown to be remarkably beneficial to mental health—but why not make more room for expressing what ails us?

Maybe because America has long emphasized rugged self-help, which is a decidedly American phenomenon, born of Puritan values. This idea of people venturing out to secure their own happiness rather than passively hoping for it goes as far back as the eighteenth century. (Indeed, a Russian adage attests that "a person who smiles a lot is either a fool or an American.") We're a country founded on meritocracy; she who works the hardest wins. Now we've applied that philosophy to our emotions.

In America, there's this idea of this great happily ever after out there on the horizon, explains Ruth Whippman, the author of *The Pursuit of Happiness* and *America the Anxious*. "That if you just keep trying and keep doing another self-help class and another wellness program, you'll eventually get to this glittering ideal." And self-help targets more women than men. We have to improve ourselves to meet an unattainable standard or a default male ideal, says Whippman, who sees gendered expectations exemplified throughout modern society. For example, many women's co-working spaces offer onsite amenities and programs which center on self-improvement: meditation sessions, fitness classes, vitamin shots, or nutrition lectures. Male-dominated clubs, on the other hand, get to have *fun*. They incorporate real leisure, with arcades or activities like ping-pong tournaments and whiskey tastings. There is simply not the same imperative for men to improve themselves in the same way.

"It's kind of ironic because all of these things which are supposed to be about relaxing and taking the pressures off modern life just end up actually piling the pressures on," says Whippman. "It's just another thing that you have to do and be and achieve. It's just an extra state that you have to get to." These are not necessarily new trends, though they are amplified by social media, which trades on the currency of perfection.

The tides are shifting. Once the COVID-19 pandemic hit, women started to question these unsustainable pressures. They couldn't do it anymore. There's a desire to understand the underlying issues at play: Why does everyone seem so utterly depleted? Why are we forcing ourselves to feel better about it all? And what do we need to feel better that doesn't add *more* pressure?

Charting a Chiller Course

The pandemic pushed Americans to reassess their priorities and aspirations. Millions quit their stressful jobs, while 42 percent of workers in a LinkedIn survey said they were taking a break for their well-being or to spend more time with loved ones.[23] More and more people recognized widespread suffering, with mental wellness growing into the dominant lens. There was a far greater honesty about stress, psychological woes, and day-to-day struggles spurring collective vulnerability. In fitness too: a 2021 survey of 16,000 Americans found that over a quarter of adults surveyed work out to reduce stress.[24] It's why, anecdotally, when you asked people why they exercised, you were more likely to hear them say it's for their "sanity" than desiring Kayla Itsines's physique.

A societal emphasis on mental health is moving the industry outside the framework of productivity and aesthetic goals, says Beth McGroarty of the Global Wellness Institute: "The new compass point is one of healing and forestalling crisis," she says, noting that serious health management is overtaking the "bionic woman model."

In her research, Whippman found that the single biggest factor affecting happiness across the board is social support. Calhoun, meanwhile, witnesses groups of women coming together to discuss long-avoided issues and reassess impossible ideals in a way that feels both constructive and therapeutic. She launched a monthly social club for women to be "in each other's presence with no filters." Attendees, she reports, find it far more healing than any spa or yoga class.

Progress is slow but growing. Young women protesting the deluge of toxic positivity on social media have turned to digital communities like Sad Girls Club, which counts more than a quarter million Instagram followers looking for authentic emotional support.[25] Even who women have turned to for advice has changed: there are influencers who advocate compassion and moderation, not a six-pack and an emotional lobotomy.

One body positivity advocate changing the face (and shape) of fitfluencers is self-described "fat femme" Jessamyn Stanley. Stanley, who is Black, tries to widen the appeal of yoga by posting intricate poses and inspirational advice on Instagram for people who feel excluded from wellness. She'll photograph herself doing the splits upside down while clothed in a sports bra, exposing her belly and stretch marks in an industry that's generally exemplified, by Stanley's account, by a "perfectly slender, usually White [woman who] obviously has some kind of money to afford all those leggings."

Stanley's repeated use of "fat" is to reclaim a word she believes undeserving of its negative connotations. "The only way you can let go of a weapon, especially in the form of a word, is to take the weapon back," she told me. Stanley took her efforts beyond social media, launching her own fitness app, The Underbelly, where she invites yoga learners to access their feelings in an authentic way. "You don't have to omit the sadness, the anger, and all of the other 'ugly' emotions that flavor our lives,"[26] Stanley wrote in her book *Every Body Yoga*, meant as an amuse-bouche for intimidated yoga beginners who "don't feel comfortable walking into a studio."

The radical fitfluencer's insistence to fight for the further inclusion of various body shapes struck a chord within the Instagram community. Fans learn, for example, how to tailor yoga poses for all body types, with tips on how to move around with larger thighs or breasts. A sweep of her account shows thousands of likes and hundreds of comments from followers comforted by her honest depictions of pursuing wellness activities in an idealized climate. Some cry watching her videos. "You are an inspiration to the ones that don't look like the so-called 'model type,'" wrote one fan.

Stanley wasn't surprised. "[People] want to see another person that's like them," she said of her 470,000 followers. She believes a large swath of Americans want to exercise but feel put off by traditional instructors and the mainstream media's unattainable depictions. "I was overwhelmed by people [who responded] 'Wow, I didn't know that fat Black people could practice yoga, I thought it was only skinny women," she said, adding, "There were a lot of people who think that I'm a unicorn."

Stanley does not consider herself any sort of mythical creature. If anything, she said, "I am the norm, I am not the minority."

• • •

You can get sucked into the culture of it all. With wellness, you'll see yourself on a constant quest of betterment, the ideal always on the horizon. We bow at the altar of excellence with our hard-earned effort, be it a meticulous meditation regimen or Olympian-level fitness classes. You would think everything should propel you to great new heights—to self-conquest—for there is no glory or virtue in the neutral. And people don't always realize it's work because of the way it's been marketed—as a "lifestyle."

But make no mistake, we are striving for perfection, not unlike our religious ancestors working toward salvation. We have an image of what perfection is in our head—it can be super fit, calm, or free of any ailment—and it is reinforced like propaganda even when built on shaky premises. I'm not against self-improvement, rather that we have internalized a silent imperative: that we must continually work to upgrade our bodies and brains.

The pressure, ironically, can have the opposite effect. Fitness enthusiasts can push themselves so hard that an entire industry sprouted *in response to it*. One of the leading industry trends, with double-digit growth, is that of recovery: big-box gyms have hired recovery coaches and set up dedicated areas with self-massage tools.[27] One-on-one assisted stretching studios— like a spa for your overworked muscles—have opened across the country.[28] This means that for some, salvation isn't always promised as much as what eventually awaits us: burnout. Then the cycle starts all over again, reverting us through the rhythms of self-care. It's one big reinforcing complex: work hard, fall apart, then buy some stuff so you can get back on the horse. A snake eating its own tail.

If it's not mental upgrades and strenuous sweat—the productivity mandate—then it's another powerful doctrine embedded into trendy wellness doctrines: level up your health with technological advances. With cutting-edge science at our fingertips, why wouldn't you want to go further? These are two sides of the same coin, assuring us we can maximize just about everything.

But can we?

Chapter 10

Chasing Golden Unicorns:
Biohacking the Future

The small back room of the InterContinental hotel in downtown L.A. was bursting at the seams. Roughly a dozen chairs were set up for a lecture. Instead, almost a hundred people showed up. Most of the casually dressed millennials at the 2017 ideas conference Summit L.A. either sat on the floor or stood shoulder to shoulder. Those in the back stood on their toes, struggling to catch a glimpse of the speaker, the biohacking leader Dave Asprey.

Other than Gwyneth Paltrow or Lacy Phillips, Asprey was the closest I've witnessed to guru status. The participants bombarded the founder with health questions: What should I eat for breakfast? Can I have a glass of wine at dinner? Should I be taking the psychedelic drug ayahuasca? What sleep tracker do you use? Fans shot their hands in the air, each competing for a morsel of his wisdom.

Asprey, a tall, elegant man dressed in leather alligator boots and a chambray shirt, handled their questions with ease. He answered all inquiries with the air of a "cool" college professor, at times readjusting his orange-tinted glasses while applauding their curiosity. Equal parts peer and educator, Asprey peppered his answers with personal anecdotes and preferred products. The crowd's iPhones lit up as they googled his advice.[1]

Popularity wasn't new to Asprey. He first catapulted to fame through his high-performance coffee brand called Bulletproof. The caffeinated drink was infused with two tablespoons of grass-fed unsalted butter and MCT oil (a supplement sourced from coconuts and made of fatty acids). Clocking in anywhere from 250 to 450 calories (based on butter added), the beverage is claimed to boost energy, increase cognitive function, and help shed pounds. Asprey came up with the unorthodox recipe after traveling to Tibet and tasting traditional yak-butter tea drinks that locals consumed to keep warm. In 2011, he sold his own version as a self-optimization tool.

Over the next few years, Asprey's fatty cup of joe received coverage in everything from top-tier business publications to morning news programs. "It's a gateway drug for taking control of your own biology," Asprey told the *New York Times*. On *The Tonight Show*, host Jimmy Fallon shared a warm mug of Bulletproof coffee with actress Shailene Woodley and declared, "It's good for your brain."[2] Bulletproof became a curious cultural phenomenon, hailed as a "miracle drink" and drawing fans ranging from Halle Berry to Tim Tebow. Today, the creamy concoction is sold at Whole Foods, among other retailers, including Bulletproof's own brick-and-mortar Santa Monica coffee shop. Bulletproof has now evolved into a lifestyle concept, expanding to books, a podcast, conferences, and a whole suite of self-enhancement products like memory strengthening supplements and "amplified energy" bottled water.

But Asprey's biggest success was popularizing the term "biohacking." It's a concept borrowing research from bodybuilding, biotech, anti-aging science, and nutrition to make you look, perform, and feel way better than the average bear. Asprey describes biohacking as "the desire to be the absolute best version of ourselves," but it's more like an attempt to use cutting-edge science to overcome physical limitations. His company's mission? To tap into the unlimited power of being human. And according to recent industry reports, biohackers will become "the new wellness pioneers," heralding a new era where we can shortcut our way to optimal health.[3]

Asprey was once a mere mortal, a cog in the American lifestyle wheel. The former cloud computing executive was unhappy with his weight, sluggish, foggy, and moody and dealt with a host of issues, including ADD, OCD, and chronic fatigue syndrome (among other diagnosed and self-diagnosed disorders). He adopted one fad diet after another. He exercised every day. But still, the scale barely budged, and he didn't feel any better. Asprey's doctors were not helpful. They assumed he was secretly munching on candy bars. The entrepreneur recalled thinking, "I'm going to troubleshoot this myself, because I am not getting help from the medical establishment."[4]

So Asprey became his own guinea pig. He imported European "smart drugs" (cognitive enhancers). He tested brain-boosting contraptions. He committed to intermittent fasting routines.

Asprey spent fifteen years and over a million dollars to reportedly lower his biological age. In the process, he lost a hundred pounds and, by his account, increased his IQ by more than 20 points.

Today, Asprey lives like a health-obsessed Iron Man. He swallows fifty supplements every morning, recovers in a cryotherapy chamber he built in his house, and plans to get an injection of stem cells every six months. He says he no longer needs the eight hours of recommended sleep, making do with precisely six hours and ten minutes.[5] Every day he does some sort of biohacking exercise: "I could do red light therapy. I could do neurofeedback. I could just do some squats on a vibrating platform. I could do a resistance band workout with blood flow restriction," he told *GQ*.[6]

At this rate, says Asprey, he'll live to be 180. He thinks you can too. "I can tell you firsthand that you're not condemned to live with the body and brain you were born with," Asprey proclaims on his website. The Bulletproof website reads like a rundown of things people can regulate: stress, energy, mitochondrial clocks, risk of cancer, biochemistry, collagen production, sexual performance, and clarity of thought. (My favorite promise-filled headline is the one on daveasprey.com: WANT TO LIVE LONGER? BREW YOUR COFFEE THIS WAY.) DIY augmentation takes the form of neurofeedback devices as well as cold showers and fasting regimens.

In some ways, Asprey sees his work as a humanitarian effort: "We're helping people—we're empowering them by giving them control of their biology so that maybe they might see their doctor less." The entrepreneur envisions a future in which individuals become their own body experts and less dependent on medical professionals.

With help from Asprey, biohacking became synonymous with Silicon Valley, a sector that welcomes disruptive experimentation in the name of productivity. This is how Asprey became a star attraction at Summit, a conference heavy with tech founders, entrepreneurs, and ambitious creatives. But I was rather surprised to see that nearly half the room were women, if only because the biohacking scene skews male. Asprey said his Bulletproof conferences boast 50 percent female attendance, a significant uptick since he started. "My experience is that women are, on average, better biohackers than men because they have far more body awareness," Asprey told me. "Women are under tremendous pressure from a career perspective, and they are often even more constrained for time than men are."

Biohacking resonates because we're all frustrated, says Asprey, noting that complaints extend beyond the scale. Its appeal is motivated by exasperation at not having enough time, and therefore not enough energy, for work, relationships, or personal pursuits. Asprey gives one such example: "You're frustrated that every day after you've finished your commute home, you just need to lie down and put your feet up, that you don't want to play with your kids . . . It all comes down to what I want my body to be—to support me and be my servant."

At the conference, I approached a few women, curious about what they were looking to take charge of. Most of the answers included ordinary grievances such as fatigue or weight loss. One petite thirtysomething told me she was intrigued by Asprey's fertility research. This was news to me. Does biohacking cover reproduction?

"It covers *everything*," she replied. Indeed, Asprey's books explain how to safeguard one's fertility in addition to sharing how he personally cured his wife, who was diagnosed with polycystic ovarian syndrome and declared infertile. He says he did so with biohacking techniques—not through medical interventions like IVF.[7] They now have two children.

"Whether or not you choose to have kids, to become Super Human you want your body to be as fertile as possible because our bodies are designed to get out of the way as soon as we can't reproduce," Asprey writes in his *New York Times* bestseller *Super Human*. "No matter how old you are, you don't want your hormones telling your body that you're past the age of reproduction. A much better signal from your hormones is that you are young enough to have kids and therefore worth taking up room on this planet."[8]

To that end, we need to reboot our bodies, hike up our supplement intake (Bulletproof's supplements, that is; "First things first, throw away your multivitamin," reads the website), and detoxify our surroundings.

I was captivated by all of these biohacking ideas. It was as if they'd come from a wizard's spellbook to magically force the body into submission. I too wanted to know how to manufacture more energy at the office (or heck, even at dinner with friends). I too am frustrated by having to work super-long days and feeling like I can't get ahead. I too wanted to extend my fertility as my biological clock thumped ever louder. I wanted it all: stamina, youth, and focus. I was just as tired and over it as everyone else in that room.

But it also made me wonder: To what extent can scientific advancement bend nature to our will?

The Illusion of Control

In 1976, two researchers set out to understand an age-old human question: How important is our sense of control?

Ellen Langer (Harvard) and Judith Rodin (Yale) conducted an experiment on older adults. They separated a nursing home into two floors. The residents on the "agency" floor were told they'd have free rein to do what they wished with their room furniture, go where they pleased, do what they wanted during their free time, and independently care for a plant given to them. The patients on the "no agency" floor were notified that the staff would take care of every last detail and decision for them, including watering their new plant.

In reality, both groups had the freedom to do as they pleased. No one would stop an individual on the "no agency" floor from seeing a friend or watering the plant. The *perception* of what was permissible was all that differed. After eighteen months, the researchers discovered that those in the group that was granted more individual control and personal responsibility were happier. They also showed improved health. The "no agency" group had more deaths.[9]

Langer eventually made groundbreaking research progress in what she called the illusion of control, which is the tendency for people to overestimate their ability to control or impact events over which they actually have no influence. This impression makes us feel more confident and at ease. We hit elevator buttons that are already lit and wear "lucky" jerseys to a baseball game for the same reason: we want to feel that we contributed to the solution, that we matter. "Our biology is set up so that we are driven to be causal agents; we are internally rewarded with a feeling of satisfaction when we are in control, and internally punished with anxiety when we are not," writes the neuroscientist Tali Sharot in her book *The Influential Mind*.[10]

Most of us know and appreciate the comfort of taking action instead of waiting around and just hoping things will pan out. In the face of chaos, you can exert some influence. Plenty of people benefit from a similar placebo effect, by which the perception that something is working provides a certain amount of relief.

When it comes to health intentions, most people would probably seek effective benefits, not just a placebo. But in making decisions, we can overestimate our odds at achieving the desired outcome. Part of this stems from what's called a positivity bias or "the Pollyanna principle": a tendency for the mind to focus on positivity more than negativity. When we think we have more influence than we do, the obvious danger is that we might fall for a solution that is easy and simple versus taking the time and effort to analyze the situation, which is likely more complex than we assumed at first glance. Pollyannas might not anticipate potential problems.[11]

The wellness industry capitalizes on this bias, similar to how casinos enhance players' perception of control over the risk of gambling. Brands know this bias is psychologically beneficial: a sense of control reduces anxiety, fear, and stress levels, all things that contribute to overall mental health. When we believe we might be more in control, we're much more likely to buy something.

It's an open industry secret. The guidebook *Marketing to the New Natural Consumer* reads, "Note that the use of natural products as a way of regaining control over one's physical and emotional self is *not* contingent upon efficacy . . . It is not necessary that a treatment (such as reflexology) or a regular maintenance plan (taking Vitamin C) necessarily works. Simply engaging in these behaviors brings a regained sense of control to the individual." The co-authors go on to deem it a coping strategy—an antidote—to the stress of modern life, similar to partaking in body-modification rituals (like tattooing) as an "attempt to reclaim part of their self from the larger institutional structure."[12] So brands may not sell you an actual solution, but rather the illusion of a solution. A psychological exercise with a sticker price.

The biohacking movement is perhaps the most brazen example of harnessing our physiology to grasp this illusion of control. Not long after hearing Asprey speak, I visited the physical embodiment of his movement: Bulletproof Labs (now called Upgrade Labs), a futuristic "human upgrade center" in Santa Monica filled with space-age pods and curious contraptions better suited to NASA astronauts than SoCal residents. Somewhere between a gym and a science lab, its mission is "to help you achieve the highest state of physical and cognitive performance."

Inside, young and fit people seated in plush leather lounge chairs quietly flipped through magazines while receiving IV nutrient infusion drips.

An "atmospheric cell trainer" resembling Superman's pod reportedly "massages cells from the inside out" to balance out stressors. An "oxygen trainer," which looked more like a gas mask hooked up to a stationary bike, supposedly increases circulation. Then there was a tanning bed–like contraption that exposes your entire body to red and infrared LED light to "boost mitochondrial function." It was a dystopian Disneyland—or an Equinox designed by Christopher Nolan.[13]

"When you apply technology to your body there are so many things you can do that have a higher return on your investment of time and energy," Asprey told me. One of his favorite machines reportedly lets him get two and a half hours' worth of cardio in just twenty-one minutes. Asprey has all these toys at his own home, but he wanted to share them with busy professionals looking to sneak in a brain tune-up or ultra-quick workout.

In much the same way, supplements claim you can quickly master your fate. Companies like Elysium Health sell "revolutionary" at-home kits that test your biological age, then suggest their line of pills to reduce it. Their tagline? "Get ready to take control of your future." This simplistic marketing works. Goop promoted the kit on Instagram, writing, "A DNA test that can determine your rate of aging? Sign us up."

The trendiest supplement label in wellness circles remains Moon Juice, which sells powdered adaptogen (that is, herb and mushroom) blends claiming to fix your brain, sleep, stress, energy, *and* love life. These pills and concoctions, aptly named Power Dust and Sex Dust, harness the "power of plants" to "deliver beauty, balance, and vitality as a daily practice." The majority of the herbs—touted to improve immune functions or reduce stress—are backed up by little or contradictory evidence. But that doesn't stop Moon Juice from claiming on the Nordstrom website that their "elite" powder fuels "your physical and entrepreneurial feats."

Here's one overall distinction worth thinking about: health versus self-improvement. Over the decades, we've dialed up self-enhancement in various sectors like beauty (plastic surgery) or fitness (steroids). We've always sought individual interventions, though not always to heal as to boost, and now that optimization creed has come for wellness. You could argue there's a big difference between contact lenses and Botox: one solves a medical problem, the other perhaps less so (depending on your beauty philosophy). And so a chunk of late-stage wellness, for all its talk of health, seems more like Botox—a nice-to-have—than anything resembling a must-have.

This is likely what Fran Lebowitz meant when she made headlines by declaring "wellness is greed" in the Netflix documentary series *Pretend It's a City.* "Extra health," is how she described it, lamenting, "It's not enough for me that I'm not sick. I have to be 'well.' This is something you can buy." She has a point: it's how we've been sold on sleep trackers and overpriced magic pills, not to mention $118 Lululemon leggings. These were all hardly necessary until they were introduced to us, then marketed ad nauseam.

It's all subjective though, no? Botox (or acne treatment, for that matter) can be part of someone's mental well-being; it can make someone feel less insecure about their appearance. Maybe it helps them leave the house with confidence. That's why so much of wellness is debatable: what you might call "improvement" might be another person's "necessity." On one hand, there's an instinct to shun anything that's overly consumerist and lacking scientific evidence. On the other hand, there's something to be said for helping people feel better, or more "like themselves."[14]

We can't solely blame marketers for offering up new modes of self-improvement. They simply respond to a consumer demand that has its origins in the (far more regulated and science-backed) healthcare industry. There is an expectation—a sense of near entitlement—that if we have the technology to elevate our well-being, why don't we?[15] *Why aren't companies doing more to enable that? Why can't they solve all of life's problems?*

People are demanding more health solutions, and that's something the pharmaceutical and medical industry hasn't fully been able to address. So they turn to the wellness industry.

It should be noted that healthcare branding, which is not to be confused with wellness marketing, helped bring awareness and legitimize ailments that long affected women. Complaints ranging from pain to mood swings might have once been discounted before the industry named and publicized them as perimenopause, anxiety, and other recognized conditions. That helped ease the stigma. But wellness doesn't function like healthcare branding—it's not beholden to the same standards of efficacy or regulations on what you can and cannot promise the consumer.[16] That's how you end up with a bunch of fantastical-sounding supplements and optimization gizmos.

But still, why do we fall for the quick and simple solutions, or as the clinical exercise physiologist and nutritionist Bill Sukala calls it, "chasing golden unicorns"?

Research shows that stressful environments and highly competitive situations spur a desire for control. This makes sense: when you need to achieve something, you spring into action mode (without necessarily thinking through all the potential outcomes). This natural reaction is precisely why biohacking gained a loyal audience in Silicon Valley. Overwhelmed tech bros were desperate for a leg up. This is a work culture where workhorses survive and leaders look up to Steve Jobs, a man who once fired 25 percent of a team with parting words such as "You guys failed. You're a B team. B players."[17] Being number one reigns supreme in this industry, so anything that offers even the slightest competitive edge can mean rising to the top or snagging that promotion. A pill or drink that promises you can work longer, harder, and with less sleep? Contraptions that will cut workout time in half? Catnip to the overworked and undersupported.

Over time, seeing how biohacking resonated with men, those same companies started coming for women, who, to be fair, are just as overwhelmed.

Asprey's female fans have the same frustrations as men, just perhaps with different origins. They were compelled by his assessment: society mandates that people either have superhuman stamina or work like a dog to keep up. In contrast, he was suggesting, *Hey, it's okay, I know a way for you to keep up with what the world demands.* Biohacking isn't necessarily about becoming Superman, I learned; it's focused on spending "more time enjoying the fruits of [one's] labor and less time sweating it out in the field."[18] So if a buttery, textured coffee promises sustained energy, women are all for it. They've undoubtedly internalized the idea that their current skills aren't enough for them to succeed in our competitive society.

If only it were guaranteed. A portion of Bulletproof's peddled lifestyle advice and product lines relies on studies conducted on animals or studies with such small test groups that it would be hard-pressed to find definitive takeaways. According to the UK's *Daily Telegraph*, these claims aren't as strong as you'd believe:

> Another paper—"Switching from refined grains to whole grains causes zinc deficiency"—is a report of a 1976 research project featuring a study group of just *two people*. A third study—"Diets high in grain fibre deplete vitamin D stores"—is a 30-year-old study of 13 people.
>
> A fourth—"Phytic acid from whole grains block zinc and other minerals"—is based on a 1971 study of people in rural Iran eating unleavened flatbread. Another is about insulin sensitivity in domestic pigs.
>
> In other words, the research upon which the Bulletproof Diet stands is not exactly cutting-edge.[19]

As for buttered coffee, it promises to give you energy. It's supposed to banish hunger pangs, jump-start fat burning, and sharpen mental focus. Bulletproof suggests having it in place of breakfast—a meal in itself—thereby competing with our treasured avocado toast.

Much of the drink's fanfare stems from the butter, which is high in omega-3s, and also in MCTs (basically coconut oil), which some studies suggest improve cognitive function in Alzheimer's patients—a promising start. But MCTs don't necessarily have an impact on the healthy, and the studies supporting MCT benefits are mixed. As critics have pointed out, there's no evidence to presume this is a superior breakfast or that its ingredients induce fat burning. In fact, critics say it's a low-nutrient replacement—yet clocking in at 450 calories and 50 grams of fat—for what could be a better-balanced meal. Nutrition experts warn that it decreases your nutrient intake by about one-third,[20] whereas you could get healthy fats from foods like avocados or salmon.

Bulletproof offers big, vague claims without always the evidence to back them up. Also, as far as I'm concerned—though clearly this isn't a study either!—their fatty coffee doesn't suppress hunger. I tried it, and by 11:00 a.m. I was aching for a bagel. By noon, I was eyeing my dog's food bowl.

Another potential downside of biohacking is that it makes people *feel* more proactive about their health than they actually are. It's a psychological effect that researchers refer to as "illusory invulnerability." If you believe you're already taking action, you may be less compelled to pursue actual healthy habits. Or you may even engage in unhealthy behavior. In one study, those who took supplements were more likely to neglect activities such as exercise or eating balanced meals than those who didn't. Consuming supplements also spurred unhealthy indulgences, like choosing an all-you-can-eat buffet over a healthy meal. Taking that magic pill gave them "license" to slack off.[21]

Sometimes individuals do see a positive effect after taking a supplement. But can they prove it's causal versus coincidental? If someone decides to commit to a healthier lifestyle and couples it with a vitamin regimen, then yes, they will likely experience physical changes and start feeling better. But who's to say the pills are doing anything?

Maybe every industry sells control, whether that's beauty, automobiles, or tech. Sure, but you can't quite equate nutrition to cosmetics. The stakes are higher. When it comes to our health, there is no place for deceptive marketing tactics or faulty science. But the promises are just so alluring: Who doesn't want to believe they can live longer, better, and stronger?

Flashback: "I'm Gonna Live to Be a Hundred"

In June 1971, health guru Jerome Irving (J. I.) Rodale appeared on *The Dick Cavett Show*. Dubbed Mr. Organic, he was a pioneer of the natural health movement, having founded *Prevention* magazine and authored books such as *Happy People Rarely Get Cancer*. Semiretired at age seventy-two, Rodale felt fit as a fiddle and ready to divulge his secret to longevity: a nutritious diet. "I never felt better in my life," exclaimed Rodale with a smile. "I'm gonna live to be a hundred."

Following a commercial break, Rodale moved over on the couch to let the next guest take center stage. Suddenly, the audience heard Rodale let out a sound that resembled a loud snore. Assuming it was a prank, the audience erupted into laughter. But this was no gag. Cavett took one look at his guest—mouth agape, head thrown back—and knew something was wrong.

Rodale was pronounced dead on the spot. He had suffered a fatal heart attack.

Years later, while recounting the incident, Cavett joked, "Who would be the logical person to drop dead on a television show? A health expert."

Jokes aside, Rodale remains an important figure in the modern wellness movement. Like his predecessors and successors, he was quick to promise an Eden of health. Rodale penned columns full of practical lifestyle advice. He sat at the forefront of healthy and organic food. Rodale also harbored a mistrust of government, medicine, and industrial powers. His dogma centered on questioning accepted health tenets both big and small.

While skepticism is warranted (and necessary), reformers can sometimes get it wrong. Rodale pushed a slew of unconventional ideas, some far more experimental than scientific. He believed in exposing the body to shortwave radio waves to boost the body's supply of electricity.[22] Sugar, in his mind, was so toxic it could severely impair judgment and even lead to crime. (Rodale even supposedly suggested that Hitler was a sugar fiend addicted to whipped-cream-topped cakes, implying that a sweet tooth turned him into a genocidal maniac.)[23] Rodale was also an anti-vaxxer, advocating a dietary cure for polio. "Isn't there a better way of conquering polio than jabbing all the children in the country with a needle?" the publisher wrote in a 1955 issue of *Prevention*.[24]

At one point, the Federal Trade Commission targeted Rodale's book *The Health Finder*, which claimed to help people add years to their lives and free themselves from colds, among other promises. The agency deemed the book not only inconsistent with modern science but engaging in deceptive advertising. The FTC took Rodale to court, and he defended himself on First Amendment grounds throughout the 1960s.

Rodale, Inc., grew to become one of the world's largest health and wellness publishers, printing popular magazines such as *Men's Health*, *Women's Health*, and *Runner's World*, before being acquired by Hearst. In addition to the empire Rodale established, he endures as the pinnacle of dissent both from centuries past and the wellness gurus yet to come.

Can I Truly "Own" My Biological Future?

In 2018, I started receiving invitations to check out a mobile clinic offering on-the-spot ovarian egg reserve testing, which measures the anti-Müllerian hormone (AMH)—just one marker of a woman's remaining egg supply. The traveling clinic was run by the femtech start-up Kindbody, dubbed "the SoulCycle of fertility" by *The Verge*. Here, I and other women could learn for free about what might convince us to buy their core service: oocyte cryopreservation, also known as egg freezing.

So one spring day, I visited an egg-yolk-yellow bus parked in a busy mid-city intersection across the street from the Los Angeles County Museum of Art. It held court among other transportation vehicles, namely food trucks, UPS trucks, and Uber pickups. This bus, however, saw a steady stream of women jumping in, then exiting fifteen minutes later to pick up free lip balm and water bottles from a nearby table. A line formed in front of the splashy vehicle—a revolving door of fashionable parishioners in high-heeled sandals and work-appropriate attire.

Unlike stuffy OB-GYN clinics, Kindbody had confidence-boosting "girl boss" mottoes like "Own your future" lining the bus's walls. In addition to free testing, the fertility buses offered a "wellness lounge" where women could indulge themselves with spa-like skin care consultations. This was no drab affair. It was all smiles, catchy hashtags, and swag—like a midday Sephora dash.

What would generally be regarded as a hard sell was rebranded as wellness. The company compared their services to other areas of proactive health care, such as nutrition or exercise. "Egg freezing is absolutely a form of self-care," declared Gina Bartasi, the founder and CEO of Kindbody.[25] In an interview with *The Verge*, she said, "What we want to do is help women live a life of no regrets, and have children when they want them, on their own timeframe." Kindbody's website read, "Freezing eggs is like freezing time."

Kindbody is one of many fertility start-ups that emerged in the last decade to counteract new societal shifts: in 2019, following a four-year downward trend, U.S. fertility rates hit a thirty-five-year low. In addition, more women in their thirties and forties are having babies, which inevitably increases the need for medical intervention for those impacted by age-related infertility. In 2009, 475 women chose to freeze their eggs. By 2017, there were 9,042 women.[26]

Egg freezing start-ups sell peace of mind from knowing that you can store your eggs this winter, then gather them when a future spring arrives. And why not learn about it with a little bit of levity? The appeal is obvious,

a staggering 2 million do not succeed, which puts the global IVF cycle failure rate at nearly 80 percent.[30]

A lot of confusion exists as to what constitutes "success" in this sector. Are we discussing the success of retrieving and storing eggs, of getting pregnant, or of actually having a baby at the end of the process? A lot of accurate but misleading numbers are floating around. Rates are hard to analyze because egg freezing is still so new—many who put their eggs on ice haven't retrieved them yet. But there's no confusion about the fact that fertility takes a nosedive as we age, something we might prefer to ignore.

In 2014, a marketing executive named Brigitte Adams graced the cover of *Bloomberg Businessweek* with the headline FREEZE YOUR EGGS, FREE YOUR CAREER. Wearing a black dress and heels, and with her hand defiantly positioned on her hip, the blond professional became the "poster child for egg freezing." At age thirty-nine, Adams spent $19,000 icing her future plans as she continued searching for Mr. Right. She later started an egg freezing educational website and digital community called Eggsurance.

Six years later, at forty-five, Adams picked a sperm donor and cashed in her coupon—to disappointing results. Some of her eleven eggs didn't survive the thawing process, while others failed to fertilize or turned out to be genetically abnormal. Only one egg produced a normal embryo. That one resulted in a chemical pregnancy, which is a very early pregnancy loss shortly after implantation. By then, there were no more eggs to retrieve.

"I never imagined that my egg freezing gamble would end this way," she wrote on her website, lamenting how long she'd waited to start the defrosting process. In an interview with the *Washington Post,* Adams noted that there wasn't enough discourse about "part two"—what happens when women try to use their thawed eggs—and that the "huge marketing hype" crumbles in the face of biological reality.[31]

Egg freezing technology is certainly improving, and doctors I interviewed note that many traditional clinics' messaging and approach differs from that of startups. Still, women are starting to take a harder look at what's a more complicated medical process than they might have initially assumed, but usually only after having invested considerable financial and emotional effort.

Grace Clarke, a marketing and content consultant in New York, spent four years saving up enough money to freeze her eggs with Kindbody at the age of thirty-two. But the experience proved less than optimal. Clarke says there wasn't nearly enough emphasis on educating her on probable outcomes—that is, how many harvested eggs might result in a live birth. In the end, she felt she did nothing more than buy uncertainty. "The biggest issue is that Instagram and social media have trained us to not dig deep and explore the truth, to take marketing slogans at face value," Clarke holds. "I would do anything, anything, anything, to help other people understand what it took me four years, nine thousand dollars, ten pounds, tons of shots, and a breakup to learn: Egg freezing is not a calendar date. It is an expensive marginal increase on your odds."[‡]

Now, I am not invalidating the miracle of modern reproductive assistance, which I myself have sought. No one can deny that reproductive technologies help couples start families. For women diagnosed with infertility, endometriosis, or undergoing chemotherapy, these new technologies have been a lifeline.

But we need more acknowledgement that many individuals put their faith in the process only to meet heartbreaking losses. There is concern that young women are not sufficiently informed about the odds they might not get a baby in the end. Success is dependent on an individual's biology; there's a lot of variability in outcomes. No one should consider it an "insurance policy"—insurance policies offer guarantees, while egg freezing does not. This misconception is also a testament to how uninformed some American women are about their own bodies, or how they're advised to brush off fertility until it's too late—or both.

[‡] The exact measure of increased odds is hard to determine because it is so individualized and impacted by age. There's also little long-term data.

Not all women are educated enough about fertility, which means they are also not armed to make the right decisions during pivotal years. So, at the very least, egg freezing start-ups are inspiring individuals to learn more about their bodies. But some might question: Should they be the ones doing this?

But also, what in our culture has led us to a point where egg-freezing clinics are rolling through cities? We've revered cultural milestones—homeownership, career success, and paying off student debt—without always aligning them with childbearing years. Our society doesn't always make it easy for many women to have kids at a biologically preferable time. America inadvertently incentivizes the delay of motherhood: women who reproduce before age thirty-five never see their pay recover relative to their partners' pay.[32] Paltry work-life support structures, as evidenced by the lack of subsidized childcare, limited parental leave, or more flexible opportunities for working moms, are designed to make women wait. But fertility won't.

There are other reasons too. Hopeful grandparents might accuse women of being workaholic careerists who won't supply them with a grandchild until they've reached the C-suite (a charge never directed at men). *Obsessed with work*, they complain about their ambitious daughters. But according to one Yale research study, the chief reason women wait is that they're still looking for a committed partner.[33] Many women report that potential mates are unwilling to settle down or are uninterested in parenthood any-time soon. Of course, they can forgo a partner and seek a family on their own, but that's not easy; raising and affording a child is hard even with two parents in the picture these days.

The reason behind the interest in egg freezing is that people feel they don't have very good options, says Josephine Johnston, a bioethicist at the Hastings Center. "They're trying to gain some modicum of control, even if it's imperfect and even if it's not a guarantee," she explains. When they don't feel they're in a position to have a child during their childbearing years, then at least they can do *something* to try to preserve their fertility.[34]

But—echoing the clean beauty issue—the impetus is on women to preplan a solution for a culture they feel isn't looking out for them. With so little support, it's up to them to empty their pockets to fix the problem, and the problem is women's bodies. When Kindbody's website includes "facts" such as "You'll never be more fertile than you are today," the company sends a rather alarmist message: a responsible woman needs to take medical action now before her fertility further declines.[35] Our biology is therefore something that must be *managed*.

Egg freezing is generally available only to those who either pay for it on their own or receive financial assistance via a top-tier workplace benefit. Companies like Apple, Facebook, and Google offer egg freezing at the request of female employees (thereby setting industry standards), but Johnston believes we need to identify the root causes of involuntary childlessness. "People say this [workplace benefit] is what women want. Well, why do they want that? Because everything else is against them. 'This is the only choice because I don't have the options I want.'"

Younger generations hear horror stories from women who waited too long and simply want to avoid any heartbreak. Their motivation is better described as future damage control. One egg freezing hopeful told the *New York Times*, "I wear sunscreen to protect myself from future sun damage. I work out to keep off my weight. Why would I not do something to prevent future emotional pain and suffering?"[36]

Others worry about how casually some marketing treats egg freezing. They're concerned that it propels younger women to believe they don't have to worry about fertility until later in life—a luxury usually afforded only to men. *Come flex your feminist muscles, flex your workplace independence* is the potential takeaway, according to Miriam Zoll, the author of *Cracked Open: Liberty, Fertility, and the Pursuit of High Tech Babies*.

Liberation—from conformity, authority, biology, or "the patriarchy"—has become a mainstay thread for the advertising and marketing industries, infusing consumerism with cherished American ideals. Carl Elliott opines in his fantastic book *Better than Well*, "Americans have a hard time resisting anything that can be phrased in terms of self-determination. Autonomy, liberty, freedom: these are among our most powerful words."[37]

Egg freezing companies by no means promise women anything, but there is legitimate concern that the nuance gets lost in translation.

This is not an argument against egg freezing or IVF. We're so very lucky to live in a time in which women have options and the ability to seek reproductive assistance. Instead, the concern is that commercialization promotes a still nascent, complex technology to women. One study published in the journal the *New Bioethics* found that many fertility clinics engaged in deceptive advertising by selling the procedure persuasively, not informatively, all while minimizing risks and the low birth rate.[38]

As most any doctor will tell you, for every success story, there are many disappointed women. Even the most promising breakthroughs can have their limits.

Enhancing Human Potential or Wielding Hope?

Hidden beneath layers of clever marketing, the wellness industry beckons with a far stronger, more seductive message than relief or escape. The carrot it dangles in front of women is the one thing they desperately desire: control. Women are promised they can manage the chaos ruling their life by following a laid-out plan: eat right, exercise, meditate, then buy or do all this stuff. This mass consumerism is a vehicle for harnessing everything that feels turbulent in their lives.

The allure of control is communicated throughout wellness. Fitfluencers transform the sluggish to the masterful. Spiritual influencers hawk crystals to help followers snag a coveted job promotion. "Clean" snacks dangle a disease-free future. Woven throughout lies the message that you can manipulate what is unruly, subpar, or standing in the way of progress. Buy it, use it, think it—and you're back in the driver's seat. All noteworthy goals. We *should* try to take control of our health. We should take responsibility, as much as possible, for what we eat, how we sleep, and how much movement we engage in. But there's a significant distinction between what we can actually manage and what is out of our hands. When it comes to new scientific advancements, at what point do we admit we're denying real limitations? Or relinquishing control to brands and leaders as a costly crutch?

We start to think anything is possible, partially because wellness ads tell us health can be attained, maintained, and elevated. "But every time you reach a milestone, the goalpost moves farther away," says Sarah Greenidge, the founder of WellSpoken, an organization committed to regulating wellness brands to ensure that they provide credible information. "It keeps you chasing wellness, which makes sense—it keeps you always consuming. You can always be more well, more in control." As the market grows bigger and ever more encompassing in all areas of life, organizations like WellSpoken attempt to course correct an industry showing signs of growing pseudoscience.

"The wellness industry has thrived on a very low-health-literate, high-disposable-income consumer," says Greenidge, who hopes to rein in brands and educate consumers. WellSpoken consultants partner with companies, content creators, and influencers to offer guidelines on how to communicate their messaging. Their goal is to crack down on false claims and exaggerated solutions to the very many issues we're now told we can manage.

Most physicians, in contrast, will rarely promise full control or guaranteed results. They won't definitively say they'll cure patients of serious cancer or that you'll live to be 180, which is why they're not the leaders of this movement. Gurus gather the masses with assurance, not probability. Or as the author and biochemist Isaac Asimov once said: "Inspect every piece of pseudoscience and you will find a security blanket, a thumb to suck, a skirt to hold."

It's comforting. When we feel overwhelmed, these rituals—like popping a morning supplement—make us feel safer. But the truth is, life is wild. You cannot control everything. Longevity, least of all from a glass bottle, is never guaranteed. Even Dave Asprey cannot control everything, despite his claims of stalling aging and plans to live past what's humanly possible. On Twitter, biohacking fans observe that the forty-seven-year-old founder is *graying*. His thick mane reveals him to be a biological normie. They ask: What's up with the "perennially haggard" look? Why wasn't he able to fully reverse his hair color? Why does he already "look 135 years old"?

While real scientific breakthroughs and advancements occur, we also need to recognize the limits of science. The way that wellness has been commodified by gurus drawing from science and then exaggerating results spreads the toxic positivity message that you can fully accomplish what is an impossible goal. But bodies, even the best bodies, eventually betray us. No one will ever be completely healthy forever. We can't stop the aging process. At a certain point, our biology breaks down. That's nature.

Chapter 11

Democratizing Wellness:
Pushing Back Against "Wellthness"

Nestled on the Sunset Strip, a block from the famous Chateau Marmont, Remedy Place is no mere gym. It is a members-only wellness social club—a place where booze is banned and health is served through IV drips.

Here, L.A.'s richest and presumably healthiest get first dibs on the hottest new workout trends. They treat themselves to "detoxifying" infrared saunas. They submerge their bodies in subzero cryotherapy chambers. They engage in power networking over yoga mats. It is, as the founder and wellness adviser to the stars Jonathan Leary told me, a space for people of a certain status to hang out and be active, not unlike a twenty-first-century country club. It is what he calls "social self-care."

But the kombucha-flowing happy hours don't come cheap. Monthly memberships start at $495, capped at two hundred members. Remedy Place doesn't have to worry about selling spots; before it even opened, celebrities, entertainment industry elites, and pro athletes came calling. Nike sent its executive team to check it out, followed by Goop. As Leary told me when I visited during the week of the club's opening, "in a place like L.A., people do love some type of exclusivity."

I reported on Remedy Place in the context of other new spaces marrying high-end fitness with elite hobnobbing. There is also L.A.'s Monarch Athletic Club, which charges $1,000 to $2,000 *per month* for access to unlimited private training along with a recovery suite, IV therapy, and a nutrition bar.

In New York, an exclusive fitness lounge called GHOST bills itself as an "architectural playground" full of art, boutique classes, live DJ sets, a marble boxing ring, and luxury amenities like Himalayan salt infrared saunas. At $3,000 a year (on top of a $400 registration fee), Ghost is, as the founder describes it, "the Soho House of fitness." It's primarily invite-only but you can try to get in: access entails a thorough application process digging into a prospect's job and lifestyle interests. An in-person interview is required. Imagine the college application process—but with your Instagram account in place of a personal essay. And just like getting into Harvard, membership connotes status, affirmation that you are good enough.

The Manhattan boutique workout studio The Ness permits a small percentage of new clients by way of a member referral system, which means newcomers are vetted and vouched for by those already accepted. "If you're hosting a dinner party at your house, would you just post flyers of the invite and say everyone come over for dinner? No, you invite your friends," co-founder Colette Dong told me of her mostly female clientele. "We feel the same way about fitness in terms of garnering a community . . . [Our clients] feel really comfortable and let loose."[1]

If wellness is already the new luxury signifier, these places have escalated it to a new echelon. It's no longer enough where you work out, but *with whom* you work out. You need to know the right people, be in the right shape, and offer something in return—social cachet—for application approval. It's the next step for those who see fitness intertwined with their personal brand. Wellness, it could be said, is now a doorway to exclusivity.

Makes sense, if only because the wellness economy now mirrors American income inequality, where the middle class gets smaller and smaller, to the point where only a disfigured hourglass remains: democratic models like the YMCA on one end and affluent boutique gyms on the other. You're either going budget or you're going luxe. But the luxe seems to be winning, the hourglass squeezed ever tighter, more lopsided. "It's much easier to target the one percent than it is to really come up with a model for the ninety-five percent," says Beth McGroarty, director of research at the Global Wellness Institute. "Community is now the entrance and aspiration."[2]

While the upper class perfects their downward dog, the communities most in need of physical exercise profoundly lack it. Apart from the limited number of gyms or recreational centers in rural areas, many can't access parks or safe outdoor spaces. A 2018 study found that three-quarters of wealthy individuals exercise on most days, compared to a quarter of lower-income populations.[3] That gap, researchers suggest, will only widen further.*

Wealth and wellness are near synonymous terms these days, morphing the idea of health as a necessity into one of indulgence. Premier health clubs are but a chia seed in the granola bowl of upscale wellness. Fitbit released fitness tracking jewelry. Beboe THC vape pens are referred to as the "Hermès of marijuana." When I did a story on Goop selling $90 vitamin packs, Clare Varga, head of beauty at trend forecasting firm WGSN, summed up the "wellthness" trend: "It's become aspirational," she said. "It's an investment and demonstration of self-value with a healthy body becoming the ultimate must-have fashion accessory." You'll see this

---

* The fix isn't simple. Even if gyms, parks, or digital health trackers are made available to underprivileged groups, it's not a given they'll have time to use them.

reflected in pop culture. If a film wants to connote an affluent Type A woman, she'll, sure enough, be shown furiously pedaling in a cycling class or dressed in head-to-toe athleisurewear.

It's not just what we buy or do, but where we live. Gated health-focused communities and condo buildings compose what will soon be a $180 billion wellness real estate market.[4] The upper crust is scooping up homes equipped with posture-supportive heat reflexology floors, mood-enhancing aromatherapy, and vitamin C–infused showers. Rounding out their in-house staff, they employ a 24/7 "personal wellness assistant" to remind them to exercise, meditate, or to tend to any "emergency" wellness needs, like, I assume, replacing an empty oat milk carton.

Take Troon Pacific, a development company selling sleep-enhanced homes with over-the-top health amenities such as built-in bedroom speakers programmed with guided meditation. It made headlines when it listed a "wellness-focused" mansion in the Bay Area. The 8,350-square-foot estate incorporated "biophilic design" (nature-inspired architecture) and an entire floor dedicated to health and fitness—a gym, yoga deck, massage room, sauna, and steam shower. (The home, of course, also came equipped with a Tesla car charger.) "The greatest luxury in life is your health," Troon Pacific CEO and co-founder Gregory Malin told me, "and so wellness became our focus."[5] The house sold for nearly $20 million.

The wealthy always take trends to the extreme. Once a specific product or idea becomes popular, then people want the fancy version. When everyone has a TV, then comes the demand for sophisticated, voice-activated home entertainment systems. So too with wellness. As the sector grows and technology advances, it ratchets up more and more.[6] That's why you start seeing ads for ethically mined 24-karat gold dildos.

Wellness is more susceptible to scrutiny because of what it stands for, which consumers presume should be afforded to all. But it does make you think: How did wellness, the pursuit of health, become associated with luxury? And though these high-end efforts generally get the most attention, they certainly are not the majority. So who are the new players expanding the reach to more communities?

Drink Your Way to a Better Life

In one Instagram post, the curvy, striped beverage bottle sits on a vanity shelf alongside luxe brands: La Mer, Chanel, and the prestige skin care line Sunday Riley. In another, a manicured and jeweled hand grasps the bottle against a designer floral dress, like the last accessory of a perfect ensemble. There it is again as a model runs with the bottle down a hotel hallway. Sometimes it's the star attraction of an afternoon spent relaxing at a luxury pool. The brightly colored bottles are constantly spotted in posts of good-looking people engaged in fun, chic activities.

Why is Dirty Lemon—a health drink—acting like a vodka brand?

It is, at the end of the day, just water, lemon juice, and a teensy bit of activated charcoal. Yet the beverage brand promises you, quite literally, the world: globe-trotting adventure, allure, mystery, beauty, and sexiness. You could say Dirty Lemon is a line of functional elixirs with big ambitions. Beyond its social media fantasy, the collection of $6.99 drinks promises to transform one's body—it claims to improve digestion, stimulate liver function, and "gently cleanse your system of impurities." Consumers vaguely know the nutritional benefits of this expensive lemon water, but that's not what matters. What matters is that *it's cool*. And cool is the currency.

Dirty Lemon founder Zak Normandin told me he was inspired by skyrocketing start-ups such as the millennial beauty brand Glossier. He wondered: Why can't we do the same for health tonics? So Dirty Lemon incorporated lifestyle photography that spoke "around" the juices. The company also purposely designed the product to stand out on a 2x3-inch screen—bright colors, minimal wording—so it could be the star of an Instagram post. Unlike other product categories—such as a vacuum cleaner— wellness beverages lend themselves to be photographed everywhere. You can shoot them in a convertible, at the beach, in the bath. A mattress, no matter how trendy, can't pull that off.[7]

Almost every wellness brand sells some sort of mythical state of bliss on Instagram, their preferred playground. Their sales pitch is less about health benefits and more about something stronger: a feeling. It's about feeling good, feeling in control, feeling attractive. Brands are counting on you buying a fantasy, not unlike the fashion industry's tactics. Kombucha, supplement brands, and collagen proteins use the same playbook, populating Instagram with imagery of smiling models seemingly enjoying a life of sugarless beverages on an empty stomach. For detox tea, it's flat tummies and opulent white marble kitchens, while collagen powder brands prefer athletic types posing in the lush outdoors.

This is partially because luxury marketers, publicists, and branding consultants now work for the wellness economy. All the PR firms that once pitched me as a journalist on fashion labels and high-end restaurants a decade ago currently represent supplement brands and "natural" food or beverage companies. But that's to be expected when the wellness industry doesn't always lead with science, but coalesces around emotion and consumerism.

Once celebrities entered the wellness fray, the aspiration factor skyrocketed. Halle Berry has a wellness site. Kristen Bell launched a premium CBD skin care brand. Miranda Kerr became an organic beauty mogul. Not to mention the slew of stars either fronting or investing in snack brands or fitness tech. They work in an ecosystem where they send their goods to their other celebrity pals, who then further promote the brand in their glossy kitchens. When you see Oprah hawking Clevr Blends, a $28 powdered instant latte brand advertised as "made with brain-boosting, mind-clearing, mood-lifting ingredients," it *might* be because she believes in all those claims. But it's also likely because her pal Meghan Markle is an investor. Celebs know an opportunity when they see one. They're businesspeople as much as they are entertainers.

The same goes for Goop. While Paltrow and her company do not

you take up running to get fit, but maybe also to keep up with your health-centric friends.[10]

If dental care became the next symbol of self-care, I assure you there would suddenly be a flush of women posting pictures of themselves flossing.

Since our culture is based in part on capitalism, the wellness industry has become, in part, reflective of our individualist and consumerist culture. (You're not going to stop Americans from buying stuff—that's how we express ourselves.) The movement may have sprung from revolutionary roots, but it has since divorced itself from an anti-establishment ethos to grow as bloated as the establishments it once rallied against.

Now, I am not one who cannot enjoy a bit of fantasy and luxury. I've subscribed to *W* and *Vogue* since I was thirteen. But what separates wellness (or what claims to be wellness) from other sectors is that health should not be associated with class, image, or five-star hotel pools. Inevitably, the messaging becomes intertwined. We start to conflate health with specific kinds of people or products because that's all we're accustomed to seeing—a very narrow *appearance* of health. If thin, wealthy, and attractive are all we're trained to see, that becomes our automatic factory setting.

Not everyone appreciates this new culture. I spoke with an executive of a popular at-home fitness equipment company that was making inroads with older consumers frustrated by millennial gym rats who made them feel insecure with their flagrant displays of body perfection and Lululemon fashion shows. At home, no one could judge their average arms, let alone a ratty college T-shirt. They said they missed the nineties, when "people weren't afraid to look like crap at the gym."

Luxury wellness marketing is most puzzling when it comes to self-care, which was stripped down to sparkly stuff to lure affluent women. Companies will make you believe that their product is crucial to achieving relaxation and therefore take advantage of your (sleep-deprived) vulnerabilities. But there is no uniformity to stress relief, as everyone has their own particular burden and their own preferred mode of relief.

Barbara Riegel, a professor of biobehavioral health sciences at the University of Pennsylvania and a leading researcher on self-care, considers most marketed solutions merely fleeting self-soothing techniques. Real self-care, by her professional definition, is more aligned with both physiological and psychological health maintenance, including nutrition, sleep hygiene, exercise, and illness symptom management. These are not things that need the snazziest device or hippest boutique class. "Self-care has been taken over by marketing," says Riegel, who adds that her fellow international researchers are confused by all this talk of facials and tech. "This is a U.S. phenomenon."

Other industry experts agree that wellness is indeed a global trend, but what's going on with American women is something else. It is a mania not replicated in certain European countries where they have better work-life balance, more communal societies, and a more attentive (or socialized) medical healthcare system. Some have policies in place that support self-care. Sweden, for example, set up a 24/7 open hotline for registered nurses to respond to citizens' non-urgent health issues. One Italian academic told me, "We take two-hour lunches with friends or coworkers to eat fresh food and we receive four weeks mandated vacation. I'm not sure my country *needs* all this wellness."

Self-care does not require a SoulCycle class, Sephora shopping spree, or Bali spa retreat. Oddly, a large percentage of these pricey solutions were thrown out the window during the COVID-19 pandemic. Women quickly learned they could sometimes get the same results with smaller, more affordable activities, like going for a hike.

On one hand, commodification skews health initiatives and intimidates those who cannot buy fancy products. But on the other hand, the aspirational aspect has inspired more people to participate. I used to go with friends to boozy brunches on weekends—now we go to yoga. It's not a zero-sum game. Whether for the right reasons or not, more women are focused on their health these days. It's fun. It's cool. It's *joyful*. It's no longer the drudgery we once thought it was. Women might buy a meditation app membership instead of a purse, or spend a Sunday at the gym instead of the mall. Maybe because of the market, they become aware of solutions that really can help them. Mental health is probably the best example of this. In the span of just a few years, mental wellness went from taboo to widespread discussion. Then, as technological advancement pushed therapy and support groups to the forefront of convenience, the category expanded well beyond the usual stakeholders.

As wellness gains more traction, more and more people demand access. They, in time, innovate solutions that fit their specific requirements. I've profiled a BIPOC-worker-owned yoga cooperative in South Central L.A. and mental health apps catering to underserved communities with diverse therapists. You can no longer say wellness is strictly for a certain person: more groups have joined the fray. Even that which starts off with upscale circles can be adapted to suit others in need. It is, as one wellness researcher described to me, "trickle-down wellness."

Take Timeshifter, a personalized jet lag app first popular with business travelers, pro athletes, and anyone keen to optimize every hour while traveling. Now Timeshifter is working to bring its wellness app to shift workers who possess unique health risks, including an increased risk of diabetes, heart disease, and even certain cancers due to circadian rhythm disruption and lack of sleep. These are people in manufacturing, construction, mining, delivery, the military, and medical care; nurses, soldiers, and truckers who are more at risk of drowsy driving, which increases the risk of fatal car crashes on the commute home. Many of these professions have a high proportion of women, such as nursing, where the night shift is par for the course.

Luxury is to *some degree* where we're at. In most media outlets, wellness is generally presented through the prism of a very specific lifestyle, potentially spurring ageism, ableism, and elitism. But the average gymgoer does not come from a "sleep-enhanced house," nor do they frequent a fitness studio to flex their superiority muscles. Gyms (and streets) are filled with people of all colors, backgrounds, and professions. Most are just looking to get in some exercise or release some tension from having been glued to an office chair all week.

Flashback: When Female Complaints Made Way for Female Pressures

What would a combination of Oprah, Gywneth, and Estée Lauder look like? Lydia Pinkham, the inventor of the most popular health tonic in nineteenth-century America. Pinkham's face graced newspapers. Her herbal concoctions sat atop every pharmacy counter. She even inspired folk songs.

In 1875, the Massachusetts native created Pinkham's Vegetable Compound. It was advertised as made with "natural" ingredients, and Pinkham claimed it was superior to whatever the medical industry was hawking. Her advice? "Let doctors alone." Each bottle contained life root, unicorn root, black cohosh, and fenugreek seed suspended in 19 percent alcohol. Pinkham was a strict temperance advocate, but the family business had no qualms about selling forty-proof bottles of booze.

Pinkham's concoction promised to cure all female "weaknesses," of which there were many: menstrual pains, headaches, kidney issues, uterine prolapse, labor pains, indigestion, faintness, addictions, "floodings," "irregularities," and flatulence. It was a broad cure-all, but some of these terms had hidden meanings. As Sarah Stage writes in *Female Complaints,* "floodings" and "irregularities" were a wink and a nod to those seeking an abortion.[11]

What separated this tonic from the competition? Each bottle featured a sophisticated profile illustration of the dignified, middle-aged Pinkham. Seemingly wise, compassionate, and sturdy, people compared her to the Mona Lisa or Lady Liberty. Pinkham came across as someone you knew, someone you could trust. Pinkham used this to her advantage when she encouraged women to write to her with their problems, which she would answer and often publish as testimonials. It was a novel concept back then: building a personal connection with a brand. Hundreds of women per month wrote in complaining of issues that Pinkham shrewdly blamed on an era ill-suited for women. Pinkham's ads described how the American woman was "expected to play a complex role of many duties, some of which are entirely incompatible with each other." A woman was made to keep order in the house, bear and raise the children, cook fine meals, do all the shopping, and potentially work outside the house . . . all while looking and acting presentable. "Sometimes a servant and always a lady," is how she put the burden foisted on women. The same copy could run today.[12]

Following Lydia's death in 1883, Pinkham's Vegetable Compound shifted its focus from health to that of appearance. Beautiful women invested in their health, read the new copy. The compound would "cleanse" and beautify the body, thereby restoring women's chief power: their looks. "There is no secret about a woman's beauty; it all lies in the care she devotes to herself, to removing from her system all poisonous impurities, and keeping at bay those fearful female diseases," read one ad.

Shortly thereafter, the marketing shifted again to exemplify upper-middle-class women of leisure. But the marketing illustrations didn't line up with the clientele: wealthy people could afford physicians. It was the working class who resorted to over-the-counter tonics. The new company owners understood that status is aspirational, and that customers would want to believe that they—alongside the gloved and stylish—were *peers* relying on the very same product. They too wanted in on what the respectable and rich possessed, "if not real, then vicarious."[13]

Branching Out Beyond a
Narrow Representation

Each morning at six o'clock, Maggie Holub begins her work tending to corn and soybean crops on her five-hundred-acre farm in Scribner, Nebraska. Born and raised here, farming is in her blood. She was raised with hogs and chickens. Tinkering with irrigation systems and fertilizing crops are second nature to her. Although, Holub didn't expect to run a farm in her twenties; her original plan was to join the family-owned farm once her father retired. Unfortunately, in 2014, he passed away from terminal brain cancer at just fifty-one, thereby accelerating the succession plan. Holub went from some-time helper to full-time third-generation farmer. Today, the friendly and approachable Holub operates and fixes all the farming equipment and hauls all of the grain with two semitrucks and trailers.

But Holub has another passion—one that she's increasingly sharing with others: fitness.

Three evenings a week, Holub packs a trailer filled with dumbbells, yoga mats, and other exercise equipment. Her destination? Anywhere that lacks organized fitness in her rural vicinity. As a trained exercise instructor, Holub runs a mobile gym that sets up shop in neighboring small towns that lack not only exercise facilities but also adequate broadband Internet service. These are people who cannot just watch a streaming fitness class or buy a Peloton. "In any large metro area, there's a gym on every corner and you can go there twenty-four hours a day," says Holub. "We don't have that." In the summer months, she leads cardio strength routines outdoors. In the winter, she scouts for indoor spaces like high school gyms or community centers.

Outsiders assume that rural populations don't need group fitness classes or gyms because they have access to the outdoors. But residents in isolated communities are often at risk for health conditions. For one thing, there are no sidewalks, bike paths, or street lamps in some areas, making safety a legitimate concern. Or it's freezing cold half the year and they cannot comfortably run or walk outside. Not to mention that many people simply don't enjoy walking or running. Some need a communal outfit to hold them accountable.

In farming communities, there can be a stigma against fitness culture. Farmers might presume exercise is unnecessary since they already move their bodies all day on the land. But there's a real need for everyone else around them, such as their partners or kids who lack adequate movement. That Holub shows up in their neighborhood and charges only $2 a class leaves few excuses for them not to participate. Lots of people, many of them women, flock to Holub's classes. They come to exercise and to socialize—interactions they crave when they're often quite isolated. "You have to go out of your way in rural Nebraska to go be with or meet somebody else," says Holub.

Farmers are one group among many trying to better represent their needs. They even have their own influencers who speak to their specific agriculture community. They might not, for example, take an interest in veganism or plant-based diets if they raise cattle and their family loves meat. Social media posts show more barbecues and beer than avocado toast and almond milk. As one dairy farmer fitfluencer put it, "I wanted to show people that you can still consume dairy, achieve the results you want, and thrive while doing so."[14]

Women on farms have concerns that differ from those of corporate career women in metropolitan areas. In place of bad bosses and meeting fatigue, they battle environmental stressors and machinery breakdowns. They juggle a hectic schedule of feeding farm animals and caring for their families. In one post detailing the importance of self-care, one woman wrote, "We pour our hearts into animal welfare, church potlucks, and [the] county fair. Our anxiety is guided by the weather, the markets and consumer demands. Most of the time we leave it in God's hands and pour another cup of coffee. But friends, no matter how many times you reheat it in the microwave . . . you cannot continue to pour from an empty cup."

Plenty of independent trailblazers are charting a new course in health initiatives. Despite a large Hispanic population, hardly any Spanish-led yoga classes were available in Miami. The bilingual yoga teacher Rina Jakubowicz recalled Hispanic women telling her, "It's for white people, it's not for us." Others expressed concern that it was a religious practice at odds with their faith. But Jakubowicz sensed interest. So she established a bilingual yoga teacher training course, which was then accredited by Yoga Alliance. Her first students included a cleaning and cooking crew who worked for her yoga studio employer. "They didn't think they could do anything else in the U.S. besides cleaning houses. It was really empowering," says Jakubowicz, who has since run several training courses. "They were really grateful to have somebody willing to spend time to teach and connect with them instead of just looking at them as labor. Now they can go out and teach."[15]

The landscape is shifting. I hear from Black women who say they're teaching yoga to rap music and not what they deem "dying whale music." They wear baggy T-shirts emblazoned with the names of hip-hop groups instead of Lululemon gear. The Black Yoga Teachers Alliance, a nonprofit and professional membership organization, counts hundreds of teachers, and its Facebook group has swelled to six thousand. Leaders believe there is still a way to go in terms of representation and access, but they sound optimistic.

These are just several of countless innovative contributions in fitness, though maybe you haven't heard of them. One reason you might associate wellness with overpriced juice bottles is because that's what clogs Instagram and mass media. Look at your local news or even hop on neighborhood Facebook groups and you'll notice a plethora of independently led initiatives working to close the health gap. I think that's important to remember before bashing the entire industry. It's nuanced: there's some good, there's some bad. A few steps forward, then one or two back.

Wellness—real wellness—doesn't require all the fancy fixings touted by glamorous stars or pricey social clubs. People are starting to recognize that.

Get Together: New Wellness Communities

What I am most excited about in wellness are the communities being brought together. I feel strongly that connection is one of the most important pieces of the wellness puzzle and not emphasized nearly enough. I think about Ganja Goddess Getaway (now called Glowing Goddess Getaway), the women's cannabis retreat I described in the introduction. At first glance, it might seem just like an outdoor house party. But that retreat has a higher aim: deep connections.

Ganja Goddess Getaway co-founder and CEO Deidra Bagdasarian began hosting the retreats following the birth of her second child. "I was kind of isolated after having a baby," she told me. "I needed a women's event." Bagdasarian wanted to recharge and connect, but not in a superficial way.

Bagdasarian believes cannabis can be used "as a creative and spiritual tool" to help women get in touch with themselves and bond more easily with others. With a joint, new friends can cut down on the small talk and get to the real talk. "Cannabis helps take down our walls and be our authentic selves right from the beginning," she explains. I saw it firsthand as the Getaway participants divulged family secrets, embraced strangers, and swapped phone numbers. As soon as I would introduce myself and extend my arm for a handshake, women would laugh and bear-hug me instead. The slightest I overheard of bad blood was someone saying in a soft, compassionate voice that another member "needed to soak in some positivity." Later I spotted them laughing together by the pool.

What started as a modest retreat series with roughly fifty participants ballooned into one averaging two hundred. Then came smaller regional gatherings—free of charge—held every Sunday at, naturally, 4:20 p.m. (consumables are brought potluck-style). Bagdasarian wants to expand the retreat once more U.S. states legalize marijuana use, with a plan to go nationwide. "We just got so much feedback about how this was something that [these women] were missing in their life," says Bagdasarian. "All women are in need of sisterhood and a safe space—and cannabis, it turns out, works for everyone."

Getting people outdoors in a low-cost, communal manner is a trend gaining traction. Many Americans have limited budgets, barring them from club memberships or expensive at-home exercise equipment. At the same time, they increasingly value experiences, particularly those that put them face-to-face with others. Many organizations engage specific communities by organizing local hikes and nature outings, including Outdoor Asian, Fat Girls Hiking, Latino Outdoors, and others.

Even wellness real estate got a more accessible makeover (or at least more accessible than a $20 million wellness mansion). Haven is a co-living compound in Venice, California, that houses ninety-six strangers brought together by their commitment to wellness. Roommates get to live in a fully furnished adult dorm with a fitness studio, healthy cooking classes, a co-working space, meditation areas, and events ranging from star energy healing ("bring your crystals and water") to sound baths.

Compared to skyrocketing apartment rental prices in L.A., Haven is a far more affordable option (by more than half the cost for a one-bedroom), especially considering the add-on amenities. But residents aren't just here for the slashed rent or a full moon circle ceremony. They want, in their words, to "find their tribe." And many do among this diverse group of yoga mat–toting millennials, most of whom are independent contractors and entrepreneurs. These are yoga instructors, meditation teachers, and cannabis founders.

Residents are equal parts health enthusiasts and spiritually enlightened. They overuse words like "experiences," "energy," and "gratitude" to describe the frustration of sharing a bathroom with a dozen other housemates. "Everything is a journey" is how they described chore duty. When I visited, an upstairs bathroom was plastered in a dozen Post-it notes with scribbled affirmations such as "I trust my intuition fully" and "My life is unfolding exactly as it is meant to be." (This is where I felt a bit concerned for them: *Let them poop in peace.*)

But overall, life at Haven seems idyllic. Residents meditate or quietly journal on a living room couch while aromatherapy vapors roam the halls like calming spirits. They flip through tarot cards or work on their Burning Man project. Small groups grab surfboards and head to the beach, just a few blocks away. Or they bike ride to a nearby health market to buy ingredients for a communal vegan dinner. Residents explained that they were "a hundred times" happier sharing a 350-square-foot pod-style room with six other strangers than when they'd lived alone in luxury condo apartments.

An unorthodox living arrangement raises eyebrows. Haven residents are subjected to inquisitive questioning by friends and family, many of whom scoff at their cramped shared living quarters. Why, they wonder, would any mature adult decide to bunk with strangers? "Most of [the time] it's like, how's the cult?" said one resident. "People don't get it."[16]

Is it a cult? Or more like modern social survival? I asked a twenty-five-year-old yoga teacher named Katie why she decided to live at Haven. Katie said she had hustled her way through school and work, but there was no one to share her success with. "We live in this world where society celebrates getting to the top as fast as you can and doing it all on your own and getting your ginormous apartment and living by yourself," said Katie, "and then sometimes you question, *Why?* Why am I here by myself?"

Katie's new living arrangement changed all that. "The best thing [about Haven] is coming home and there's always somebody here," she said. There was one particular element that sealed the deal for Katie, and when she mentioned it, I realized how crucial something seemingly so small could be. It's likely something many of us who live with others—be it parents, spouses, or friends—take for granted: "You come home and they say 'Hey, how was your day?'" That, to her, was real wellness.

Chapter 12

Guides for the Perplexed

You don't hear much about Food Babe Vani Hari in the press anymore. Mainstream news networks seemingly stopped booking her. She's not as prevalent in women's outlets. Blogs criticized her up the wazoo.

Since her reputation's descent, grassroots efforts have sprung up to combat misinformation and aggressive marketing claims. One influencer who has more than three hundred thousand Instagram followers is a food scientist who has positioned herself as the anti–Food Babe. For safety and privacy reasons, the public knows only her first name, Erin, and she goes by the handle Food *Science* Babe. On social media platforms, you'll find Erin posting in-depth explanations as well as entertaining TikTok videos debunking food myths—everything from outsized concerns about GMOs to why certain ingredients are banned in Europe but not in the United States. "So many times an ingredient is actually not banned in Europe, it's just called something different," she told me with a twinge of exasperation. "In some cases, yes, *it is* banned in Europe, but that doesn't necessarily mean that it's unsafe."

Other times she's called upon to weigh in on whether secreted beaver butt goo is, as Vani Hari suggests, "lurking" in your vanilla ice cream.[1]

That gem keeps circulating on social media, prompting Erin to address it more than once. "I'm really sick of talking about beaver butts, but here we go again," she remarks in one video. Having worked in the food industry for over a decade—in both the organic and conventional sectors—Erin knows precisely when influencers are peddling pseudoscience or fabricating fears. "It's not very obvious sometimes that [Food Babe] is spreading misinformation," says Erin. "So much of it is not outwardly apparent to somebody that might not know. That's why I feel like it's even more harmful."

Approachable and funny, Food Science Babe Erin has converted a mass of women who were once like her. Before taking on her cheeky moniker, she was a strict organic devotee who shopped in accordance with the Dirty Dozen list, ate "clean," and excluded whole food groups. "It is a part of your belief system and almost like your identity to some extent," she says. Erin never questioned her beliefs because the messaging was so rampant. She just assumed it was true. She was so committed she went to work for an organic snack company to craft new products. But in helping this brand secure organic and non-GMO certifications, Erin saw firsthand how food marketing claims often have little or muddled scientific evidence. "I realized how arbitrary certifications were—just submitting paperwork, paying them, and then you get to put this label on your product," Erin told me. "This doesn't really mean it's healthier."

Erin also participated in marketing meetings that singularly focused on one target group: moms of young kids. "[Marketers would say] 'they're looking for these labels, they'll spend more for these labels.' It was never 'we want to make sure it's healthier' because that's not what those labels mean." Erin repeats what all those toxicologists told me about clean beauty: "It's really just marketing."

At the same time, the anxiety over what to feed her family was taking a toll on her health. As a working mom of a young child, Erin wondered: Why make shopping or eating tougher than it already is? Why are we torturing women? "It's just causing such unnecessary stress and fear . . . making somebody think that what they're feeding their kid is going to make them get cancer is just ridiculous." Erin often hears from scientists butting heads with their marketing teams that want to push fantastical packaging claims. "It's difficult when [the marketers] don't have the science background and it's the marketing that's being conveyed to consumers."

Erin quit her job and redirected her efforts to share what she knows with a thirsty public. An increasing number of women have turned their backs on the fearmongers of the Web to flock to her well of knowledge. Food Science Babe has racked up over 3 million likes on TikTok, where she posts hilarious videos of why it's absurd, for example, to say "I don't eat anything with chemicals." She's made inroads with parenting circles by explaining why orange juice cartons with a "non-GMO" label are a scam. (There are no GMO oranges, so *all* orange juice is automatically non-GMO.) "Anytime you create a label that says 'non' or 'free-of,' consumers are obviously going to think whatever isn't in there is somehow bad, because why else would you have that label?" says Erin. "But in reality, GMO crops are just as safe and at least as nutritious as their non-GMO counterparts."[2]

Her motto? "Facts, not fear."

Medical experts also attempt to educate the public on social media, proving: If you can't beat 'em, join 'em. Physicians are going so far as to establish their own influencer groups, which function much like talent agencies. Dr. Austin L. Chiang, an assistant professor of medicine at Thomas Jefferson University Hospital, co-founded the Association for Healthcare Social Media—the first nonprofit society for health professionals on social media. He believes the best way to counter misinformation is to transform doctors into the very thing threatening their authority. "In our medical training, we don't have any sort of marketing or communications training," says Dr. Chiang, "and yet we're expected to impact our communities and the general public."[3]

This rings true. Americans need to schedule an appointment to see a doctor, and few have a daily relationship with their primary care physician. In comparison, they can easily build a relationship with wellness

influencers who share tips, then leave their DMs open for two-way communication. So if doctors once were siloed off in medical journals, now
they're sharing evidence-based medicine in funny TikTok and Instagram
clips. Why should influencers hold all the influential power?

Dr. Chiang believes that if medical professionals are trained as story-
tellers, it'll be easier to spread accurate science and challenge disinforma-
tion. If they need to learn some TikTok dance moves, so be it. During
the COVID-19 vaccine rollout, Dr. Chiang could be found dancing in a
white coat to "Good Day" by Nappy Roots as he explained the differences
between the Pfizer and Moderna vaccines on TikTok. "Won't stop pandemic if not enough people get it," Dr. Chiang explained as he tossed his
hair back and forth.[4]

The need for more scientific influencers became evident during the
pandemic. Bizarre conspiracy theories about the vaccine—that they contain microchips, alter DNA, or enlarged Nicki Minaj's cousin's friend's
balls—grew stronger by the day. Influencers got bolder. And they didn't
need mainstream media acceptance to continue their work on social media.

Vani Hari, for one, was busy launching attacks on the FDA and spinning her wheels about . . . sanitizer. Hari worried that disinfectant booths
were coming to your local school, airport, stores, and public places. She
asked, What are these chemicals going to do to your skin? What do disinfectants do to the microbiome? Food Babe urged followers not to conform
to this "madness," to protest those ushering in oversanitization. "If you
don't want to be subjected to disinfectant spray booths everywhere you go,
it's time to make your voice heard!" she wrote on Facebook. "Please tag
your friends and family to warn them what might be coming. Now is the
time to speak up, before it is too late."[5]

Hari plays up her unorthodox "outsider" status, no doubt appealing to
those looking to join a passionate crusade or community. She consistently
plays up the "us versus the rest of the world" rhetoric (literally the title of
one of her book chapters), which undoubtedly makes readers feel they're a
part of something revolutionary. In a public response to critics, she quoted

Mahatma Gandhi: "First they ignore you, then they laugh at you, then they fight you, then you win."[6] Except it wasn't Gandhi who said that; it was an early-twentieth-century trade union activist.

Aggravating the issue of how to best communicate scientific truth, the Internet serves up the more popular characters, like Vani Hari, with little to no vetting. Online, popularity wins. Algorithms are tailored to our individual biases, which means we read what we want to read. It gets hard to communicate with others because we all absorb different sources of information, says Sheril Kirshenbaum, the co-author of *Unscientific America*. "In many ways, we're all living on the same planet, but we are living in very different realities based on who we're listening to or coming into contact with." We can now, in effect, design our own reality, a kind of magical thinking suited to our desires. A modern-day Tower of Babel.

People also overestimate just how much they *think* they know in science. Kirshenbaum points to the drama over genetically modified foods that have parents clutching their pearl onions. She co-directed a national survey that revealed that despite fears over demonized GMOs, 45 percent of American adults did not even know that all food contains DNA.[7] "That's wild to me," says Kirshenbaum.

When it comes to affluent Americans, misinformation is sometimes even worse, thanks to rampant inaccuracies elevated in Facebook groups, marketing campaigns, or group texts. One survey asked people whether they avoid buying products containing "chemicals" at the grocery store, with 73 percent of higher-income participants responding yes, compared to 65 percent of those from lower-income households.[8] Researchers concluded, "We also observed that even though higher earners have more access to information about food, they are also more likely to be influenced by misinformation and pseudoscience."

It's not that these people aren't smart. It's that they weren't properly trained to understand the scientific process and how to be critical thinkers. "If we give everybody a much more solid understanding of how data gets collected and what's good methodology, what's cherry-picking . . . they would be a little more adept at recognizing when they're being manipulated or when something being reported might not reflect reality," says Kirshenbaum, "because it's very easy to fall for something, especially if you want to believe it."

Science illiteracy does far more damage than inducing stress and unnecessary shopping sprees. By mid-2020, I—as well as plenty of the science experts cited in this book—noticed a growing group of women falling prey to chemophobia. Some women were taught to fear all "chemicals," and in time, that philosophy poisoned their logical thinking. The fear migrates: If "chemicals" are bad in food, then what else are they bad in? Should I not get the vaccine? Should I shun all "unpronounceable" medicines? Should I just eat vegetables instead?

Digital communities help feed these fixations. Countless social media posts repeat "facts" that distort science and scare women. "I'm very nature-oriented and always strive for an organic vibe. [A vaccine] doesn't deliver on that front," wrote one "self-taught physician" on Twitter. Another pleaded, "Let's take our health back from these people who seek to fill our bodies with man-made chemicals."

"In some ways, COVID made [access to information] better, as far as science communicators realizing, 'I need to get out there and debunk stuff.' But at the same time, I feel like a lot of it got worse too," Erin told me. Pseudoscience pushers have gotten more confident, more vocal. It's difficult for science communicators such as Erin because their work is time-consuming: "It's easier to create content when you're just making stuff up and you're not actually having to double-check it or do research." Science communicators generally don't make a lot of money off these educational efforts, nor do they partner with supplements brands or sell a juice detox guide.

Erin is mixed on where we stand moving forward. "I feel like with every new science communicator that decides to start a page, ten more wellness influencers decide to start a page," she laughs. "I'm not sure if it is getting better or not!" And yet she's still out there every day as Food

Science Babe, answering women's questions and debunking ridiculous Pop-Tart ingredient claims. She receives messages "all the time" from women who say they stumbled upon her content, forcing them to rethink their beliefs. They're eager to learn. "I hope that people are seeking out more science communicators, and maybe it's easier for them to find us when we are on social media . . . Hopefully, it's getting better."

How can you, on your own, ensure that you are more scientifically literate when it comes to wellness? There's no easy guide to this ever-growing industry, or to one's health. But here are some takeaways I like to keep in mind:

Remember that wellness isn't one-size-fits-all. It's great that Moon Juice guru Amanda Chantal Bacon starts her morning with calendula tea, green juice, three tablespoons of bee pollen, a shot of pressed turmeric root in freshly squeezed grapefruit juice, and something called "activated cashews." But that might leave one a little hangry. It might not be for you.

Health is specific to an individual's needs. Know that it's quite hard to quantify a lot of preventative medicine because it's based on individual factors, so you shouldn't believe anyone who says a product or modality will definitely work for *you* just because it worked for *them*.

Check your biases. We are all partial to ideas or products that reflect something we already believe in, be it political, cultural, or religious. But the more you practice challenging your biases, the better you get at it. When you see a product (or influencer) claiming "natural" or "chemical-free," ask yourself, Am I buying in to this because I presume natural is better? Do I sincerely want to try this or do I just want to *feel* more aligned with something I value?

Be wary of emotionally manipulative language. Influencers yodeling about how an ingredient will nuke your body are trying to arouse an emotion. The same goes if they say an item will transport you to a purer era, appealing to our desire to run away and live on a farm. Take a step back to consider whether you believe the product's purported benefits (or harm).

Demand evidence. If someone has a striking claim, they better back it up. They can't just make statements like "Your child's American Girl doll is hiding toxins in its ponytail" without evidence. The onus is on them to *prove* that.

Consider your sources. Who are you taking your health advice from? Is it someone with established credentials? What is their expertise? Are they someone other experts refer to and quote? Now that wellness has seeped into the general culture, you'll see it touted by fashion bloggers, celebrities, and (some unqualified) podcasters. Consider rounding out your information diet for a fuller picture.

Analyze intentions. When someone promotes an idea or a product, ask: Is this person or organization beholden to a corporation, brand, or lobbying group? Are they trying to sell me something? For those who blur the line between health and business growth, take their product suggestions with a grain of Himalayan salt.

Is it necessary? Think if you need something or if it's just a shiny "extra" pulling you into the cult of self-improvement. We often make wellness purchases from a place of lack, says the WellSpoken founder Sarah Greenidge. "Explore where that feeling of lack comes from," she advises. "Check in with your body and think about: Is this something that's going to serve me right now?"

Evaluate the root stressors. Analyze what causes you stress, pain, or unhappiness. It could be work, social media, or an overpacked schedule. Before masking complaints with self-care rituals, see whether there's any way you can weed out the fundamental causes. (You can't always: there's only so much we can influence.)

Understand that science is always evolving. Scientists are constantly reevaluating health science research, pursuing further studies that might change what we once accepted in the past. That doesn't necessarily mean that past scientists were sloppy or reckless, rather that science is a continual journey of attaining more knowledge. We do the best we can with the information available at the current time.

Loosen the grip. Control—or the semblance of it—is very much a part of our mental health. We will do anything to possess it, including summoning the spirits to help us nab a dream job. It's the same reason we watch the Weather Channel; we want to manage what we can't predict. But that doesn't get you far down the line. Inevitably, something will come undone. Take a cue from meditation: relinquish a bit.

Much of this also applies to our understanding of how science works, or more aptly, *should* work. As the mathematician John Allen Paulos explains in *Innumeracy*, nearly every activity carries some risk. The question is: How much? And in comparison to what alternative? We're made to believe that science is absolute and iron-clad, thus any shaky ground has us reconsider the whole thing. When in reality, "there are always uncertainties in any live science, because science is a process of discovery."

There are always some uncertainties and elements out of our control.

Conclusion

There's a bigger consideration about our pursuit of health through wellness that goes beyond the science literacy of it all. It comes back to one of the main issues we've covered, which is that with millions and millions of dollars backing the marketing of the wellness industry, it can sometimes be difficult to tell whether our efforts make any difference at all. I'm often asked point-blank: *Is wellness working?* It's a tough question to answer. For one thing, it's too early to tell. We don't have any metrics to make a definitive judgment call on how all these trends impact greater public health. But I'd like to think we're on our way to smoothing the path forward, to distinguishing between the effective and the ineffective.

Granted, the pursuit of wellness is as old as time. Greek philosophers openly extolled the benefits of integrating mind and body—it was Pythagoras who advocated for soulful "me time" in the morning to center oneself before socializing. Ancient Jews observed the Sabbath to reflect and recharge for the week of labor ahead. Buddhist meditation dates back centuries. And America didn't only inherit the political traditions of ancient thinkers, we also got their penchant for wellness gurus.

Our American version of wellness went into high gear alongside the Industrial Revolution, when the rich got healthier and the poor less so. In today's information revolution, we Americans say we can't keep up with modern life. We say technology has moved too fast, the healthcare system is broken, and workplace productivity burns us out. Eating well, moving around, connecting with nature, and even just sleeping normally have been taken away from us. Those things used to be easier, public, or commonly held, but now if we want those things we have to pay for them. And you know what? We will because we're desperate for it.

In the summer of 2021, I revisited The Class. This time, the cardio workout was held outdoors on the Santa Monica Pier. Dozens of women assembled at 8:30 a.m. for a "heart-clearing" session set against the backdrop of the rough Pacific Ocean waves. A peppy blond instructor named Pixie sermonized on gratitude and the importance of expressing emotions between bouts of jumping jacks. After asking us to "pound out" resentment by gently beating our thighs, she told us to get loud when others try to silence us. "You don't need anyone's permission but your own," she firmly instructed. I once again witnessed women showing weighted emotion. They danced with abandon and breathed heavily with intention.

Later, I chatted with one fellow classmate who said The Class was just as relevant then as it had been years earlier. "It's only gotten more stressful," she laughed. There was a raging new COVID variant, a torn country at each other's throats, and so on and so on. The world, it seemed, was irreparably out of balance. The Class, for a moment, helped calm that anxiety.

Like her, I had to admit I was thrilled to be back among my emotional jumpers. Maybe it wasn't a cure-all or the community I had envisioned, but it sure did *something*. That's about as much as I expect these days from most wellness pursuits.

Wellness was initially introduced as a symbol of empowerment and a better way of life, and to some degree it is. If we're talking real wellness—

good nutrition, disease management, and such—then yes. You can't discount the myriad of ways we can live a healthier lifestyle. Quickie marts sell bagged carrots and display as many water varieties as soft drinks. Tech platforms democratize access to streaming fitness classes. Terms like "prevention" and "being active" are part of the American vernacular now.

We openly discuss mental health, far more than our parents' generation did. Look at the sophisticated offerings ranging from affordable therapy apps to inclusive digital support groups. Maybe it's not perfect, but it's progress. Do I wish there was more of an emphasis on community and less on personal intervention? Could we focus more on systemic issues? Of course. But what's the alternative right here and now in our highly individualistic society? You have to appreciate that which is, at the very least, making modern life a bit more manageable.

In the same breath, I must say that there are issues within the greater wellness industry, as covered throughout this book. So much of the wellness movement is built upon critique—a pushback against a disappointing health system, revulsion at pharmaceutical scandals, and a distrust of Big Food. Those are all warranted concerns, but they can come at a cost. Obsessing over "natural" or overvaluing alternatives can obstruct clear thinking. Doctors and manufacturers undoubtedly harmed women in the past, but we can't ignore science or evidence-based medicine in the name of defying authority. The romanticization of fighting the establishment does just that.

Pseudoscience and quacks have always been a mainstay of American culture. But we've entered a new era of uncritically accepting them and their charcoal-infused nonsense. Once supplements and "detox" kits overtook store shelves, we blindly embraced them. Herbal Essences now sells "gluten-free" shampoo, which is ludicrous considering that no one drinks their hair product. (Perhaps the company knows they can make a buck off those who have been taught to fear gluten, presumably, in all forms.) We started going with the flow instead of following the research.

I've seen far too many women—myself included—adopt new rituals and debatable products with nary an ounce of skepticism.

While we might want to just brush off problematic issues in the name of the free market, there is a societal impact to consider. Deceptive marketing has deeper ramifications. It starts small, then gets larger, until eventually it overtakes an entire industry. Even the word "wellness" has become an ambiguous, amorphous term—untethered to anything concrete, with more and more products shoved under its umbrella every day. It's dulling our bullshit detectors.

Wellness is paraded as something anyone can achieve if they just commit to their health destiny. Then, as Arthur J. Barsky writes in *Worried Sick*, "everything seems either healthful or harmful, and life becomes a series of prescribed and proscribed behaviors. Personal habits, diets, leisure activities are all modified to conform to the orthodoxy of the healthy lifestyle, as if there was only one way of life that could assure us of complete and endless health."[1]

So much of the current messaging serves to control women's time and role in society. Our health becomes a catalyst for investment, one demanding negotiations, sacrifice, and performance. We need to purge our figures of excess fat, rid our minds of angry thoughts, cleanse our organs of "toxins," fix whatever is "wrong" with us. It's fueling what can only be called self-absorption, revering our body to unhealthy proportions.

This is why it's difficult to discuss wellness in generalized, absolute terms. There is good, bad, and a whole lot in between. You cannot fully denounce it, nor can you disregard its growing problems. Often you need to discuss each sector individually, since this industry is ever expanding, encompassing more than a dozen subindustries. But overall, experts express optimism. "I feel we're marching in the right direction in terms of awareness and people acknowledging that it's multidimensional," says Ophelia Yeung, a senior research fellow at the Global Wellness Institute. "You can't just fix [everything] with medicine. You have to live [healthily]. I think that message is really out there now."

Wellness will continue to grow because the inherent sentiment remains the same: the status quo isn't cutting it. We shop at farmers' markets to cut back on overprocessed food. We wear a Fitbit because we recognize our lives are too sedentary. We go to yoga because we need a moment to slow down. Those activities in turn help define us—and what we want our lives to be.

· · ·

A 2020 Ogilvy study of seven thousand consumers discovered that a majority of shoppers now expect most brands to provide wellness offerings. Car manufacturers, for example, are reportedly incorporating wellness into vehicle design with features that measure stress levels or emit mood-altering scents (which may be helpful—we'll see). "Every brand can be a wellness brand now," noted Marion McDonald, Ogilvy's Global Health and Wellness Practice Lead. It sounds as if wellness will soon be part of pretty much every aspect of everyday life, in the way that religion was back in the day.

The title of this book is not meant to be taken literally. I am not suggesting that women engage in wellness practices or join a gym as a way to replicate the role of organized religion. That would certainly be pushing the comparison. But I do see ways in which wellness functions as deconstructed religion, a regulatory system instructing us how to move through our lives. It's almost as if it's cementing a new moral order. Wellness has ethical values (healthism). People follow laws dictating what they must ("organic") and must not ("toxic") consume—a quest for purity to sanctify the body. Nature is armed with godlike powers, which then assumes sickness is thereby attributed to the unnatural or synthetic. Wellness has its symbols (a yoga mat) and high priest (Gwyneth), if not false idols (supplements). Rituals can be picking up a turmeric latte before a workout class or instituting a daily gratitude practice.

Wellness even has many of the same sins (gluttony, sloth) and self-denials (food again) as religion. There are significant differences, though: this clergy sermonizes not about the devil but rather the daily environmental threats against which we require amulets (clean beauty).

Worshippers are provided with belonging, whether that's via an identity or community. Eating "right" or working out are imbued with sacred meaning because they all funnel into a promised salvation: a life free of stress, aging, and sickness. True believers—the hardest-working, that is—can gain entrance to this Eden of control. The belief is not necessarily based on science, but psychology.

How are we to interpret this? Well, it depends on how it's used and who's in charge. When the gospel is embraced by well-intentioned, scientific entities, then maybe it can be beneficial. But when it's adopted by the Goops of the world, less so. Pursuing healthy habits in itself is good. It's the pseudoscience, hyperconsumerist ethos that is muddying the waters. That's the distinction I hope I made throughout this book.

The religious treatment of wellness might also be because we've made it harder for people to find aspects of a fulfilling life in modern society. I think a lot about Oprah's Stanford University speech in which she implored students to find meaning. There's one question after she says "You must have a spiritual practice," and it's *What is yours?* I think about those young adults staring at what is essentially a very difficult, existential homework assignment: How do I find fulfillment in this culture? What is the meaning of my life? How do I define myself? It's not easy, especially in a society so obsessed with identity yet in which the familiar road map—with guardrails like religious orthodoxy or strict gender roles—no longer necessarily applies. That people gravitate toward overly marketed wellness makes sense in this day and age if only because the existential dilemma facing us can be overwhelming.

Many want meaning and a guide directing them how to get it. The acclaimed late author David Foster Wallace may have put it best when he said atheism doesn't exist in our culture:

There is no such thing as not worshipping. Everybody worships. The only choice we get is what to worship. And the compelling reason for maybe choosing some sort of god or spiritual-type

thing to worship [. . .] is that pretty much anything else you worship will eat you alive. If you worship money and things, if they
are where you tap real meaning in life, then you will never have
enough, never feel you have enough. It's the truth. Worship your
own body and beauty and sexual allure and you will always feel
ugly, and when time and age start showing, you will die a million
deaths before they finally plant you. On one level, we all know
this stuff already—it's been codified as myths, proverbs, clichés,
bromides, epigrams, parables: the skeleton of every great story. The
trick is keeping the truth up front in daily consciousness."[2]

If we crave belonging and we increasingly worship good health, how
do we ensure wellness is the best it can be? Redirecting the private sector economy is one part of the equation. For what wellness truly sets to
cure, we also need systemic solutions and public infrastructure. We need
more medical research, improved doctor-patient relationships, policies to
support women, and better consumer product regulatory oversight. We
need stronger communities. In our individualistic society, we are told that
everything is our responsibility (and then often directed toward an app).
But we're not supplied with enough support, even financially, to pursue
healthier habits. Wellness, therefore, becomes everything that insurance
and medicine won't touch. But if institutions want to change the landscape—as they publicly claim—why not incentivize fitness, nutrition, and
connection?

Public investment is building. Fitness is a good example: A few state
parks now advertise the mental health benefits of nature and attempt to
widen access to recreation. Some physicians "prescribe" nature-based treatments, like recommending that patients join organized social hikes. Local
governments are building more walking and biking trails to encourage
daily physical activity.

Granted, the public sector is generally divided in that parks and rec is
separate from the health department, which is separate from social services.

And maybe we need a wellness czar at the city, state, or federal level to coordinate them all. Or perhaps we should look to other countries for innovative ideas. New Zealand adopted a "well-being budget," while the United Arab Emirates employs a minister of happiness. Ophelia Yeung told me there's no one successful model that the United States can readily replicate. "[Wellness] is such a nascent emerging field, and there is no one really thinking about it from such a perspective yet," she said. "Thought leadership is needed." Although, even if there was a model, it would hardly be a copy-and-paste situation: each population is unique in its needs and experiences.

Insurers and employers are shifting too. It's not uncommon for health insurance plans to include gym membership discounts and stress management programs. ClassPass, the fitness class subscription platform, teamed up with Kaiser Permanente to offer thousands of free online workouts and reduced rates for live exercise classes. These are just several initiatives proving, at the very least, that society increasingly recognizes that citizens need help to live healthier lifestyles.

• • •

Early in the writing of this book, I called up Don Ardell, considered one of the architects of modern wellness. In 1977, he wrote a book titled *High Level Wellness*, which was groundbreaking for its time. Ardell wanted to educate the public about the actions they could take to promote their well-being. The individual was meant to ask: How can I feel better? What tools are at my disposal to ensure health and happiness? None of the answers, except for injury or disease, included a visit to the doctor. But his book wasn't *anti-doctor*. "Modern medicine is a wonderful thing," he wrote, "but there are two problems: people expect too much of it, and too little of themselves."[3]

A manifesto for personal responsibility, the book focuses on the stripped-down core pillars of the movement. "Wellness was never meant as an advertising gimmick, a brand, a treatment, a market, industry, or service," he stresses more than forty years later. Self-responsibility and community were equally emphasized. "Making a decision that you want to live a healthy life is not the same as being able to do it," says Ardell. "If you don't have a supportive culture—friends, family members, and your environment . . . your chances are next to zero to be able to pull off."

Voices like Ardell's get lost amid the noise, especially as we elevate the wild and pricey. But I notice pockets of consumers questioning their newfound habits. In much the same way that women pondered the status quo, they now seek to understand why they've gravitated to wellness. I believe consumers want to return to evidence-based solutions, of which there are plenty. They are floating around out there, in the same communities where they drink cold-pressed celery juice.

As for me? I threw out my supplements. I welcomed Neutrogena back into my bathroom. I've learned to pause before buying the hype on a new product, while simultaneously permitting myself to enjoy many products lacking scientific evidence. I still buy kombucha, though I drink it for the taste, not because I believe in some kind of magical gut healing. And though I still spend a fortune on my favorite boutique fitness classes (because they're fun), I try to remind myself that I don't need the fittest of bodies.

Wellness didn't solve all my problems. Stress, lackluster medical care, and image-related pressures are still prevalent issues. But it sure did inspire a framework to better deal with some of them. Learning to embrace mental health solutions put me on the road to finding personalized solutions that worked for me.

It didn't happen overnight, but over the years, I've witnessed an improvement in how I feel and how my body and mind react. That's worth something.

Wellness, as Goop would rightly say, is a journey. And I can't disagree with that.

Notes

Introduction

1. Rina Raphael, "Namaste En Masse: Can Wellness Festivals Grow as Big as Coachella?," *Fast Company*, Jan. 30, 2017, fastcompany.com/40421458/namaste-en-masse-can-wellness-festivals-grow-as-big-as-coachella.

2. Rina Raphael, "Why This Feminist Weed Camp Isn't Just for White Women," *Fast Company*, Oct. 17, 2017, fastcompany.com/40474705/why-this-feminist-weed-camp-isnt-white-women.

3. Elaine Stone and Sheryl A. Farnan, *The Dynamics of Fashion*, 5th ed. (New York: Fairchild Books, 2018), 180.

4. "An Inside Look into the 2021 Global Consumer Health and Wellness Revolution," *NielsenIQ*, Oct. 28, 2021, nielseniq.com/global/en/insights/report/2021/an-inside-look-into-the-2021-global-consumer-health-and-wellness-revolution/.

5. Adi Menayang, "Millennials Are 'the Most Health-Conscious Generation Ever,' Says Report by the Halo Group," *FoodNavigator-USA*, March 27, 2017, foodnavigator-usa.com/Article/2017/03/27/Millennials-scrutinize-health-claims-more-than-other-generations.

Chapter 1: Why the Hell Is the Advice Always Yoga?

1. Erin Donaghue, "New FBI Data Shows Rise in Anti-Semitic Hate Crimes," CBS News, Nov. 13, 2018, cbsnews.com/news/fbi-hate-crimes-up-new-data-shows-rise-in-anti-semitic-hate-crimes/.

27. Patti Neighmond, "Yo-Yo Dieting May Pose Serious Risks for Heart Patients," *Shots* (blog), NPR, May 1, 2017, accessed Aug. 8, 2021, npr.org/sections/health -shots/2017/05/01/526048767/-yo-yo-dieting-poses-serious-risks-for-heart -patients.

28. Stuart Wolpert, "Dieting Does Not Work, UCLA Researchers Report," UCLA Newsroom, April 3, 2007, newsroom.ucla.edu/releases/Dieting-Does-Not -Work-UCLA-Researchers-7832.

29. Keith Devlin, "Top 10 Reasons Why the BMI Is Bogus," NPR, July 4, 2009, npr.org/templates/story/story.php?storyId=106268439.

30. Tessa E. S. Charlesworth and Mahzarin R. Banaji, "Research: How Americans' Biases Are Changing (or Not) over Time," *Harvard Business Review*, Aug. 14, 2019, hbr.org/2019/08/research-on-many-issues-americans-biases-are -decreasing.

31. Alexandra Owens, "Allure Cover Girl Olivia Wilde's Beauty Secrets," *Allure*, Sept. 18, 2013, allure.com/story/allure-olivia-wilde-beauty-secrets.

Chapter 3: Is My Face Wash Trying to Kill Me?

1. Beautycounter, "Beautycounter in DC 2018," April 1, 2018, YouTube video, 2:47, youtube.com/watch?v=i9URKZvP-MQ.

2. Alix Tunell, "Forget Cadillacs, These Beauty Consultants Want Political Change," *Refinery29*, March 15, 2018, refinery29.com/en-us/beautycounter -political-action.

3. U.S. Food and Drug Administration, "Claire's Stores, Inc., Announces Voluntary Recall of Three Make-up Products," March 11, 2019, fda.gov/safety/recalls -market-withdrawals-safety-alerts/claires-stores-inc-announces-voluntary -recall-three-make-products.

4. David Gelles, "Selling Shampoo, Eye Cream and a Chemical Crackdown," *New York Times*, Oct. 8, 2016, nytimes.com/2016/10/09/business/selling-shampoo -eye-cream-and-a-chemical-crackdown.html.

5. Nancy Tomes, *The Gospel of Germs: Men, Women, and the Microbe in American Life* (Cambridge, MA: Harvard University Press, 2002), 10.

6. "Life Story: Ellen Swallow Richards (1842–1911)," *Women & the American Story*, June 23, 2021, wams.nyhistory.org/modernizing-america/modern-womanhood /ellen-swallow-richards/.

7. Barbara Ehrenreich and Deirdre English, *For Her Own Good: 150 Years of the Experts' Advice to Women* (New York: Doubleday, 1989), 198–99.

8. Sarah Stage and Virginia B. Vincenti, *Rethinking Home Economics: Women and the History of a Profession* (Ithaca, NY: Cornell University Press, 1997), 259–60.

9. "Personal Care Products," Environmental Working Group, ewg.org/areas-focus/personal-care-products.

10. Norah MacKendrick, *Better Safe Than Sorry: How Consumers Navigate Exposure to Everyday Toxics* (Oakland: University of California Press, 2018).

11. The Honest Company, "A Message from Our Founder, Jessica Alba," *Honest* (blog), March 10 2016, www.honest.com/blog/lifestyle/purpose/a-message-from-our-founder-jessica-alba/19793.html.

12. Abbie Boudreau and Aude Soichet, "Jessica Alba Leads Mommy War on Synthetic Chemicals," ABC News, Dec. 3, 2013, abcnews.go.com/US/jessica-alba-leads-mommy-war-synthetic-chemicals/story?id=21084997.

13. Roland Marchand, *Advertising the American Dream: Making Way for Modernity, 1920–1940* (Berkeley: University of California Press, 1985), 66.

14. John Muir, *The Complete Works of John Muir* (Hastings, UK: Delphi Classics, 2017).

15. Rina Raphael, "The Global Beauty Business Goes Au Naturel," *Fast Company*, Sept. 20, 2018, fastcompany.com/90227521/the-global-beauty-business-goes-au-naturel.

16. Rina Raphael, "Herbivore's Moldy Face-Cream Recall at Sephora Underscores an Ugly Issue for Natural Beauty," *Fast Company*, April 12, 2019, fastcompany.com/90334490/herbivores-moldy-face-cream-recall-at-sephora-underscores-an-ugly-issue-for-natural-beauty.

17. Carolyn Crist, "'Clean' Beauty Products Not Always Safe, Dermatologists Say," Reuters, Oct. 2, 2019, reuters.com/article/us-health-cosmetics-clean-safety-idUSKBN1WH2AC.

18. Fred Fedler, *Media Hoaxes* (Ames: Iowa State University Press, 1989), 199.

19. Jessica Bibby et al., "Transitioning to Transparency," Fashion Institute of Technology, 2018, fitnyc.edu/documents/transitioning-to-transperancy.pdf.

20. Douglas Atkin, *The Culting of Brands: Turn Your Customers into True Believers* (New York: Portfolio, 2004), 17.

21. "Lead in Your Lipstick? The Facts on Heavy Metals in Cosmetics," Beautycounter, Dec. 9, 2016, beautycounter.com/blog/better-beauty/lead-in-your-lipstick-the-facts-on-heavy-metals-in-cosmetics.

22. Tasha Stoiber, "What Are Parabens, and Why Don't They Belong in Cosmetics?," Environmental Working Group, April 9, 2019, ewg.org/what-are-parabens.

23. P. D. Darbre et al., "Concentrations of Parabens in Human Breast Tumours," *Journal of Applied Toxicology* 24, no. 1 (2004): 5–13, doi:10.1002/jat.958.

24. Leigh Krietsch Boerner, "Blue Shift: Why Parabens Shouldn't Scare You," Wirecutter, *New York Times*, Oct. 3, 2016, nytimes.com/wirecutter/blog/why-parabens-shouldnt-scare-you/.

25. Dorota Błędzka et al., "Parabens: From Environmental Studies to Human Health," *Environment International* 67 (2014): 27–42, doi:10.1016/j.envint.2014.02.007.

26. "Antiperspirants/Deodorants and Breast Cancer," National Cancer Institute, cancer.gov/about-cancer/causes-prevention/risk/myths/antiperspirants-fact-sheet.

27. "Do Plastics, Body Care Products or Deodorant Play a Role in Breast Cancer Risk?—Komen Perspectives," *The Komen Blog*, April 1, 2010, blog.komen.org /blog/komen-perspectives-do-plastics-body-care-products-or-deodorant-play-a -role-in-breast-cancer-risk/.

28. "Antiperspirants and Breast Cancer Risk," American Cancer Society, cancer.org /cancer/cancer-causes/antiperspirants-and-breast-cancer-risk.html.

29. "Is Deodorant Harmful for Your Health?" Penn Medicine, June 6, 2019, penn-medicine.org/updates/blogs/health-and-wellness/2019/june/deodorant.

30. "Antiperspirants," American Cancer Society.

31. Anthony F. Fransway et al., "Parabens," *Dermatitis* 30, no. 1 (2019): 3–31, doi:10.1097/der.0000000000000429.

32. "Advocacy for Clean Beauty and a Better Future," Beautycounter, beautycounter .com/advocacy.

33. Scott Faber, "Cosmetics Safety Bill Gains Support from Industry and Advo-cates," Environmental Working Group, July 5, 2017, ewg.org/news-insights /news/cosmetics-safety-bill-gains-support-industry-and-advocates.

34. Katie M. O'Brien et al., "Association of Powder Use in the Genital Area with Risk of Ovarian Cancer," *JAMA* 323, no. 1 (2020): 49–59, doi:10.1001 /jama.2019.20079.

35. Julia Horowitz, "Jessica Alba's The Honest Company Can't Catch a Break," *CNNMoney*, June 12, 2017, money.cnn.com/2017/06/12/news/companies/honest -company-problems/index.html.

36. Thomas C. O'Brien, Ryan Palmer, and Dolores Albarracin, "Misplaced Trust: When Trust in Science Fosters Belief in Pseudoscience and the Benefits of Critical Evaluation," *Journal of Experimental Social Psychology* 96 (2021): 104184, doi:10.1016/j.jesp.2021.104184.

37. Alex Berezow, "Dear EWG, This Is Why Real Scientists Think Poorly of You," American Council on Science and Health, June 1, 2017, acsh.org/news/2017/05 /25/dear-ewg-why-real-scientists-think-poorly-you-11323.

38. Berezow, "Dear EWG."

Chapter 4: Gym as Church

1. Peloton, 30 Min Sundays with Love, Nov. 22, 2020, members.onepeloton.com /profile/workouts/bb7de32e8cca49b1b78679f828360f27.

2. "Sundays with Love," *The Output* (blog), Peloton, Oct. 18, 2020, blog.onepeloton.com/sundays-with-love-peloton/.

3. Jalen Rose, "Peloton Star Ally Love Tells Jalen Rose About Almost Dying at Age 9," *New York Post*, July 1, 2021, nypost.com/2021/07/01/peloton-star-ally-love-tells-jalen-rose-about-almost-dying-at-age-9/.

4. Ally Love, "Peloton's Ally Love Almost Died in a Car Accident at Age 9 and Was Told She'd Never Run Again," *Women's Health*, Oct. 20, 2020, womenshealthmag.com/fitness/a34041498/ally-love-peloton-dance/.

5. "Peloton Interactive (PTON) Q4 2021 Earnings Call Transcript" *Motley Fool*, Aug. 27, 2021, fool.com/earnings/call-transcripts/2021/08/27/peloton-interactive-pton-q4-2021-earnings-call-tra/.

6. Recode, "Full Video: John Foley, Founder and CEO of Peloton | Code Commerce," Sept. 15, 2017, YouTube video, 14:45, youtube.com/watch?v=-g5Y-Dp5kDw.

7. Wade Clark Roof, *Spiritual Marketplace: Baby Boomers and the Remaking of American Religion* (Princeton, NJ: Princeton University Press, 2001), 79.

8. "United States Securities and Exchange Commission, Peloton Interactive, Inc.," sec.gov/Archives/edgar/data/1639825/000119312519230923/d738839ds1.htm.

9. Casper ter Kuile and Angie Thurston, "How We Gather (Part 2): SoulCycle as Soul Sanctuary," The On Being Project, July 9, 2016, onbeing.org/blog/how-we-gather-part-2-soulcycle-as-soul-sanctuary/.

10. Kathryn Romeyn, "How an Ex–Talent Manager Co-founded SoulCycle and Sold for $90M," *Hollywood Reporter*, July 3, 2017, hollywoodreporter.com/lifestyle/style/how-an-talent-manager-founded-soulcycle-sold-90m-1015009/.

11. Tim Ferriss, "#372: Julie Rice—Co-founding SoulCycle, Taming Anxiety, and Mastering Difficult Conversations," *The Tim Ferriss Show*, Apple Podcasts, June 5, 2019, podcasts.apple.com/us/podcast/372-julie-rice-co-founding-soulcycle-taming-anxiety/id863897795?i=1000440479706.

12. Sarah Lacy, "Scaling Your Startup . . . with Soul," Startups.com, Aug. 11, 2020, startups.com/library/founder-stories/julie-rice-elizabeth-cutler.

13. TheLeapTV, "Julie & Spencer Rice | SoulCycle | USC Interview," Feb. 28, 2020, YouTube video, 1:25:28, youtube.com/watch?v=lU6vhAq331s, accessed Feb. 7, 2022.

14. Ferriss, "#372: Julie Rice."

15. "Q&A with SoulCycle's Julie Rice: A Local Gym That Helped Spawn an Exercise Craze," *West Side Rag*, March 10, 2013, westsiderag.com/2013/03/10/qa-with-soulcycles-julie-rice-a-local-spinning-gym-that-helped-spawn-an-exercise-craze.

16. Lacy, "Scaling Your Startup."

17. Romeyn, "How an Ex–Talent Manager."

18. TheLeapTV, "Julie & Spencer Rice."

19. Ferriss, "#372: Julie Rice."

20. Steven Kotler and Jamie Wheal, *Stealing Fire: How Silicon Valley, the Navy SEALs, and Maverick Scientists Are Revolutionizing the Way We Live and Work* (New York: Dey Street Books, 2018), 141.

21. "Researchers Discover a Completely Legal Performance Enhancer: Friends," University of Oxford, Aug. 31, 2015, ox.ac.uk/news/2015–08–31-researchers -discover-completely-legal-performance-enhancer-friends.

22. Ter Kuile and Thurston, "How We Gather."

23. Aziz Angari, Twitter post, Dec. 13, 2019, 9:43 p.m., twitter.com/AzizAngari /status/1205679604406607872.

24. Wendy Simonds, *Women and Self-Help Culture: Reading Between the Lines* (New Brunswick, NJ: Rutgers University Press, 1992), 42–43.

25. Rina Raphael, "Namaste En Masse: Can Wellness Festivals Grow as Big as Coachella?" *Fast Company*, June 30, 2017, fastcompany.com/40421458 /namaste-en-masse-can-wellness-festivals-grow-as-big-as-coachella.

26. "Your Posture, Right or Wrong, Is Up to You," *Life*, April 12, 1937, 52–56.

27. Karl Toepfer, *Empire of Ecstasy: Nudity and Movement in German Body Culture, 1910–1935* (Berkeley: University of California Press, 1997), 39.

28. Carey Dunne, "The Emperor's New Corsets," *The Baffler* 34, Spring 2017, the baffler.com/salvos/emperors-new-corsets-dunne.

29. Warwick Maloney, "Dr. Bess Mensendieck," *Movement Health*, Dec. 8, 2017, movementhealth.com.au/news/dr-bess-mensendieck/.

30. Dunne, "The Emperor's New Corsets."

31. "Finds Beauty Lies in Muscle Control," *New York Times*, March 9, 1924, times machine.nytimes.com/timesmachine/1924/03/09/101583907.html?pageNumber =63Them.

32. Susan Pinker, *The Village Effect: How Face-to-Face Contact Can Make Us Healthier and Happier* (Toronto: Vintage Canada, 2015), 36.

33. Karen Turner, "Secularism Is on the Rise, but Americans Are Still Finding Community and Purpose in Spirituality," *Vox*, June 11, 2019, vox.com/first -person/2019/6/4/18644764/church-religion-atheism-secularism.

34. "For Mindfulness Programs, 'with Whom' May Be More Important Than 'How,'" Brown University, Feb. 16, 2021, brown.edu/news/2021–02–16 /mindfulness.

35. Nicholas K. Canby et al., "The Contribution of Common and Specific Therapeutic Factors to Mindfulness-Based Intervention Outcomes," *Frontiers in Psychology*

(Jan. 14, 2021): 11:603394, doi:10.3389/fpsyg.2020.603394; PMID: 33584439; PMCID: PMC7874060.

36. Michelle Ruiz, "A Conversation with Cody Rigsby, Peloton's 'King of Quarantine,'" *Vogue*, Nov. 25, 2020, vogue.com/article/cody-rigsby-on-becoming -pelotons-king-of-quarantine.

37. Robert D. Putnam, *Bowling Alone: The Collapse and Revival of American Community* (New York: Simon & Schuster Paperbacks, 2000), 184.

38. Ferriss, "#372: Julie Rice."

39. Maxwell Strachan, "SoulCycle Lays Off Long-Time Employees with Zero Severance," *Vice*, May 18, 2020, vice.com/en/article/m7jaqq/soulcycle-lays-off -long-time-employees-with-zero-severance.

40. Alex Abad-Santos, "How SoulCycle Lost Its Soul," *Vox*, Dec. 23, 2020, vox.com /the-goods/22195549/soulcycle-decline-reopening-bullying-bike-explained.

41. Katie Warren, "SoulCycle's Top Instructors Had Sex with Clients, 'Fat-Shamed' Coworkers, and Used Homophobic and Racist Language," *Business Insider*, Nov. 17, 2020, businessinsider.com/soulcycle-instructors-celebrities -misbehavior-2020-11.

42. Catherine Saint Louis, "In New York, a Rivalry Shifts into High Gear," *New York Times*, Oct. 8, 2010, nytimes.com/2010/10/10/fashion/10Spin.html.

43. Warren, "SoulCycle's Top Instructors."

44. Mallory Schlossberg, "I Used to Be Obsessed with SoulCycle—until I realized How Much Is Wrong with the Class," *Business Insider*, April 8, 2016, businessin sider.com.au/why-i-stopped-going-to-soulcycle-2016-4.

45. Saint Louis, "In New York."

46. Abad-Santos, "How SoulCycle Lost Its Soul."

47. Richard P. Feynman, *"Surely You're Joking, Mr. Feynman!"* (New York: W. W. Norton, 1985), 343.

Chapter 5: A Plea to Be Heard

1. Rina Raphael, "Gwyneth Paltrow's Goop Conference Was as Kooky as You Expected It to Be—and That's Exactly What Fans Wanted," *Fast Company*, June 12, 2017, fastcompany.com/40430244/gwyneth-paltrows-goop-conference-was -as-kooky-as-you-expected-it-to-be-and-thats-exactly-what-fans-wanted.

2. Ann Anderson, *Snake Oil, Hustlers and Hambones: The American Medicine Show* (Jefferson, NC: McFarland Publishers, 2004).

3. Jamie Ballard, "Women Are More Likely Than Men to Be Open to Alternative Medicine," YouGov America, Aug. 20, 2018, today.yougov.com/topics/health /articles-reports/2018/08/20/alternative-medicine-men-women.

4. Catherine Thorbecke, Jennifer Pereira, and Eric Jones, "Selma Blair Reveals She Cried with Relief at MS Diagnosis After Being 'Not Taken Seriously' by Doctors," *GMA*, Feb. 26, 2019, goodmorningamerica.com/culture/story/selma -blair-opens-tears-relief-ms-diagnosis-61310469.

5. Julie Miller, "'There's No Tragedy for Me': Selma Blair's Transformation," *Vanity Fair*, March 2019, vanityfair.com/hollywood/2019/02/selma-blairs-transformation.

6. *Nightline*, season 40, episode 41, "Selma Blair Describes the Moment She Received Her Multiple Sclerosis Diagnosis," ABC, Feb. 26, 2019, abc.com /shows/nightline/episode-guide/2019-02/26-022619-selma-blair-describes-the -moment-she-received-her-multiple-sclerosis-diagnosis, accessed Nov. 15, 2021.

7. Pat Anson, "Women in Pain Report Significant Gender Bias" *National Pain Report*, Nov. 8, 2015, nationalpainreport.com/women-in-pain-report-significant -gender-bias-8824696.html.

8. Bernard L. Harlow and Elizabeth Gunther Stewart, "A Population-Based Assessment of Chronic Unexplained Vulvar Pain: Have We Underestimated the Prevalence of Vulvodynia?" *Journal of the American Medical Women's Association* 58, no. 2 (2003): 82–8.

9. Tracy Jarrett, "Endometriosis Increases Risk of Heart Disease in Young Women," NBC News, March 29, 2016, nbcnews.com/health/womens -health/endometriosis-increases-risk-heart-disease-young-women-n547381.

10. Full Frontal with Samantha Bee, "All You Get Is Birth Control | March 21, 2018 Act 2, Part 1 | Full Frontal on TBS," March 22, 2018, YouTube video, 3:53, youtube.com/watch?v=X2FS0s95o_Q.

11. Esther H. Chen et al., "Gender Disparity in Analgesic Treatment of Emergency Department Patients with Acute Abdominal Pain, *Academic Emergency Medicine* 15, no. 5 (May 2008): 414–18, doi:10.1111/j.1553–2712.2008.00100.x, PMID: 18439195.

12. K. L. Calderone, "The Influence of Gender on the Frequency of Pain and Sedative Medication Administered to Postoperative Patients," *Sex Roles* 23 (1990): 713–25, doi.org/10.1007/BF00289259.

13. Sarah Klein, "5 Ways to Make Your Next Ob-Gyn Appointment a Little Less Terrible," *Prevention*, Nov. 4, 2016, prevention.com/health/g20486679/make -your-ob-gyn-visit-less-terrible/.

14. Springer, "Wait, Just a Second, Is Your Doctor Listening?" *ScienceDaily*, July 19, 2018, sciencedaily.com/releases/2018/07/180719112209.htm.

15. Ming Tai-Seale, Thomas G. McGuire, and Weimin Zhang, "Time Allocation in Primary Care Office Visits," *Health Services Research* 42, no. 5 (2007): 1871– 94, doi:10.1111/j.1475–6773.2006.00689.x.

16. David Ollier Weber, "How Many Patients Can a Primary Care Physician Treat?" American Association for Physician Leadership, Feb. 11, 2019, phy sicianleaders.org/news/how-many-patients-can-primary-care-physician-treat.

17. Lisa A. Cooper et al., "The Associations of Clinicians' Implicit Attitudes About Race with Medical Visit Communication and Patient Ratings of Interpersonal Care," *American Journal of Public Health* 102, no. 5 (2012): 979–87, doi:10.2105/ajph.2011.300558.

18. "Discrimination in America: Experiences and Views of African Americans," NPR, Oct. 2017, media.npr.org/assets/img/2017/10/23/discriminationpoll -african-americans.pdf.

19. Nina Martin and Renée Montagne, "Nothing Protects Black Women from Dying in Pregnancy and Childbirth," ProPublica, Dec. 7, 2017, propublica .org/article/nothing-protects-black-women-from-dying-in-pregnancy-and -childbirth.

20. Danielle Ofri, *What Doctors Feel: How Emotions Affect the Practice of Medicine* (Boston: Beacon Press, 2013), 155.

21. Susan Kelly, "Emergency Physicians' Level of Burnout Jumped Last Year," *Healthcare Dive*, Jan. 24, 2022, healthcaredive.com/news/burnout-emergency -physicians-rising/617554/.

22. Elisabeth Rosenthal, *An American Sickness: How Healthcare Became Big Business and How You Can Take It Back* (New York: Penguin Books, 2018), 252.

23. Rina Raphael, "A Shockingly Large Majority of Health News Shared on Facebook Is Fake or Misleading," *Fast Company*, Feb. 4, 2019, fastcompany.com/90301427/a -shockingly-large-majority-of-health-news-shared-on-facebook-is-fake.

24. Paul Bergner, "Lobelia: Legal Considerations in the Samuel Thomson Trial," *Medical Herbalism: Journal for the Clinical Practitioner*, medherb.com/Materia _Medica/Lobelia_-_Legal_considerations_in_the_Samuel_Thomson_trial.htm.

25. Theodore W. Ruger, "The Thomsonian Movement and the Structures of American Health Law," Petrie-Flom Center for Health Law Policy, Biotechnology, and Bioethics at Harvard Law School, Dec. 28, 2009, petrieflom.law.harvard .edu/assets/publications/Ruger_Thomsonian_Movement_and_Structures_of _American_Health_Law.pdf.

26. Samuel Thomson, *A Narrative of the Life and Medical Discoveries of Samuel Thomson* (Columbus, OH: Pike, Platt, 1832), 24.

27. Peter Maisel, Erika Baum, and Norbert Donner-Banzhoff, "Fatigue as the Chief Complaint—Epidemiology, Causes, Diagnosis, and Treatment," *Deutsches Ärzteblatt International* 118, no. 33–34 (2021): 566–76, doi:10.3238/arztebl.m2021.0192.

28. Emily Laurence, "Gwyneth Paltrow Goop Wellness Supplements Line Suffered from Adrenal Fatigue—and It Helped Inspire a New Goop Business," *Well+Good*, March 16, 2017, wellandgood.com/gwyneth-paltrow-goop-wellness-supplements-adrenal-fatigue/.

29. "TINA.org Takes Gwyneth Paltrow's Goop-y Health Claims to Regulators," Truth in Advertising, Aug. 22, 2017, truthinadvertising.org/tina-takes-goop-claims-to-regulators/.

30. Rae Paoletta, "NASA Calls Bullshit on Goop's $120 'Bio-Frequency Healing' Sticker Packs," *Gizmodo*, June 22, 2017, gizmodo.com/nasa-calls-bullshit-on-goops-120-bio-frequency-healing-1796309360.

31. Daniel Morgan, "What the Tests Don't Show," *Washington Post*, Oct. 5, 2018, washingtonpost.com/news/posteverything/wp/2018/10/05/feature/doctors-are-surprisingly-bad-at-reading-lab-results-its-putting-us-all-at-risk/.

32. Erin Blakemore, "1,800 Studies Later, Scientists Conclude Homeopathy Doesn't Work," *Smithsonian Magazine*, March 11, 2015, smithsonianmag.com/smart-news/1800-studies-later-scientists-conclude-homeopathy-doesnt-work-180954534/.

33. Jonathan Jarry (biological scientist and science communicator, McGill Office for Science and Society), in discussion with the author, January 2022.

34. Jonathan Jarry, January 2022.

35. Dr. David Scales (sociologist, physician, and assistant professor of medicine, Weill Cornell Medical College), in discussion with the author, January 2022.

36. The Body of Evidence, "Anecdotes (The Body of Evidence)," July 18, 2016, YouTube video, 7:42, youtube.com/watch?v=QDlPoSSVPuA, accessed Jan. 16, 2022.

37. Klaus Linde et al., "Acupuncture for the Prevention of Tension-Type Headache," *Cochrane Database of Systematic Reviews* 4, no. 4, April 19, 2016, CD007587, doi:10.1002/14651858.CD007587.pub2.

38. Michael Stenger, Nicki Eithz Bauer, and Peter B. Licht, "Is Pneumothorax After Acupuncture So Uncommon?" *Journal of Thoracic Disease* 5, no. 4 (2013): E144–46, doi:10.3978/j.issn.2072–1439.2013.08.18.

39. Skyler B. Johnson et al., "Complementary Medicine, Refusal of Conventional Cancer Therapy, and Survival Among Patients with Curable Cancers," *JAMA Oncology* 4, no. 10 (2018): 1375, doi:10.1001/jamaoncol.2018.2487.

40. Ned Potter, "Steve Jobs Regretted Delaying Cancer Surgery 9 Months, Biographer Says," ABC News, Oct. 20, 2011, abcnews.go.com/Technology/steve-jobs-treatment-biographer-jobs-delayed-surgery-pancreatic/story?id=14781250#.

41. Federal Trade Commission, "In the matter of Easybutter, LLC, a limited liability company, also doing business as Hempme," ftc.gov/system/files/documents/cases/2023047hempmecbdcomplaint.pdf.

42. McGill Office for Science and Society, "Functional Medicine (CS31)," April 13, 2019, YouTube video, 10:44, youtube.com/watch?v=3EDW_upV3ZU.

43. David Gorski, "Dr. Robin Berzin, Functional Medicine Concierge Practices, and the Marketing of Medical Pseudoscience," *Respectful Insolence*, Sept. 5, 2018, respectfulinsolence.com/2018/09/05/robin-berzin-functional-medicine-concierge/.

Chapter 6: Can't Treat What You Don't Know

1. Elisabeth Brooke, *Women Healers: Portraits of Herbalists, Physicians, and Midwives* (Rochester, VT: Healing Arts Press, 1996), 69.

2. Maya Dusenbery, *Doing Harm: The Truth About How Bad Medicine and Lazy Science Leave Women Dismissed, Misdiagnosed, and Sick* (New York: HarperOne, 2019), 7–8.

3. Judith Walzer Leavitt, *Women and Health in America: Historical Readings* (Madison: University of Wisconsin Press, 1999), 53.

4. Patrick Boyle, "Nation's Physician Workforce Evolves: More Women, a Bit Older, and Toward Different Specialties," Association of American Medical Colleges, Feb. 2, 2021, aamc.org/news-insights/nation-s-physician-workforce-evolves-more-women-bit-older-and-toward-different-specialties, accessed Aug. 5, 2021.

5. Mirjam J. Curno et al., "A Systematic Review of the Inclusion (or Exclusion) of Women in HIV Research: From Clinical Studies of Antiretrovirals and Vaccines to Cure Strategies," *Journal of Acquired Immune Deficiency Syndromes* 71, no. 2 (2016): 181–88, doi:10.1097/qai.0000000000000842.

6. "Here's Why Women Are More Likely to Have Chronic Pain," Cleveland Clinic, May 30, 2019, health.clevelandclinic.org/women-are-more-likely-to-have-chronic-pain-heres-why/.

7. Pietro Invernizzi et al., "Female Predominance and X Chromosome Defects in Autoimmune Diseases," *Journal of Autoimmunity* 33, no. 1 (August 2009): 12–16, doi: 10.1016/j.jaut.2009.03.005.

8. Anna Nowogrodzki, "Inequality in Medicine," *Nature*, Oct. 5, 2017, nature.com/articles/550S18a.

9. Chloe E. Bird, "Increased Funding for Research in Women's Health Issues Could Unleash Staggering Returns," *Fortune*, Feb. 11, 2022, fortune.com/2022/02/11/women-health-medical-research-underfunding-equity-rand/.

10. Sergey Feldman et al., "Quantifying Sex Bias in Clinical Studies at Scale with Automated Data Extraction," *JAMA Network Open* 2, no. 7 (2019): e196700, doi:10.1001/jamanetworkopen.2019.6700.

11. Gabrielle Emanuel, "Preterm Birth: Months Early—and a Century Behind," GBH News, wgbh.org/news/preterm-birth-months-early-and-a-century-behind.

12. "Women in Healthcare Leadership 2019," OliverWyman, oliverwyman.com /our-expertise/insights/2019/jan/women-in-healthcare-leadership.html.

13. "Global Female Technology (Femtech) Market: Analysis & Forecast," *Globe-Newswire*, July 29, 2020, globenewswire.com/news-release/2020/07/29/2069355 /0/en/Global-Female-Technology-Femtech-Market-Analysis-Forecast.html.

14. Rina Raphael, "Can Silicon Valley Get You Pregnant?" *Fast Company*, Jan. 30, 2018, fastcompany.com/40521525/fertility-tech-is-worth-billions-and -investors-are-finally-paying-attention.

15. Neal Dempsey, "Venture Capital Is Still a 'Boys' Club.' Let's Start to Change That." *Crunchbase News*, August 16, 2021, news.crunchbase.com/news/venture -capital-female-gender-diversity/.

16. Collin West and Gopinath Sundaramurthy, "Women VCs Invest in Up to 2x More Female Founders," *Kauffman Fellows Journal*, March 25, 2020, kauff manfellows.org/journal_posts/women-vcs-invest-in-up-to-2x-more-female -founders.

17. Laura Lovett, "Femtech Market Has Potential but Struggles to Score Investor Dollars," *MobiHealthNews*, Aug. 28, 2020, mobihealthnews.com/news/femtech -market-has-potential-struggles-score-investor-dollars.

18. Sheila Kaplan and Matthew Goldstein, "F.D.A. Halts U.S. Sales of Pelvic Mesh, Citing Safety Concerns for Women," *New York Times*, April 16, 2019, nytimes.com/2019/04/16/health/vaginal-pelvic-mesh-fda.html#.

19. Susan Berger, "Vaginal Mesh Has Caused Health Problems in Many Women, Even as Some Surgeons Vouch for Its Safety and Efficacy," *Washington Post*, Jan. 20, 2019, washingtonpost.com/national/health-science/vaginal-mesh-has-caused -health-problems-in-many-women-even-as-some-surgeons-vouch-for-its-safety -and-efficacy/2019/01/18/1c4a2332-ff0f-11e8-ad40-cdfd0e0dd65a_story.html.

20. "Transvaginal Mesh Revision Surgeries," *Drugwatch*, drugwatch.com /transvaginal-mesh/revision-surgeries/.

21. Carl Heneghan, "What Next for Transvaginal Mesh?" *BMJ Opinion*, June 5, 2019, blogs.bmj.com/bmj/2019/06/05/carl-heneghan-what-next-for -transvaginal-mesh/.

22. "FDA Takes Action to Protect Women's Health, Orders Manufacturers of Surgical Mesh Intended for Transvaginal Repair of Pelvic Organ Prolapse to Stop Selling All Devices," U.S. Food and Drug Administration, April 16, 2019, fda.gov/news-events/press-announcements/fda-takes-action-protect-womens -health-orders-manufacturers-surgical-mesh-intended-transvaginal.

23. Jonathan Stempel, "Boston Scientific in $189 Million Settlement with U.S. States over Surgical Mesh Devices," Reuters, March 23, 2021, reuters.com

/article/us-boston-scientific-settlement/boston-scientific-in-189-million -settlement-with-u-s-states-over-surgical-mesh-devices-idUSKBN2BF29D.

24. Carl J. Heneghan et al., "Trials of Transvaginal Mesh Devices for Pelvic Organ Prolapse: A Systematic Database Review of the US FDA Approval Process," *BMJ Open* 7 (2017): e017125. doi:10.1136/bmjopen-2017-017125.

25. Jonathan Gornall, "How Mesh Became a Four Letter Word," *BMJ* (2018): 363, doi:10.1136/bmj.k4137.

26. "Statement on Agency's Efforts to Increase Transparency in Medical Device Reporting," U.S. Food and Drug Administration, June 21, 2019, fda.gov/news -events/press-announcements/statement-agencys-efforts-increase-transparency -medical-device-reporting.

27. Neil Vargesson, "Thalidomide-Induced Teratogenesis: History and Mecha- nisms," *Birth Defects Research*, part C, *Embryo Today: Reviews* 105, no. 2 (2015): 140–56, doi:10.1002/bdrc.21096.

28. James Meikle, "Thalidomide 'Caused up to 10,000 Miscarriages and Infant Deaths in UK,'" *The Guardian*, Mar. 6, 2016, theguardian.com/society/2016 /mar/06/thalidomide-caused-up-to-10000-miscarriages-infant-deaths-uk.

29. Robert D. McFadden, "Frances Oldham Kelsey, Who Saved U.S. Babies from Thalidomide, Dies at 101," *New York Times*, Aug. 7, 2015, nytimes .com/2015/08/08/science/frances-oldham-kelsey-fda-doctor-who-exposed -danger-of-thalidomide-dies-at-101.html.

30. Ingrid Peritz, "Frances Oldham Kelsey Averted a Thalidomide Tragedy Because She Wouldn't Be Rushed," *Globe and Mail*, Aug. 14, 2015, theglobe andmail.com/life/health-and-fitness/health/frances-oldham-kelsey-averted-a -thalidomide-tragedy-because-she-wouldnt-be-rushed/article25976972/.

31. Leila McNeill, "The Woman Who Stood Between America and a Generation of 'Thalidomide Babies,'" *Smithsonian Magazine*, May 8, 2017, smithsonianmag .com/science-nature/woman-who-stood-between-america-and-epidemic-birth -defects-180963165/.

32. John Mulliken, "A Woman Doctor Who Would Not Be Hurried," *Life*, Aug. 10, 1962, 28–29.

33. Gardiner Harris, "The Public's Quiet Savior from Harmful Medicines," *New York Times*, Sept. 13, 2010, nytimes.com/2010/09/14/health/14kelsey.html.

34. Emily Olsen, "Femtech Startups Nearly Double Funding Dollars from Last Year, but Still Make up Small Percent of Market," *MobiHealthNews*, Sept. 30, 2021, mobihealthnews.com/news/femtech-startups-nearly-double-funding -dollars-last-year-still-make-small-percent-market.

Chapter 7: Nutritionmania: Why Are We Confused About What We Eat?

1. *Keeping Up with the Kardashians*, season 17, episode 9, "Hard Candy," E!, Nov. 10, 2019.

2. Margaret L. Westwater, Paul C. Fletcher, and Hisham Ziauddeen, "Sugar Addiction: The State of the Science," *European Journal of Nutrition* 55 (2016): 55–69, doi.org/10.1007/s00394-016-1229-6.

3. "Tenfold Increase in Childhood and Adolescent Obesity in Four Decades: New Study by Imperial College London and WHO," World Health Organization, Oct. 11, 2017, who.int/news/item/11–10–2017-tenfold-increase-in-childhood -and-adolescent-obesity-in-four-decades-new-study-by-imperial-college-london -and-who.

4. "Nearly Two-Thirds of Mothers 'Shamed' by Others About Their Parent- ing Skills," *ScienceDaily*, June 19, 2017, sciencedaily.com/releases/2017/06 /170619092158.htm.

5. Ellen Wallwork, "Reese Witherspoon Food Shamed After Sharing Photo of Her Son's Breakfast," *HuffPost UK*, Dec. 3, 2015, huffingtonpost.co.uk/2015/03/12 /reese-witherspoon-food-shamed-over-sons-breakfast-photo_n_6855780.html.

6. Janet Forgrieve, "The Growing Acceptance of Veganism," *Forbes*, Nov. 2, 2018, forbes.com/sites/janetforgrieve/2018/11/02/picturing-a-kindler-gentler-world -vegan-month/?sh=30074c722f2b.

7. Sophie M. Balzora, "One-Third of Americans Are Trying to Avoid Gluten–but Is It the Villain We Think It Is?," *NYU Langone Health NewsHub*, nyulangone .org/news/one-third-americans-are-trying-avoid-gluten-it-villain-we-think-it-is.

8. Martha C. White, "Recipe for Success: Cookbook Sales Survive Shift to Dig- ital Media," NBC News, Aug. 14, 2018, nbcnews.com/business/consumer /recipe-success-cookbook-sales-survive-shift-digital-media-n900621.

9. Vani Hari, "Healthy Meal Plans for Looking and Feeling Your Best!," *Food Babe*, Oct. 10, 2017, foodbabe.com/healthy-meal-plans/.

10. Vani Hari, "You'll Never Guess What's in a Starbucks Pumpkin Spice Latte (Hint: You Won't Be Happy)," *Food Babe*, April 6, 2015, foodbabe.com/starbucks-pumpkin -spice-latte/.

11. Nina Teicholz, *The Big Fat Surprise: Why Butter, Meat, and Cheese Belong in a Healthy Diet* (New York: Simon & Schuster, 2015), 43–61.

12. Dustin Moore (registered dietitian and writer) in discussion with the author, April 2022.

13. Centers for Disease Control and Prevention, "Trends in Intake of Energy and Macronutrients—United States, 1971–2000," *Morbidity and Mortality Weekly Report* 53, no. 4 (2004): 80–82.

14. Camila Domonoske, "50 Years Ago, Sugar Industry Quietly Paid Scientists to Point Blame at Fat," NPR, Sept. 13, 2016, npr.org/sections/thetwo-way /2016/09/13/493739074/50-years-ago-sugar-industry-quietly-paid-scientists -to-point-blame-at-fat.

15. "How Much Is Too Much?" SugarScience, University of California, San Francisco, April 27, 2018, sugarscience.ucsf.edu/dispelling-myths-too-much.html# .YYnDStnMLeo.

16. Paul Zane Pilzer, *The Next Trillion: Why the Wellness Industry Will Exceed the $1 Trillion Healthcare (Sickness) Industry in the Next Ten Years* (Lake Dallas, TX: VideoPlus, 2001), 8.

17. Belinda S. Lennerz et al., "Effects of Dietary Glycemic Index on Brain Regions Related to Reward and Craving in Men," *American Journal of Clinical Nutrition* 98, no. 3 (September 2013): 641–47, doi:10.3945/ajcn.113.064113.

18. Wendy Scinta, "The History of Portion Sizes: How They've Changed Over Time," *Your Weight Matters*, April 28, 2016, yourweightmatters.org/portion -sizes-changed-time/.

19. Larissa Galastri Baraldi et al., "Consumption of Ultra-Processed Foods and Associated Sociodemographic Factors in the USA Between 2007 and 2012: Evidence from a Nationally Representative Cross-Sectional Study," *BMJ Open* 8, no. 3 (March 2018), ncbi.nlm.nih.gov/pmc/articles/PMC5855172/.

20. Linda Searing, "The Big Number: Only 7 Percent of Adults Are Consuming the Right Amount of Fiber," *Washington Post*, June 21, 2021, washington post.com/health/fiber-weight-control-heart/2021/06/18/2ff37134-cf7f-11eb -8cd2-4e95230cfac2_story.html.

21. Michael F. Jacobson, "Burying the Snackwell Myth," *Medium*, Dec. 11, 2015, medium.com/@CSPI/burying-the-snackwell-myth-4b6e9dff6d07.

22. "Food Marketing," UConn Rudd Center for Food Policy & Health, April 20, 2020, uconnruddcenter.org/research/food-marketing/#f(1).

23. Warren James Belasco, *Appetite for Change: How the Counterculture Took on the Food Industry* (Ithaca, NY: Cornell University Press, 2007), 28.

24. Marion Nestle, "Food Lobbies, the Food Pyramid, and U.S. Nutrition Policy," *International Journal of Health Services* 23, no. 3 (1993): 483–96, doi:10.2190/32F2–2PFB-MEG7–8HPU. PMID: 8375951.

25. Robert H. Lustig, *Fat Chance: Beating the Odds Against Sugar, Processed Food, Obesity, and Disease* (New York: Plume, 2014), 252.

26. Marion Nestle, *Food Politics: How the Food Industry Influences Nutrition and Health* (Berkeley: University of California Press, 2013), 123.

27. Camila Domonoske, "DNA Tests Find Subway Chicken Only 50 Percent Meat, Canadian News Program Reports," NPR, March 1, 2017, npr.org/sections /thetwo-way/2017/03/01/517920680/dna-tests-find-subway-chicken-only-50 -percent-meat-canadian-media-reports.

28. Ben Quinn, Sarah Butler, and Rebecca Smithers, "Mars Recalls Chocolate Bars in 55 Countries After Plastic Found in Product," *The Guardian*, Feb. 23, 2016, theguardian.com/lifeandstyle/2016/feb/23/mars-chocolate-product-recalls -snickers-milky-way-celebrations-germany-netherlands.

29. "Food Safety in America—Time to Bolster Consumer Confidence," *C.O.nxt*, May 5, 2021, co-nxt.com/blog/food-safety-in-america-time-to-bolster -consumer-confidence/.

30. "We Are What We Eat: Healthy Eating Trends Around the World," Nielsen, January 2015, nielsen.com/wp-content/uploads/sites/3/2019/04/Nielsen20Glob al20Health20and20Wellness20Report20-20January202015-1.pdf.

31. Roland Marchand, *Advertising the American Dream: Making Way for Modernity, 1920–1940* (Berkeley: University of California Press, 1985), 297–98.

32. Catherine Price, *Vitamania: Our Obsessive Quest for Nutritional Perfection* (New York: Penguin Press, 2015), 77.

33. Marchand, *Advertising the American Dream*, 296.

34. Price, *Vitamania*, 71.

35. "2. Americans' Views About and Consumption of Organic Foods," Pew Research Center, Dec. 1, 2016, pewresearch.org/science/2016/12/01/americans -views-about-and-consumption-of-organic-foods/.

36. Benjamin L. Campbell et al., "U.S. and Canadian Consumer Perception of Local and Organic Terminology," *International Food and Agribusiness Management Review* 17, no. 2 (May 2014): 1–20.

37. "EWG's 2021 Shopper's Guide to Pesticides in Produce," EWG, ewg.org /foodnews/summary.php and https://www.healthkick.info/pesticides-in-produce -the-clean-15-and-the-dirty-dozen/.

38. Food Science Babe, "Food Science Babe: The Dirty Deception of the 'Dirty Dozen,'" *AgDaily*, March 18, 2021, agdaily.com/insights/dirty-deception-ewg -dirty-dozen/.

39. Food Science Babe, "I really want to bring attention to the deceptive games the EWG plays all in the name of scaring consumers over safe foods to raise money for their organization. This needs to stop. Please share." Facebook photo, March 18, 2021, facebook.com/foodsciencebabe/photos/a.350962359061846 /950422905782452/?type=3.

40. "FY2019 Pesticide Report: Consistent with Trends Over the Past 8 Years, Pesticide Residue Levels Remain Low," U.S. Food and Drug Administration, Oct. 20, 2021, fda.gov/food/cfsan-constituent-updates/fy-2019-pesticide-report -consistent-trends-over-past-8-years-pesticide-residue-levels-remain-low.

41. "Americans' Views," Pew Research Center.

42. Crystal Smith-Spangler et al., "Are Organic Foods Safer or Healthier Than Conventional Alternatives?: A Systematic Review," *Annals of Internal Medicine* 157, no. 5 (2012): 348, doi:10.7326/0003–4819–157–5–201209040–00007.

43. Marcin Barański et al., "Higher Antioxidant and Lower Cadmium Concentrations and Lower Incidence of Pesticide Residues in Organically Grown Crops: A Systematic Literature Review and Meta-analyses," *British Journal of Nutrition* 112, no. 5 (2014): 794–811, doi:10.1017/S0007114514001366.

44. Kenneth Chang, "Study of Organic Crops Finds Fewer Pesticides and More Antioxidants," *New York Times*, July 11, 2014, nytimes.com/2014/07/12/science/earth /study-of-organic-crops-finds-fewer-pesticides-and-more-antioxidants-.html.

45. Peter Whoriskey, "Is Organic Food Safer and Healthier? The Guy in Charge of U.S. Organics Won't Say," *Washington Post*, April 30, 2015, washingtonpost .com/news/wonk/wp/2015/04/30/is-organic-food-safer-and-healthier-the-guy -in-charge-of-u-s-organics-wont-say/.

46. Joanna Schroeder et al., "Organic Marketing Report," *Academics Review* (2016), ww1.prweb.com/prfiles/2014/04/07/11743859/Academics-Review_Organic %20Marketing%20Report.pdf.

47. Michael Pollan, "Naturally," *New York Times*, May 13, 2001, nytimes.com/2001 /05/13/magazine/naturally.html.

48. Vanessa Apaolaza et al., "Eat Organic—Feel Good? The Relationship Between Organic Food Consumption, Health Concern and Subjective Wellbeing," *Food Quality and Preference* 63 (Jan. 2018): 51–62, doi:10.1016/j.foodqual.2017.07.011.

49. "When It Comes to Buying Organic, Science and Beliefs Don't Always Mesh," NPR, Sept. 7, 2012, npr.org/transcripts/160681396.

50. "Individuals May Consider Organic an Important Factor When Defining Healthy Food," Johns Hopkins Bloomberg School of Public Health, public health.jhu.edu/2015/individuals-may-consider-organic-an-important-factor -when-defining-healthy-food.

51. Yancui Huang, Indika Edirisinghe, and Britt M. Burton-Freeman, "Low-Income Shoppers and Fruit and Vegetables: What Do They Think?" *Nutrition Today* 51, no. 5 (2016): 242–50, doi:10.1097/NT.0000000000000176.

52. Cara Rosenbloom, "A Diet Rich in Fruits and Vegetables Outweighs the Risks of Pesticides," *Washington Post*, Jan. 18, 2017, washingtonpost.com

/lifestyle/wellness/a-diet-rich-in-fruits-and-vegetables-outweighs-the-risks-of
-pesticides/2017/01/13/f68ed4f6-d780-11e6-9a36-1d296534b31e_story.html.

53. Anna Vlasits, "The Growing Diet Divide Between Rich and Poor in America," *STAT*, June 21, 2016, statnews.com/2016/06/21/growing-diet-divide/.

54. James Temple, "Sorry—Organic Farming Is Actually Worse for Climate Change," *MIT Technology Review*, Oct. 22, 2019, technologyreview.com/2019/10/22 /132497/sorryorganic-farming-is-actually-worse-for-climate-change/.

55. Ocean, Inc., "Oceana Report: Plastic Pollution from Amazon Deliveries Grows by 29% in Just One Year," *GlobeNewswire*, Dec. 15, 2021, globenewswire .com/news-release/2021/12/15/2352262/0/en/Oceana-Report-Plastic-Pollution -From-Amazon-Deliveries-Grows-By-29-in-Just-One-Year.html.

56. "2018 Food & Health Survey," International Food Information Council, food insight.org/wp-content/uploads/2018/05/2018-FHS-Report-FINAL.pdf.

57. Meg Greenfield, "Give Me That Old-Time Cholesterol," *Washington Post*, June 20, 1984, washingtonpost.com/archive/politics/1984/06/20/give-me-that-old -time-cholesterol/303be7f3-fd49-4911-ad5b-bb8a9faaa742/.

58. Vani Hari, "Join Me! Investigate Your Food," *Food Babe*, foodbabe.com/about-me/.

59. Susan Donaldson James, "Subway Takes Chemical Out of Sandwich Bread After Protest," ABC News, Feb. 5, 2014, abcnews.go.com/Health/subway -takes-chemical-sandwich-bread-protest/story?id=22373414.

60. Mark Alsip, Kavin Senapathy, and Marc Draco, *The Fear Babe: Shattering Vani Hari's Glass House* (n.p.: Senapath Press, 2015), 28–31.

61. Vani Hari, "Should I Get the Flu Shot?," *Food Babe*, April 16, 2015, foodbabe .com/should-i-get-the-flu-shot/.

62. James Hamblin, "The Food Babe: Enemy of Chemicals," *The Atlantic*, February 11, 2015, theatlantic.com/health/archive/2015/02/the-food-babe-enemy-of -chemicals/385301/.

63. "Dietary Supplement Use Reaches All Time High," Council for Responsible Nutrition, crnusa.org/newsroom/dietary-supplement-use-reaches-all-time-high.

64. David J. A. Jenkins et al., "Supplemental Vitamins and Minerals for CVD Prevention and Treatment," *Journal of the American College of Cardiology* 71, no. 22 (2018): 2570–84, doi:10.1016/j.jacc.2018.04.020.

65. Francis Collins, "Study Finds No Benefit for Dietary Supplements," *Director's Blog*, National Institutes of Health, April 16, 2019, directorsblog.nih.gov/2019 /04/16/study-finds-no-benefit-for-dietary-supplements/.

66. Fan Chen et al., "Association Among Dietary Supplement Use, Nutrient Intake, and Mortality Among U.S. Adults: A Cohort Study," *Annals of Internal Medicine* 170, no. 9 (2019): 604, doi:10.7326/m18–2478.

67. Serena Gordon, "Dietary Supplements Do Nothing for You: Study," *Health-Day*, Consumer Health News, April 8, 2019, consumer.healthday.com/vitamins-and-nutrition-information-27/vitamin-and-mineral-news-698/dietary-supplements-do-nothing-for-you-study-744827.html.

68. Paul Offit, "The Vitamin Myth: Why We Think We Need Supplements," *The Atlantic*, July 19, 2013, theatlantic.com/health/archive/2013/07/the-vitamin-myth-why-we-think-we-need-supplements/277947/.

69. Robert H. Shmerling, MD, "What's in Your Supplements?" *Harvard Health* (blog), Feb. 15, 2019, health.harvard.edu/blog/whats-in-your-supplements-2019021515946.

70. Nikhil Sonnad, "All the 'Wellness' Products Americans Love to Buy Are Sold on Both Infowars and Goop," *Quartz*, qz.com/1010684/all-the-wellness-products-american-love-to-buy-are-sold-on-both-infowars-and-goop/.

71. Andrew Weil, "Cured by Kombucha?," June 20, 2018, drweil.com/health-wellness/balanced-living/healthy-living/cured-by-kombucha/.

72. "Dannon Agrees to Drop Exaggerated Health Claims for Activia Yogurt and DanActive Dairy Drink," Federal Trade Commission, Dec. 15, 2010, ftc.gov/news-events/press-releases/2010/12/dannon-agrees-drop-exaggerated-health-claims-activia-yogurt.

73. "2020 Food & Health Survey," International Food Information Council, foodinsight.org/wp-content/uploads/2020/06/IFIC-Food-and-Health-Survey-2020.pdf.

74. "US Sugar and Alternative Sweeteners Market Report 2020," Mintel, May 25, 2021, store.mintel.com/us-sugar-and-alternative-sweeteners-market-report.

75. Max Knoblauch, "Americans Feel Guilty About Almost a Third of the Food They Eat," *New York Post*, March 13, 2019, nypost.com/2019/03/13/americans-feel-guilty-about-almost-a-third-of-the-food-they-eat/.

Chapter 8: Crystal-Clear Futures: A New Take on New Age Spirituality

1. Thomas G. Plante, "What Do the Spiritual and Religious Traditions Offer the Practicing Psychologist?" *Pastoral Psychology* 56, no. 4 (2008): 429–44, doi:10.1007/s11089–008–0119–0.

2. Claire Gecewicz, "'New Age' Beliefs Common Among Both Religious and Nonreligious Americans," Pew Research Center, Oct. 1, 2018, pewresearch.org/fact-tank/2018/10/01/new-age-beliefs-common-among-both-religious-and-nonreligious-americans/.

3. Anne Harrington, *The Cure Within: A History of Mind–Body Medicine* (New York: W. W. Norton, 2009), 111–12.

4. James C. Whorton, *Nature Cures: The History of Alternative Medicine in America* (New York: Oxford University Press, 2004), 125–30.

5. Anne Harrington, *Cure Within*, 118–19.

6. Marianne Williamson, *A Course in Weight Loss: 21 Spiritual Lessons for Surrendering Your Weight Forever* (Carlsbad, CA: Hay House, 2012), 15–21.

7. Steve Salerno, *SHAM: How the Self-Help Movement Made America Helpless* (New York: Crown, 2005), 248.

8. Rina Raphael, "Is There a Crystal Bubble? Inside the Billion-Dollar 'Healing' Gemstone Industry," *Fast Company*, May 5, 2017, fastcompany.com/40410406 /is-there-a-crystal-bubble-inside-the-billion-dollar-healing-gemstone -industry.

9. Rina Raphael, "Silicon Valley's Quest to Build the Wellness Community of the Future," *Fast Company*, Aug. 9, 2019, fastcompany.com/90387422/how-silicon -valleys-elite-are-trying-to-building-the-wellness-community-of-the-future.

10. Jeane Dixon and Rene Noorbergen, *Jeane Dixon: My Life and Prophecies* (Boston: G. K. Hall, 1971), 12–13.

11. Ruth Montgomery, *A Gift of Prophecy: The Phenomenal Jeane Dixon* (Toronto: Bantam Books, 1965), 13.

12. Michael Isikoff, "Terror Watch: Nixon and Dixon," *Newsweek*, March 22, 2005, newsweek.com/terror-watch-nixon-and-dixon-114707.

13. Montgomery, *Gift of Prophecy*, 34.

14. John Allen Paulos, *Innumeracy: Mathematical Illiteracy and Its Consequences* (New York: Hill and Wang, 2001), 71.

15. Krista Tippett, *Becoming Wise: An Inquiry into the Mystery and Art of Living* (New York: Penguin Books, 2017), 11.

16. Krista Tippett, "My Grandfather's Faith: Contradictions and Mysteries," *The On Being Project*, July 18, 2010, onbeing.org/blog/my-grandfathers-faith -contradictions-and-mysteries/.

17. Tippett, *Becoming Wise*, 170.

18. "In U.S., Decline of Christianity Continues at Rapid Pace," Pew Research Center's Religion and Public Life Project, Oct. 17, 2019, pewforum.org/2019/10/17 /in-u-s-decline-of-christianity-continues-at-rapid-pace/.

19. Chad Day, "Americans Have Shifted Dramatically on What Values Matter Most," *Wall Street Journal*, Aug. 25, 2019, wsj.com/articles/americans-have -shifted-dramatically-on-what-values-matter-most-11566738001.

20. Jeffrey M. Jones, "U.S. Church Membership Falls Below Majority for First Time," Gallup, Mar. 29, 2021, news.gallup.com/poll/341963/church-membership -falls-below-majority-first-time.aspx.

21. Wade Clark Roof, *Spiritual Marketplace: Baby Boomers and the Remaking of American Religion* (Princeton, NJ: Princeton University Press, 1999), 159.

22. Dalia Fahmy, "Key Findings About Americans' Belief in God," Pew Research Center, April 25, 2018, pewresearch.org/fact-tank/2018/04/25/key-findings-about-americans-belief-in-god/.

23. Travis Mitchell, "The Gender Gap in Religion Around the World," Pew Research Center's Religion and Public Life Project, March 22, 2016, pewforum.org/2016/03/22/the-gender-gap-in-religion-around-the-world/.

24. Christian Smith, *Religion: What It Is, How It Works, and Why It Matters* (Princeton, NJ: Princeton University Press, 2019), 200–202.

25. Kathleen J. Sullivan, "A Spiritual Practice Is the Foundation of a Meaningful Life, Oprah Winfrey Tells Stanford Audience," Stanford University, April 21, 2015, news.stanford.edu/news/2015/april/oprah-rathbun-lecture-042115.html.

26. Jamie Ballard, "Exercising More and Saving Money Are the Most Popular 2020 New Year's Resolutions," YouGov America, Jan. 2, 2020, today.yougov.com/topics/lifestyle/articles-reports/2020/01/02/new-years-resolutions-2020-health-finance.

27. Hannah Ewens, "The 'Goop Effect': The Women Who Spend Hundreds Seeking Spirituality," *Vice*, Feb. 18, 2020, vice.com/en/article/jgejj3/spirituality-luxury-upper-class-goop-lab-healing-treatmentss.

28. Robert D. Putnam, *Bowling Alone: The Collapse and Revival of American Community* (New York: Simon & Schuster Paperbacks, 2000), 74–79.

Chapter 9: You're Not Working Hard Enough

1. Rina Raphael, "This Ex-Convict Created New York's New Prison-Themed Fitness Empire," *Fast Company*, Aug. 25, 2017, fastcompany.com/40452499/this-ex-convict-created-new-yorks-new-prison-themed-fitness-empire.

2. Jeff Haden, "Internal Documents Reveal the Marketing Strategy Peloton Used to Become a $1.8 Billion Company," *Inc.*, Mar. 30, 2021, www.inc.com/jeff-haden/internal-documents-reveal-marketing-strategy-peloton-used-to-become-a-18-billion-company.html.

3. Rina Raphael, "How Orangetheory Grew to Dominate the Boutique Fitness Industry," *Fast Company*, July 17, 2018, fastcompany.com/90201967/how-orangetheory-grew-to-dominate-the-boutique-fitness-industry.

4. "The Effectiveness of Activity Trackers and Rewards to Encourage Physical Activity," Duke University, Oct. 5, 2016, duke-nus.edu.sg/allnews/the-effectiveness-of-activity-trackers-and-rewards-to-encourage-physical-activity.

5. Jordan Etkin, "The Hidden Cost of Personal Quantification," *Journal of Consumer Research* 42, no. 6 (April 2016): 967–84, doi:10.1093/jcr/ucv095.

6. Tara Isabella Burton, "Football Really Is America's Religion," *Vox*, Sept. 27, 2017, vox.com/identities/2017/9/27/16308792/football-america-religion-nfl-protests-powerful.

7. James F. Fixx, *The Complete Book of Running* (New York: Random House, 1977), 24.

8. Elise Rose Carrotte, Ivanka Prichard, and Megan Su Cheng Lim, "'Fitspiration' on Social Media: A Content Analysis of Gendered Images," *Journal of Medical Internet Research* 19, no. 3 (2017), doi:10.2196/jmir.6368.

9. Angela S. Alberga, Samantha J. Withnell, and Kristin M. von Ranson, "Fitspiration and Thinspiration: A Comparison Across Three Social Networking Sites," *Journal of Eating Disorders* 6, no. 1 (2018), doi:10.1186/s40337-018-0227-x.

10. Denise Prichard, "Trend Report: How You Can Expect Your Workout to Change in 2021," *Mindbody*, Jan. 7 2021, explore.mindbodyonline.com/blog/fitness/trend-report-how-you-can-expect-your-workout-change-2021.

11. Zoe Weiner, "Is It Time to Phase Out the #FitFluencer Once and for All?," *Well+Good*, Sept. 22, 2021, wellandgood.com/fitness-influencer-fitfluencer-responsibility/.

12. Stephanie Easton et al., "Young People's Experiences of Viewing the Fitspiration Social Media Trend: Qualitative Study." *Journal of Medical Internet Research* 20, no. 6 (2018), doi:10.2196/jmir.9156.

13. Baine B. Craft, Haley A. Carroll, and M. Kathleen B. Lustyk, "Gender Differences in Exercise Habits and Quality of Life Reports: Assessing the Moderating Effects of Reasons for Exercise," *International Journal of Liberal Arts and Social Science* 2, no. 5 (2014): 65–76.

14. Kim Parker, Juliana Menasce Horowitz, and Renee Stepler, "2. Americans See Different Expectations for Men and Women," Pew Research Center, Social and Demographic Trends Project, Dec. 5, 2017, pewresearch.org/social-trends/2017/12/05/americans-see-different-expectations-for-men-and-women/.

15. Rina Raphael, "Burned-out Americans Are Helping Wellness Tourism Flourish," *Fast Company*, Oct. 29, 2016, fastcompany.com/3064971/burned-out-americans-are-helping-wellness-tourism-flourish.

16. Rina Raphael, "Travelers Are Abandoning Spas to Join Fitfluencer Retreats," *Fast Company*, Dec. 11, 2017, fastcompany.com/40504343/travelers-are-abandoning-spas-to-join-fitfluencer-retreats.

17. Kasandra Brabaw, "An Eating Disorder Survivor Opened Up About Vacation Weight Gain," *Refinery29*, May 24, 2017, refinery29.com/en-us/2017/05/156020/vacation-weight-gain-body-positivity.

18. Maggie Lange, "Don't Even Think About Working Out on Vacation," *The Cut*, July 16, 2021, thecut.com/2021/07/dont-work-out-on-vacation.html.

19. Jason Kelly, *Sweat Equity: Inside the New Economy of Mind and Body* (Hoboken, NJ: Bloomberg Press, 2016), 99.

20. "Three out of Four Women Are Suffering from Burnout, According to New Harris Poll Commissioned by Meredith Corporation," Dotdash Meredith, Oct. 3, 2019, meredith.mediaroom.com/2019-10-03-American-Women -Confronting-Burnout-At-Epidemic-Levels-According-To-New-Harris-Poll -Commissioned-By-Meredith-Corporation.

21. Rina Raphael, "Yoga Class While Waiting for Refills? CVS Tests New 'Health Hubs,'" *Fast Company*, May 4, 2019, fastcompany.com/90343800/yoga-class -while-waiting-for-refills-cvs-tests-new-health-hubs.

22. Tamara Lush, "Poll: Americans Are the Unhappiest They've Been in 50 Years," Associated Press, June 16, 2020, apnews.com/article/0f6b9be04fa0 d3194401821a72665a50.

23. David Brancaccio, Chris Farrell, and Daniel Shin, "'The Big Quit' Isn't Going Away Anytime Soon," *Marketplace*, Oct. 27, 2021, marketplace.org/2021/10/27 /the-big-quit-isnt-going-away-anytime-soon/.

24. Katherine Wernet, "Stressed Out in America," *Mindbody*, mindbodyonline .com/business/education/blog/stressed-out-america.

25. Mary Pilon et al., "The Influencers Fighting Instagram's Perfection," *Outside*, Sep. 20, 2017, outsideonline.com/health/wellness/backlash-instagram -influencer-culture/.

26. "'Every Body Yoga' Encourages Self-Love and Everyone to Get on the Mat," *Here & Now*, WBUR, July 13, 2017, wbur.org/hereandnow/2017/07/13/every -body-yoga-jessamyn-stanley.

27. Jen Murphy, "The Hot New Class at Your Gym? Resting," *Wall Street Journal*, Mar. 27, 2022, wsj.com/articles/the-hot-new-class-at-your-gym-resting -11648336639.

28. Rina Raphael, "Stretching Studios Are the Next Big Boutique Fitness Trend," *Fast Company*, Nov. 27, 2018, fastcompany.com/90269526/stretching-studios -are-the-next-big-boutique-fitness-trend.

Chapter 10: Chasing Golden Unicorns: Biohacking the Future

1. Rina Raphael, "Cell Massages to Cryotherapy: Inside the 'Biohacking' Gym of the Future," *Fast Company*, Nov. 16, 2017, fastcompany.com/40492979/cell -massages-to-cryotherapy-inside-the-biohacking-gym-of-the-future.

2. Courtney Rubin, "The Cult of the Bulletproof Coffee Diet," *New York Times*, Dec. 12, 2014, nytimes.com/2014/12/14/style/the-cult-of-the-bulletproof -coffee-diet.html.

3. "Wellness 2030: The New Techniques of Happiness," Global Wellness Institute, June 16, 2021, globalwellnessinstitute.org/industry-research/wellness-2030/.

4. Rachel Monroe, "The Bulletproof Coffee Founder Has Spent $1 Million in His Quest to Live to 180," *Men's Health*, Jan. 23, 2019, menshealth.com/health /a25902826/bulletproof-dave-asprey-biohacking/.

5. Jade Scipioni, "These 2 Habits Can Help You Live Longer, Says Bulletproof Coffee Creator (Who Plans to Live to 180)," *CNBC Make It*, Nov. 20, 2019, cnbc.com/2019/11/20/bulletproof-coffee-founder-dave-asprey-how-to-live -longer.html.

6. Emily Abbate, "The Real-Life Diet of Dave Asprey, Who Thinks Coffee Is a Superfood," *GQ*, Jan. 28, 2021, gq.com/story/real-life-diet-dave-asprey.

7. Tasbeeh Herwees, "I 'Biohacked' My Body—but My Body Hacked Me Back," *Good*, March 7, 2017, good.is/food/bulletproof-diet-biohack.

8. Dave Asprey, *Super Human: The Bulletproof Plan to Age Backward and Maybe Even Live Forever* (New York: Harper Wave, 2019), 170.

9. Judith Rodin and Ellen J. Langer, "Long-Term Effects of a Control-Relevant Intervention with the Institutionalized Aged," *Journal of Personality and Social Psychology* 35, no. 12 (1977): 897–902, doi:10.1037/0022–3514.35.12.897.

10. Tali Sharot, *The Influential Mind: What the Brain Reveals About Our Power to Change Others* (Boston: Little, Brown, 2018), 102.

11. "Why We Believe We Have More Control Over the World Than We Actually Do," The Decision Lab, thedecisionlab.com/biases/illusion-of-control/.

12. Harvey Hartman and David Wright, *Marketing to the New Natural Consumer: Understanding Trends in Wellness* (Bellevue, WA: Hartman Group, 1999), 34–35.

13. Raphael, "Cell Massages to Cryotherapy."

14. Vince Parry (president and chief branding officer, Parry Branding Group), email message to the author, October 2021.

15. Vince Parry, *Identity Crisis: Health Care Branding's Hidden Problems and Proven Strategies to Solve Them* (n.p.: Parry Branding Group, 2017).

16. Vince Parry (president and chief branding officer, Parry Branding Group), in discussion with the author, October 2021.

17. Walter Isaacson, *Steve Jobs* (New York: Simon & Schuster, 2018), 181.

18. Dave Asprey, *Head Strong: The Bulletproof Plan to Activate Untapped Brain Energy to Work Smarter and Think Faster—in Just Two Weeks* (New York: Harper Wave, 2017), introduction.

19. Alex Hannaford, "The Bulletproof Diet: Simplistic, Invalid and Unscientific," *The Telegraph*, Nov. 27, 2014, telegraph.co.uk/books/what-to-read/the -bulletproof-diet-simplistic-invalid-and-unscientific/.

20. Kris Gunnars, "3 Potential Downsides of Bulletproof Coffee," *Healthline*, Feb. 7, 2022, healthline.com/nutrition/3-reasons-why-bulletproof-coffee-is-a-bad-idea#2.-High-in-saturated-fat.

21. James MacDonald, "How Dietary Supplements Can Cause More Harm Than Good," *JSTOR Daily*, Aug. 5, 2019, daily.jstor.org/how-dietary-supplements-can-cause-more-harm-than-good/.

22. Wade Greene, "Guru of the Organic Food Cult," *New York Times*, June 6, 1971, nytimes.com/1971/06/06/archives/guru-of-the-organic-food-cult-guru-of-the-organic-food-cult.html.

23. Joe Schwarcz, "The Right Chemistry: J. I. Rodale Was an Early Opponent of Sugar," *Montreal Gazette*, July 15, 2020, montrealgazette.com/opinion/columnists/the-right-chemistry-j-i-rodale-was-an-early-opponent-of-sugar.

24. Maria McGrath, "The Bizarre Life (and Death) of 'Mr. Organic,'" *New Republic*, Aug. 8, 2014, newrepublic.com/article/119007/bizarre-life-and-death-mr-organic.

25. Rebecca Grant, "How Egg Freezing Got Rebranded as the Ultimate Act of Self-Care," *The Guardian*, Sept. 30, 2020, theguardian.com/us-news/2020/sep/30/egg-freezing-self-care-pregnancy-fertility.

26. Michelle J. Bayefsky, Alan H. DeCherney, and Louise P. King, "Respecting Autonomy—a Call for Truth in Commercial Advertising for Planned Oocyte Cryopreservation," *Fertil Steril* 113, no. 4 (Apr. 2020): 743–44, 10.1016/j.fertnstert.2019.12.039.

27. Kaitlyn Tiffany, "The SoulCycle of Fertility Sells Egg-Freezing and 'Empowerment' to 25-Year-Olds," *The Verge*, Sept. 11, 2018, theverge.com/2018/9/11/17823810/kindbody-startup-fertility-clinic-egg-freezing-millennials-location.

28. Rina Raphael, "Unable to Afford IVF, Millennials Turn to Hopeful Grandparents," *Fast Company*, July 17, 2019, fastcompany.com/90376652/with-ivf-too-expensive-millennials-turn-to-a-motivated-source-of-funding-hopeful-grandparents.

29. Angel Petropanagos et al., "Social Egg Freezing: Risk, Benefits and Other Considerations," *Canadian Medical Association Journal* 187, no. 9 (2015): 666–69, doi:10.1503/cmaj.141605.

30. Romualdo Sciorio et al., "One Follicle, One Egg, One Embryo: A Case-Report of Successful Pregnancy Obtained from a Single Oocyte Collected," *JBRA Assisted Reproduction* 25, no. 2 (April 2021): 314–17, doi:10.5935/1518-0557.20200087.

31. Ariana Eunjung Cha, "The Struggle to Conceive with Frozen Eggs," *Washington Post*, Jan. 27, 2018, washingtonpost.com/news/national/wp/2018/01/27

/feature/she-championed-the-idea-that-freezing-your-eggs-would-free-your
-career-but-things-didnt-quite-work-out/.

32. Claire Cain Miller, "The 10-Year Baby Window That Is the Key to the Women's
Pay Gap," *The Upshot* (blog), *New York Times*, April 9, 2018, nytimes.com/2018
/04/09/upshot/the-10-year-baby-window-that-is-the-key-to-the-womens-pay
-gap.html.

33. Heather Murphy, "Lots of Successful Women Are Freezing Their Eggs. But
It May Not Be about Their Careers," *New York Times*, July 3, 2018, nytimes
.com/2018/07/03/health/freezing-eggs-women.html.

34. Emily Jackson, "The Ambiguities of 'Social' Egg Freezing and the Challenges
of Informed Consent," *Biosocieties* 13 (2018): 21–40, 10.1057/s41292-017-
0044-5.

35. Lucy van de Wiel, *Freezing Fertility: Oocyte Cryopreservation and the Gender Politics of Aging* (New York: New York University Press, 2020), 51.

36. Ruth La Ferla, "These Companies Really, Really, Really Want to Freeze
Your Eggs," *New York Times*, Aug. 29, 2018, nytimes.com/2018/08/29/style
/egg-freezing-fertility-millennials.html.

37. Carl Elliott, *Better Than Well: American Medicine Meets the American Dream*
(New York: W. W. Norton, 2004), 188.

38. Christopher Barbey, "Evidence of Biased Advertising in the Case of Social Egg
Freezing," *New Bioethics* 23, no. 3 (2017): 195–209, doi.org/10.1080/20502877
.2017.1396033.

Chapter 11: Democratizing Wellness: Pushing Back Against 'Wellthness'

1. Rina Raphael, "Inside the $2,000-a-Month, Invite-Only Fitness Clubs," *Ele-
mental*, Jan. 3, 2020, elemental.medium.com/inside-the-2–000-a-month-invite
-only-fitness-clubs-b44dc031bf54.

2. Raphael, "Inside the $2,000-a-Month, Invite-Only, Fitness Clubs."

3. Tom Corley, "Author Who Studies Millionaires: 240 Minutes a Day
Separates the Rich from Everyone Else," CNBC, June 22, 2018, cnbc.
com/2018/06/21/tom-corley-240-minutes-a-day-separates-the-rich-from-ever
yone-else.html.

4. Rina Raphael, "Utopic Wellness Communities Are a Multibillion-Dollar Real
Estate Trend," *Fast Company*, Jan. 24, 2018, fastcompany.com/40512467/utopic
-wellness-communities-are-a-multibillion-dollar-real-estate-trend.

5. Rina Raphael, "You Might Get the Best Sleep of Your Life in This House—if
You Can Afford It," *Fast Company*, Sept. 6, 2019, fastcompany.com/90398249
/is-this-the-worlds-most-sleep-optimized-home.

6. Paul Zane Pilzer, *The Next Trillion: Why the Wellness Industry Will Exceed the $1 Trillion Healthcare (Sickness) Industry in the Next Ten Years* (Lake Dallas, TX: VideoPlus, 2001), 50.

7. Rina Raphael, "Fitter, Healthier, Happier? How Wellness Drinks Took Over Instagram," *Fast Company*, Dec. 19, 2018, fastcompany.com/90276523/fitter -healthier-happier-how-wellness-drinks-took-over-instagram.

8. Rina Raphael, "Gwyneth Paltrow Wants to Put Her Goop Inside You," *Fast Company*, March 27, 2017, fastcompany.com/3069237/gwyneth-paltrow-wants -to-put-her-goop-inside-you.

9. Douglas Atkin, *The Culting of Brands: Turn Your Customers into True Believers* (New York: Portfolio, 2004), 31.

10. "Social Networks Push Runners to Run Further and Faster Than Their Friends," *Nature* 544, no. 270 (2017), nature.com/articles/544270a.

11. Sarah Stage, *Female Complaints: Lydia Pinkham and the Business of Women's Medicine* (New York: W. W. Norton, 1981), 102.

12. Stage, *Female Complaints*, 108.

13. Stage, *Female Complaints*, 123.

14. Jaclyn Krymowski, "Fitness and Farming—it's No Surprise They Go So Well Together," *AgDaily*, July 1, 2020, agdaily.com/features/fitness-and-agriculture -a-likely-pair/.

15. Rina Raphael, "Wellness Has a Diversity Issue—These Women Are Changing That," *Fast Company*, Feb. 21, 2018, fastcompany.com/40531531/wellness-has -a-diversity-issue-these-women-are-changing-that.

16. Rina Raphael, "This Home Comes with Yoga, Sound Baths, Star Energy Healing—and 95 Roommates," *Los Angeles Times*, Oct. 24, 2019, latimes.com /lifestyle/story/2019–10–24/haven-venice-yoga-sound-baths-95-roommates.

Chapter 12: Guides for the Perplexed

1. Vani Hari, "Food Babe TV: Do You Eat Beaver Butt?," *Food Babe*, Jan. 31, 2018, foodbabe.com/food-babe-tv-do-you-eat-beaver-butt/.

2. Lynzy Coughlin, "Debunking Food Industry Myths with Erin from Food Science Babe," *Motherhood Meets Medicine*, Apple Podcasts, Oct. 6, 2021, podcasts .apple.com/us/podcast/debunking-food-industry-myths-with-erin-from-food /id1553782780?i=1000537708777.

3. Rina Raphael, "'It's Sort of the Wild West': How Instagram Influencers Are Disrupting Healthcare," *Fast Company*, Nov. 20, 2019, fastcompany.com /90427946/as-the-healthcare-industry-increasingly-relies-on-influencers -concerns-mount.

4. Austin Chiang (@austinchiangmd), "Comparing the vaccines #science #learnontiktok #tiktokpartner," TikTok, Nov. 17, 2020, tiktok.com /@austinchiangmd/video/6896305106917149957, accessed Jan. 29, 2022.

5. Food Babe, "New investigation . . . This may be coming to a school near you. We'll likely see disinfectant booths like this in airports, stores, and other public places too," Facebook post, Aug. 12, 2020, facebook.com/permalink.php?story _fbid=3487462847955068&id=132535093447877.

6. Food Babe, "Food Babe Scam: My Response to the Attacks on Me and Our Movement," *Food Babe* (blog), Apr. 16, 2015, foodbabe.com/food-babe-critics/.

7. Holly Whetstone, "Inflation, Pandemic, War Reflect Consumers' Wariness on Grocery Prices," *AgBioResearch*, Apr. 4, 2022, canr.msu.edu/news/inflation -pandemic-war-reflect-consumers-wariness-on-grocery-prices.

8. Douglas Buhler and Sheril Kirshenbaum, "From GMOs to BPA, Why the Wealthy Are More Likely to Fall for Food Pseudoscience," *Genetic Literacy Project*, Sept. 20, 2019, geneticliteracyproject.org/2019/09/20/from-gmos-to -bpa-why-are-the-wealthy-more-likely-to-fall-for-food-pseudoscience/.

Conclusion

1. Arthur J. Barsky, *Worried Sick: Our Troubled Quest for Wellness* (Boston: Little, Brown, 1988), 8.

2. David Foster Wallace, "David Foster Wallace on Life and Work," *Wall Street Journal*, Sept. 19, 2008, wsj.com/articles/SB122178211966454607.

3. Donald B. Ardell, *High-Level Wellness: An Alternative to Doctors, Drugs, and Disease* (Emmaus, PA: Rodale Press, 1977), 3.

Acknowledgments

This book would never have been written had it not been for my patient agent Sarah Fuentes and supportive editor Amy Einhorn. Both were instrumental in getting this project off the ground and steering me in the right direction. Also, the entire team at Henry Holt: Julia Ortiz, Marian Brown, Molly Bloom, Laura Flavin, Christopher Sergio, Omar Chapa, Nicolette Seeback, and everyone else who got this baby out the door.

This book would never have been completed without the guidance, help, and advice of Dedi Felman. Dedi worked with disastrous early drafts and held my hand throughout this process. Not only that, she made working on a research-heavy book ... fun? I still miss our midday therapy sessions.

So many people devoted their time, expertise, and thoughts: Perry Romanowski, Esther Olu, Bill Sukala, Kelly Dobos, Carl Winter, Jen Novakovich, Steven Loy, Miriam Zoll, Rachel Bloom, Ruthie Schulder, Dr. David Scales, Renée DiResta, Sheril Kirshenbaum, Michelle Wong, Julie Rehmeyer, Don Ardell, Ophelia Yeung, Vincent Parry, Barbara Riegel, and many, many more.

The fact-checking and review process was a team effort. Many thanks to all those who contributed: Dustin Moore, Leah McGrath, Dr. Maude

Carmel, Laury Frieber, Jenny Splitter, Greta Moran, Alison Bernstein, Lea Urpa, Dr. Benjamin Mazer, Dr. Sophie Bracke, Kate Gallagher, Sarah Wassberg Johnson, Bram Berntzen, Dr. Danielle Ofri, Cadence Bambenek, Cody Musselman, Jay Gooch, Kathleen Meehan, Stephen Alain Ko, Mindy Levine, and Tamika Sims.

Plenty of friends got me to this point and helped in various ways. Huge thanks to Tali Malina, Merisa Brod Fink, Beth McGroarty, Rachel Krupa, Dan Gregor, Nick Bilton, Shayndi Raice, and the Mooney Method crew. A special shout-out to Susan Houriet, who gave me some of my first big opportunities in journalism, as well as Anjali Khosla for being such an encouraging and diligent editor at *Fast Company*.

I'm incredibly blessed to have a family that has always been there for me. I'm so very grateful for my Ema (Esther Raphael) and Abba (Dr. David Raphael Z"L), who instilled in me a love of books, science, and debate. I also have amazing, loving siblings: Abraham, Deborah, Nechama, Miriam, and Fred. My in-laws Marion and Dennis Spiegelman were always quick with words of encouragement.

I'm also lucky to have my East Coast family, Gina and Phil Vinick, who looked after me throughout all my years in New York. You treated me like I was your own daughter. I'll never forget that.

Last but not least, I'm forever indebted to my husband Eric Spiegelman, who knows that real wellness is a supportive partner (and a good-looking dog). I'm sorry I was such a nightmare to live with while writing this. I love you. And I promise I'll start getting out of PJs before noon.

Thank you.

About the Author

Rina Raphael is a journalist who specializes in health, wellness, tech, and women's issues. She was a features contributor for *Fast Company* magazine and has also written for the *New York Times*, the *Los Angeles Times*, CBS, NBC News, and Medium's *Elemental*, among other publications. Her wellness industry newsletter, *Well To Do*, covers trends and offers market analysis. Previously, Raphael served as a senior producer and lifestyle editor at Today.com and NBCNews.com. She lives in Los Angeles.